# The
# Messiah
# in Ancient
# America

# "And it came to pass. . ."

The left-hand Maya glyph means "and then it came to pass." The right-hand Maya glyph means "it had come to pass." These glyphs date to the seventh century A.D. (See pages 62-64.)

The stepped fret symbolically represents the stepped temple and tree of life or fountain of living waters from Mitla, Oaxaca, Mexico about 1,000 A.D. (See pages 95-106.)

# The Messiah in Ancient America

Bruce W. Warren
Thomas Stuart Ferguson

Book of Mormon Research Foundation
Provo, Utah

ISBN: 0-936860-49-9

First Printing November 1987
Second Printing January 1988

Printed in the United States of America

The Messiah In Ancient America
# TABLE OF CONTENTS

"We can not but think the Lord has a hand in . . . proving the *Book of Mormon* true in the eyes of all people. . . . Surely 'facts are stubborn things.' It will be as it ever has been, the world will prove Joseph Smith a true prophet by circumstantial evidence, . . ." (Joseph Smith, *Times and Seasons*, Volume 3, p. 921-922, September 15, 1842)

# INTRODUCTION

*"It will not be a bad plan to compare Mr. Stephens' ruined cities with those in the* Book of Mormon: *light cleaves to light, and facts are supported by facts. The truth injures no one. . . ."* (Joseph Smith, *Times and Seasons,* 1 October 1842, 3.927-28)

*"Mr. Stephens' great development of antiquities are made bare to the eyes of all the people by reading the history of the Nephites in the* Book of Mormon. *They lived about the narrow neck of land, which now embraces Central America, with the cities that can be found"* (Joseph Smith, Nauvoo, Ill.: *Times and Seasons,* vol. 3, no. 22, September 15, 1842, p. 915; see page 263 for more information on "Mr. Stephens' ruined cities" in Mesoamerica. The area of Mesoamerica includes central and southern Mexico and northern Central America).

Darrell Stoddard, a former archaeology student at Brigham Young University and ardent student of the *Book of Mormon,* related the following enlightening story:

In about 1970 in Espanola, New Mexico, I met Tony Shearer (a noted author and lecturer of ancient Mesoamerican civilizations). At that point in his life, he was involved in giving Hispanics and Indian people a sense of self-esteem by revealing to them their glorious past, i.e., the high cultures of Mesoamerica from which they came. When he learned I was a Latter-day Saint (he was not), he went into his bedroom and brought out a *Book of Mormon* that he kept on the nightstand by his bed.

He then related a fascinating incident which

occurred while he was at an archaeology site in Mexico with one of Mexico's foremost archaeologists. He explained they had just unearthed a doorway to a Mayan temple. They discovered on the lintel over the doorway a sculpted figure of an old man with a long beard (long beards are not typical of American Indians). The archaeologist then turned to Shearer and exclaimed, "Oh no, what will the Mormons do when they see this?"

Shearer added, "Archaeologists make fun of the *Book of Mormon*, while nearly everything they uncover confirms it. I keep the *Book of Mormon* next to my bed and read it almost daily. I take it with me to Mexico while studying archaeology and history there."

This book describes many new discoveries from a variety of well documented sources which, as Shearer stated, "confirm" the *Book of Mormon*. These new discoveries are startling. The overwhelming evidences known today regarding this volume of ancient scripture are striking. New discoveries by archaeologists and other scholars are occurring at an increasing rate.

Spencer W. Kimball said, "The Lamanite-Nephite culture means much more to the people of the Church, and properly so. Here at BYU, should we not have the greatest collection of artifacts, records, writings, concerning them in the world?" (Faculty Address, September 12, 1967, Brigham Young University).

Joseph Smith said, "It will be seen that the proof of Nephites and Lamanites dwelling on this continent, according to the account in the *Book of Mormon,* is developing itself in a more satisfactory way than the most sanguine [optimistic] believer in that revelation could have anticipated" (Joseph Smith, *Times and Seasons*, Vol. 3, pp. 921-22, September 15, 1842).

The prophet Nephi said, "God sendeth more witnesses, and he proveth all his words. Behold, my soul delighteth in proving unto my people the truth of the coming of Christ" (2 Nephi 11:3-4).

*The Messiah in Ancient America* is another witness that the *Book of Mormon* is the word of God as revealed to the prophet Joseph Smith.

Larry S. Ferguson
Son of Thomas Stuart Ferguson

# FOREWORD

In 1958, Thomas Stuart Ferguson published his book *One Fold and One Shepherd*. In his introduction he outlines the purposes of his book: To shed some light upon the mysterious origins of these once-great and glorious Mesoamerican civilizations. He suggests that part of the answer lies in the migrations recorded in the Book of Mormon.

This book includes substantial new evidences which support and sustain the contents of the Book of Mormon. In preparing this manuscript, Dr. Warren has taken the latest archaeological findings and interspersed them with scriptures from the Bible and the Book of Mormon. He also includes new interpretations of other Mesoamerican documents.

Another fascinating feature is an impressive list of ancient cultural parallels between the Old and New Worlds. These similarities provide the reader with evidences of the origins of some of the ancient civilizations in the Americas before Columbus, one interesting example being the parallelism between the Old and the New World on the subject of ancient temple towers.

The chapter on symbolism sheds additional light on this mysterious and intriguing study. The treatment of the topics of ancient calendars and astronomy will also prove enlightening to the reader.

In regard to Christian studies, it is emphasized that God is not a respecter of persons (Acts 10:34), but is indeed the Lord of the entire earth, who would also visit the New World and establish His teachings here. The authors also address the subject of the great fair god, a familiar personage mentioned in many of the oral legends of the major Indian tribes of the Americas.

The records of the Chroniclers enhance the credibility and importance of the Book of Mormon as an authentic document. The writings of these ancient historians become especially illuminating in reference to the phrase "and it came to pass," used profusely throughout the Book of Mormon.

This material concerning the ancient codices (books) alludes to the birth, death and resurrection of the Savior. Another unique chapter includes quotes from LDS leaders in a blending of scholarly findings with *Book of Mormon* scriptures.

This new publication culminates in a biography of Thomas Stuart Ferguson and an account of how he founded the New World Archaeological Foundation. The appendix also contains a particularly detailed explanation, by V. Garth Norman, of the prophet Zenos' allegory of the Tame Olive Tree (Jacob 5).

With the recent additions by Dr. Bruce W. Warren, this book should reinstate Thomas Stuart Ferguson as a source of enrichment in the fields of study concerning Mesoamerica and the *Book of Mormon.*

*Paul R. Cheesman,*
*Professor Emeritus*
*Brigham Young University*

# PREFACE

One pleasant day in the spring of 1983 I had an unexpected visit from Larry S. Ferguson. Larry is the son of Thomas Stuart Ferguson and Ester Israelsen Ferguson. After introducing himself, Larry explained that his father had begun to revise his book *One Fold and One Shepherd* when he suffered a heart attack and passed away. Since I had worked for the New World Archaeological Foundation founded by his father and was experienced with the materials contained in the book, Larry wanted to know if I would be interested in completing the revision of his father's publication. Feeling deeply indebted to his father for the opportunities he had given me to do archaeological field work in southern Mexico for nine years, I promptly agreed to complete the revision of *One Fold and One Shepherd.*

In the four years since that spring day in 1983 the scope of the book has been modified and extensively updated, so much so that the book is now titled *The Messiah in Ancient America.* The Ferguson family wanted the new book to be a tribute to Thomas Stuart Ferguson and his abiding testimony of the Book of Mormon and the divinity of the Messiah, Jesus the Christ.

Researching the theme of the Messiah in Mesoamerica has all the elements of a good detective story or a complex puzzle with many missing pieces. The information used in the book represents a preliminary and still very fragmented treatment of the theme. A number of problem areas still need to be researched. One of the major unresolved problems concerns the manner in which the first Spanish missionaries to Mesoamerica in the sixteenth century A.D. correlated the teachings of Christianity with the native belief systems of the Aztecs, Mixtecs, Zapotecs, Mayas, and other Indian groups. The Papal edict of 1503 had declared that American Indians were human beings, and thus it became necessary for Europeans to connect them with the Bible. We don't know enough about the Dominican and Franciscan missionary orders to have adequate controls over what the Spanish missionaries were teaching the Indians and what information these same missionaries were receiving from their native informants. Until we have more complete knowledge on these matters they will remain controversial issues.

The careful separation of information relating to the god Quetzalcoatl from the various priests of Quetzalcoatl must be insisted upon in future discussions of this deity.

This book still depends too much on lists of words and technological traits that are removed from the proper language and cultural contexts necessary for final acceptance by the scholarly community. However, time and research funds can correct this type of methological weakness. Meanwhile, I am convinced that the bulk of the evidence used in this book does point to the historical authenticity of the *Book of Mormon.*

There are many variations of the chronological periodization used for Mesoamerica. The scheme used in this book is as follows: Early Preclassic, 2500-1500 B.C.; Middle Preclassic, 1500-500 B.C.; Late Preclassic, 500 B.C.-A.D. 100; Protoclassic, A.D. 100-250; Early Classic, A.D. 250-600; Late Classic, A.D. 600-800; Terminal Classic, A.D. 800-950; Early Postclassic, A.D. 950-1300; Late Postclassic, A.D. 1300-1524; Colonial, A.D. 1524-1810; and Modern, A.D. 1810-present. It should be pointed out that all specific dates used throughout the book are in the Gregorian calendar system, which does not use an "o" year between B.C. dates and A.D. dates, as is the case in the Julian calendar system.

The reader needs to be aware that when archaeologists use the term "Olmec" they apply it to a specific style of remains dating between 1500 and 600 B.C. When these same scholars use the term "Ulmeca-Xicalanca" it refers to peoples who lived in or were from the southern Gulf Coast of Mexico and involves events much later in time than the archaeological "Olmecs."

Several individuals need acknowledgment in the production of this book. Lorna Billat, Ann Ferguson, Paula Ferguson, Suzanne Milne, and Arlene Robinson all helped with the word processing of the text. We appreciate the extensive reorganization and editing that Richard R. Hart so willingly performed. Additional editing services were performed by Lavina Fielding Anderson and Michael Rutter. Charlotte A. Colley made the text press ready. Larry Ferguson, Don E. Norton, V. Garth Norman, Howard Senior and Garr Cranney performed necessary proofreading services. Lee Nelson gave much valuable advice and designed the promotional materials for the book. We wish to thank Steven White and Kirk Magleby for their assistance. We want to thank Stephen Hales for designing the cover and poster for this book. Special thanks must go to Darrell J. Stoddard for his material on the "stepped fret" design and to V. Garth Norman for Appendix B on an allegory of the House of Israel found in Jacob, chapter 5, of the *Book of Mormon*. Finally, the driving force behind the book was Larry Ferguson, with the initial financing for the project coming from his brother, Thomas A. Ferguson.

Bruce W. Warren

## Chapter One
# THE FAIR GOD OF MESOAMERICA

---

*I feel certain that if, in our homes, parents will read from the Book of Mormon prayerfully and regularly, both by themselves and with their children, the spirit of that great book will come to permeate our homes and all who dwell therein. The spirit of reverence will increase; mutual respect and consideration for each other will grow. The spirit of contention will depart. Parents will counsel their children in greater love and wisdom. Children will be more responsive and submissive to that counsel. Righteousness will increase. Faith, hope, and charity — the pure love of Christ — will abound in our homes and lives, bringing in their wake peace, joy, and happiness.*

Marion G. Romney
General Conference, April 1960

Quoted by President Ezra Taft Benson
General Conference, October 1986

(*Ensign*, November 1986, p. 7)
Used by permission

Juan de Cordova, a Spanish friar in Oaxaca, recorded the following account just a few years after the coming of Cortes. As part of a discussion of one of the day signs in the ritual calendar of ancient Mesoamerica, he describes the eighteenth one, a flint blade which is sometimes called the solar beam. This passage has recently been translated into English in Tony Shearer's *Beneath the Moon and Under the Sun,* which introduces it with this commentary:

>Here is one of the strangest glyphs among the twenty. It is, if investigated, one of the best clues for superior beings reaching us from another planet.

>Among the oldest glyphs, this one comes to earth from another planet. The tenochs [a term which refers to the Aztecs] thought it came from the sun. Earlier uses of it suggest that it came from the northern sky, perhaps from the northeastern sky, and could be seen in broad daylight; so the story goes.

>A story was told to the Spaniards shortly after the conquest in Oaxaca. . . . On the day we call Tecpatl [the Aztec name for the day sign flint knife] a great light came from the northeastern sky. It glowed for four days in the sky, then lowered itself to the rock; the rock can still be seen at Tenochtitlan de Valle in Oaxaca. From the light there came a great, very powerful being, who stood on the very top of the rock and glowed like the sun in the sky. There he stood for all to see, shining day and night. Then he spoke, his voice was like thunder, booming across the valley. Our old men and women, the astronomers and astrologists, could understand him and he could understand them. He (the solar beam) told us how to pray and fixed for us days of fast and days of feasting. He then balanced the "Book of Days" (sacred calendar) and left vowing that he would always watch down upon us his beloved people. (71-72)

When Cortes landed on the east coast of Mexico in 1519, the inhabitants of the land thought he was their benevolent, personal God, Quetzalcoatl, who had appeared to their ancestors centuries before Columbus and had promised to return. Like Cortes, Quetzalcoatl had been bearded and white-skinned, and he was associated with the cross.

An American scholar of the last century, Daniel Brinton, states that "Whenever the personal appearance of this hero-God is described, it is, strangely, enough, represented to be that of one of the white race, a man of fair complexion, with long flowing beard, with abundant hair, and clothed in ample and loose robes."

Brinton reports that when messengers from the Gulf of Mexico brought descriptions of the bearded, white-skinned Cortes to Montezuma (or, more correctly, Moctezuma), the emperor said, "This truly is the *Quetzalcoatl* we expected, he who lived with us of old in Tula."

Quetzalcoatl was, in the understanding of Moctezuma, an anthropomorphic God in the image of a bearded white man, whose return had been predicted in ancient Mexico.

Any confusion was only temporary. The ruthless and murderous conduct of the Spanish conquerors convinced the Aztecs that Cortes was not their ancient God and Lord returned. Cortes executed 6,000 Aztecs in Cholula alone.

Bernadino Sahagun, a Spanish priest, wrote: "And when Don Hernando Cortes came [to Mexico] they thought it was He *[Quetzalcoatl]* and they received Cortes as such until his conversation, and that of those Spaniards who came with him, undeceived them" (Sahagun Book 8:21).

Juan de Torquemada, a Catholic priest born about 1564, arrived in Mexico from Spain early in the seventeenth century and describes Quetzalcoatl as a :

> white man, large of body, wide of forehead, large eyes, long and black hair, large and round beard. . . . They held him in great esteem, . . . and in spiritual and ecclesiastical matters this *Quetzalcoatl* was supreme, a great priest. . . . They say about this God, *Quetzalcoatl,* that while living in this mortal life, he dressed in long clothes down to his feet, through modesty, with a cloak on top, scattered with red crosses. He was perfect in moral virtues and they say that He is alive and He is to return. (Fig 1)

The name Quetzalcoatl is derived from two Nahuatl/Aztec language words: *quetzal*, the name of a nearly-extinct beautiful bird with long, undulating green tail feathers (the word also means "precious"), and *coatl,* meaning "serpent" or "twin." Both this bird and the serpent appear as art motifs associated with Quetzalcoatl. Several sixteenth-century documents written by both native and Catholic priest-historians contain word-pictures

Fig. 1: Quetzalcoatl wearing his cloak with red crosses. From Lord
Kingsborough's *Antiquities of Mexico,* Volume 2.

of this figure.

The Fair God of ancient Mexico and Central America was
known by many symbolic names. But in central Mexico the most
common symbolic name for him was *Quetzalcoatl.* Two symbols,
the Quetzal bird and the serpent, identify this ancient deity as the
"Life of the World." In Guatemala this ancient god was
commonly called Gucumatz—a Quiche Maya term identical in
meaning to the Aztec name Quetzalcoatl.

A belief in his divine power as creator and in his second
coming was general throughout the ancient Mesoamerican
(central and southern Mexico and northern Central America)

world. It was clear to the ancients of Mexico and Central America that this Messiah, who had been co-creator of the world, had appeared on earth in the flesh and was to return. In his ante-mortal existence, it was he, and not the Father, who had appeared to Abraham and Jacob and the other prophets and patriarchs of Israel.

In Yucatan the Messiah was known as Itzamna, the Son. Itzamna was invoked by the Mayas in their New Year rituals. It is significant that the ancient New Year ritual of southern Mexico was virtually identical to the ancient New Year ritual of the Israelites. The New Year's festival, widespread throughout Bible lands, is described in detail by Henri Frankfort in *Kingship and the Gods*. The Mesoamerican New Year festival is described by Bishop Landa in his monumental work written in 1566 and published by Professor Tozzer at Harvard University in 1941. (See his book *Relaciones de las Cosas de Yucatan* 133 ff.) In both regions, the ceremony was a festive celebration of a new beginning in the annual cycle. In both regions, the renewal of life for the current year was involved. Jewish, Babylonian, and Maya traditions also connected the New Year festival with the creation of the world. There was an appeal to God for a new period of agricultural fruitfulness. It was a time of atonement and purification in the Old World, and Landa tells us it was a time of fasting, abstinence, and atonement to the Mayas (152). A part of the festival in both Bible lands and Mesoamerica was a victory banquet. The Jewish Talmud (63) states that "destinies" are determined at the beginning of the New Year. "The books are opened" at the New Year. The destiny of society for the ensuing year was determined at the festival in Israel and Mesoamerica. Landa tells us the gods were asked by the Mayas to supply remedies for any calamities which they feared might come during the year, and the priest would give predictions for the year.

The worship of the Messiah of ancient Mexico and Guatemala was in harmony with worship of God in ancient Israel. According to the Christian scriptures, God the Father has remained somewhat aloof from the world and has left direct and

close contact with inhabitants of the world to the Son and
Messiah.

Hubert H. Bancroft, the prolific nineteenth-century
historian of western America and Mexico, admits that
Quetzalcoatl taught Christian virtues. In his five-volume work
*Native Races,* he summarizes the teaching of Quetzalcoatl. He
exhorted the people "to practice brotherly love and other
Christian virtues, introducing a milder and better form of
religion" (5, 23-24).

Much research will be required to clarify the development of
Quetzalcoatl as a deity, particularly in sorting out the priests who
took his name at various time periods. The earliest illustrations of
Nine Wind Quetzalcoatl as an ancestral culture hero show his
birth and subsequent ritual activities in the third millennium B.C.
(Figures 2, 3, and 4). A sixth century B.C. Olmec monument at

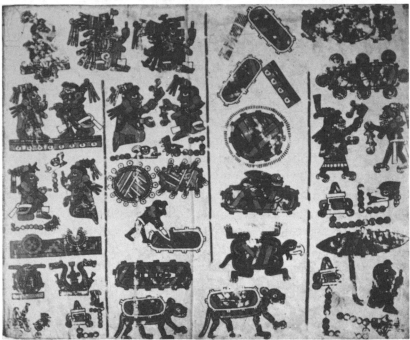

**Fig. 2: Birth of Nine Wind Quetzalcoatl, the Cultural Hero, from page 49, lower right
corner, of Codex Vienna in 2896 B.C. This Mixtec codex or screenfold book was painted
about 1350 A.D.**

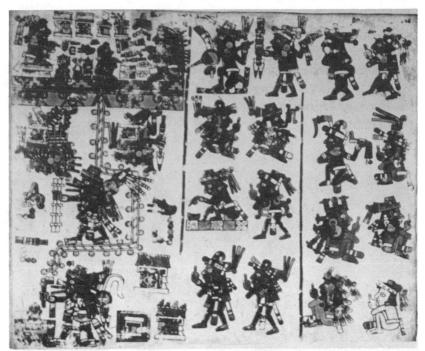

Fig. 3: The culture Hero, Nine Wind Quetzalcoatl, receiving his divine insignias in 2887 B.C. (Codex Vienna page 48). Nine Wind is shown three times in the left-hand column.

La Venta, Tabasco, Mexico shows the graphic symbolism of the "feathered serpent" (Figure 5). Around 500 B.C. shell earplug pendants from burial 74 at Chiapa de Corzo (Figure 6) depict the "feathered serpent." Also in Chiapa de Corzo in tomb 1, dating to the time of Christ, was found carved bone 3 with the symbolism of the "feathered serpent" (Figure 7). The Codex Nuttall on page 4 depicts a death and resurrection scene in A.D. 30 connected with a Quetzalcoatl calendar date. Two Codex Vienna scenes deal with a fourth century A.D. priest of Quetzalcoatl (Figures 8 & 9). The famous Toltec priest-king from Tula, Hidalgo, fled eastward to Yucatan, where he is shown at Chichen Itza (Figures 10 & 11) as Kukulcan (Maya name for Quetzalcoatl) in the tenth century A.D. The Toltecs, in the tenth century A.D. and later, show a shift toward idolatry, with Quetzalcoatl appearing first in a mask (Figure 12). Some of the

Aztecs, in the thirteenth century A.D. and later, painted him in their codices as a monster (Figure 13).

Also, the Christian background of the Spaniards could have influenced their interpretation of the Indian legends. Diane E. Wirth's book, *A Challenge to the Critics: Scholarly Evidences of the Book of Mormon,* has a fine discussion of Quetzalcoatl in the 14th chapter.

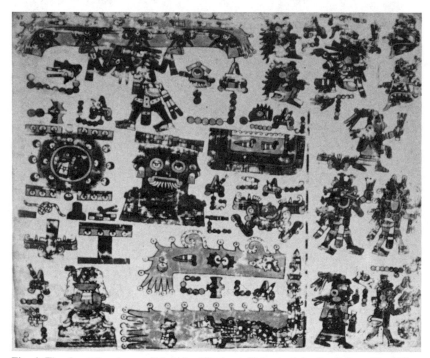

**Fig. 4: The sky and water symbols being lifted up off the earth by the Culture Hero Nine Wind Quetzalcoatl in 2844 B.C. shown in the upper left-hand corner (Codex Vienna page 47).**

Fig. 5: Large feathered serpent with priest and bucket carved on Monument 19 at the Olmec site of La Venta, Tabasco, Mexico (sixth century B.C.). (Photo by Daniel Bates. Courtesy David A. Palmer and the Society for Early Historic Archaeology.)

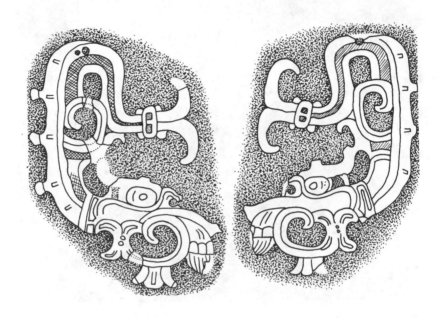

**Fig. 6: Shell earplug pendants in the shape of the feathered serpent from Burial 74 at Chiapa de Corzo, Chiapas, Mexico (fifth century B.C.).**

**Fig. 7a: Drawing of Bone 3 from Tomb 1 at Chiapa de Corzo (first century B.C.).**

**Fig. 7b: Feature F on Bone 3, emphasizing the feathered serpent.**

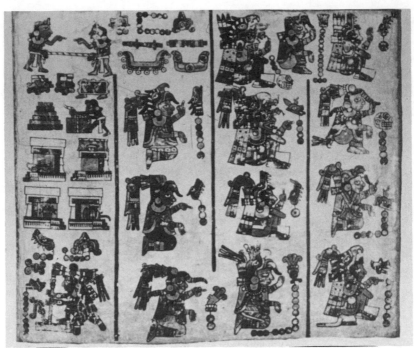

Fig. 8: Fourth century A.D. priest/scribe of Quetzalcoatl (Huematzin?), lower left corner, performing a "fire-drilling" ritual (Codex Vienna page 32).

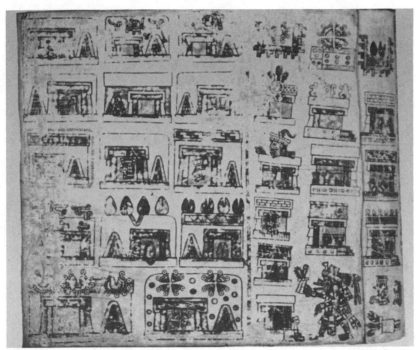

Fig. 9: Quetzalcoatl (Huematzin?) associated with the "sweat houses" of several communities in southern Mexico in the fourth century A.D. shown in lower right corner (Codex Vienna page 31).

**Fig. 10a: Ce Acatl (1 Reed) Quetzalcoatl from a stone box of the Toltec horizon (A.D. 1000).**

**Fig. 10b: Ce Acatl Quetzalcoatl from a rock-carving near Tula, Hidalgo, Mexico (the Early Postclassic capital of the Toltecs).**

**Figure 11:  The bearded Ce Acatl Quetzalcoatl or Kukulcan from the doorway of the El Castillo temple at Chichen Itza, Yucatan, Mexico (tenth century A.D.)**

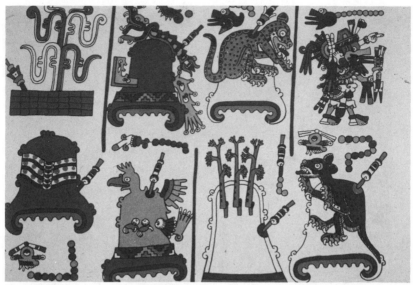

**Figure 12: The upper right hand figure from page 46 of the Mixtec Codex Nuttall, depicting the god Quetzalcoatl with the "wind mask" in the eleventh century A.D. The Codex Nuttall was painted about 1350 A.D.**

## Baptism

Bishop Diego de Landa, who arrived in Yucatan on the heels of Cortes and before the smoke of battle had cleared away, was surprised to learn that baptism had been practiced, as a "rebirth," for many centuries prior to the time of Columbus. Baptisms were performed in the name of the Messiah or Fair God.

Frans Blom, a pioneer Mesoamerican archaeologist, explorer, map-maker, and author, and his wife operated a museum and retreat for scholars in the picturesque town of San Cristobal de las Casas on the Pan-American Highway in southernmost Mexico. In his book *The Conquest of Yucatan,* Blom says that the ancient Mayan baptismal rite "was in some ways more elaborate than Christian baptism, but contained the same fundamental ideas" (79).

Dr. M. Wells Jakeman translated the writings of the learned Antonio Chi, of sixteenth-century Yucatan. Chi wrote that his pre-conquest Mayan ancestors:

Fig. 13: The god Quetzalcoatl back-to-back with the Death god. This scene is from the Codex Borgia from Cholula, Puebla, Mexico. The Codex Borgia was painted in Prehistoric times (Late Postclassic) and is now located in the Vatican library.

baptized in this manner; the chief priest of the idols took water and he threw certain flowers, and he said some words over it, and moistened a stick and brought it with him to the forehead and eyes and over the face of [the child], saying three times, "ah, ah, ah," which appears to signify and mean "revive" or "recover." And they could not marry or be priests unless they were baptized, and if any died without baptism, they held that he had to have more punishments in hell than the baptized. (103)

The use of the terms "revive" and "recover" in the ceremony, as set out by Antonio Chi, is further corroboration of the point that the baptismal rite of the Maya symbolized being "born again," "a new birth," or a regeneration, exactly as was the case with the Old World rite.

From Mexico's central mesa comes an entirely independent account concerning baptism. Whereas the accounts of Diego de Landa and Antonio Chi come from Yucatan, Padre Sahagun wrote in central Mexico. Sahagun states that the following words were in the baptismal ceremony after the child was washed with water: "Evil, wheresoever thou art, be gone, depart—for the child *lives anew* and is *born again*—once more it is purified" (6.202).

In the Cholula-Puebla region of Mexico the Tlaxcalans baptized infants by immersing and bathing them in a sacred spring. Among the Zapotec at Mexico's narrow neck of land, Tehuantepec, both the mother and the child were washed in a stream.

That knowledge of baptism—a special symbol of the cleansing, rebirth, and regeneration of the individual—was widespread in Mesoamerica. Tomas Lopez Medel, in a document written in 1612 concerning Mesoamerica, also mentions the ancient baptismal rite:

> There was also practiced and used among the Yucatecan Indians a certain kind of baptism which although it was not obligatory nor general among all, was held in repute. . . . And when they had already attained to six or seven years, the time when they were to be baptized was discussed with the priest, and the day . . . appointed. By this and other similar ceremonies which had been observed in the Yucatecan Indians and in others, some of our Spaniards have taken occasion to persuade themselves and believe that in times past some of the apostles or a successor to them passed over to the West Indies and that ultimately those Indians were preached to. (226)

It would have been difficult for the Spaniards to conclude that Christ had appeared in Mesoamerica following the crucifixion. That would not have been tolerated in the days of the Inquisition. So they granted that power to one of his apostles.

In both the Old and New Worlds the rite symbolized being

born again or spiritual rebirth. The Maya term for the ceremony, *caput sihil,* means "to be born anew." The meaning of this Maya term is confirmed from the central-mesa account of Sahagun (see notes). This "rebirth" in water was one of two requisites to the attainment of "glory" of the kingdom of God in Mesoamerica. Bishop Landa said that by baptism and by "a well ordered life" the Mayas hoped to attain the kingdom.

## Teachings of the Messiah

The Padre Torquemada, who arrived in Mexico from Spain about the middle of the sixteenth century, wrote of Mexico's Messiah:

> He was perfect in *moral virtues* and they say that He is alive and that He is to return.
>
> He never wanted nor permitted sacrifices of blood of dead men, nor of animals, but only of bread and roses and flowers and perfumes and other smells. He very efficiently prohibited and forbade wars, robberies, and deaths and other harm they inflicted on each other. They say that whenever they mentioned deaths or wars or other evils in front of Him, He would turn his head and stop His ears in order not to see or hear them. Also, in Him is praised the fact that He was very chaste and very honest, and very moderate in many other things.
>
> This God was held in such reverence and devotion, and so revered with vows and pilgrimages in all these kingdoms, on account of His prerogatives, that even the very enemies of the City of Cholula would promise to come in pilgrimage to fulfill their covenants and devotions, and they came secure [in safety], and the lords of the other provinces or cities had their chapels, oratories, and their idols and images, and only this one, among all the Gods, was called in that city "Lord par excellence"; so that when they took an oath or said, "By our Lord," it was understood they referred to Quetzalcoatl, and not to any other god, although there were many others who were very esteemed gods. All of this

was because of the great love they had for Him and
continued to have for Him for the reasons mentioned. Also,
it is true that the lordship of Quetzalcoatl was gentle, and he
asked of them in service but light things as distinguished
from painful things, and He taught them those things which
were virtuous, prohibiting them those things which were
evil, noxious and harmful, teaching them also to hate evil
things. . . . For this reason it seems that the Indians who
made and make human sacrifices were not following the will
[of Quetzalcoatl]. . . . And among other doctrines He gave
them, was to tell them that the inhabitants of the city of
Cholula were to hold as certain that in future times there
were to come by sea, from whence the sun rises, some white
men, with beards like His, and that they were His brothers.
Thus, these Indians always expected that prophecy to be
fulfilled, and when they saw the Christians, they
immediately called them "son of Gods" and "brothers of
Quetzalcoatl," although after knowing them [the Spaniards]
and experiencing their deeds, they did not hold them as
heavenly, because the slaughter the Spaniards perpetrated in
that city [Cholula] was outstanding [no other like it up to
that time in the Indies nor, perhaps, in other parts of the
world].

   This [Quetzalcoatl] was the God of the Wind, and His
temple was round and very sumptuous. . . . The Indians
applied the name to Quetzalcoatl, on account of His
gentleness and tenderness toward everybody, not wanting
the harsh and disagreeable things that others esteemed and
prized. . . . These said Tultecs were good men and friends of
virtue. They did not tell lies, and their way of speaking and
greeting each other was "Sir" and "Sir, brother" . . . and
"Sir, older brother" and "Sir, younger brother." Their speech,
instead of swearing, was "It is true," "thus it is," "it is
ascertained," and "yes" for yea, and "no" for nay (II. 50-51).


   Don Fernando de Alva Ixtlilxochitl was a prince of the royal
dynasty of Texcoco. That city and kingdom was located in the
eastern part of the Valley of Mexico, not far from the Aztec
capital, Tenochtitlan, modern Mexico City.

Ixtlilxochitl was educated in a Spanish school. Between A.D. 1600 and 1625 he wrote in the Spanish language a 945-page history of his ancestors called *Obras Historicas,* compiled from the royal archives of Texcoco (Warren 1986:1).

And finally, with respect to the teachings of the New World Messiah, the learned Ixtlilxochitl (pronounced Eesh-tleel-sho-cheetl) wrote:

> And when they were in the height of their power [in the fourth century A.D.], there arrived in this land a man whom they called Quetzalcoatl and others Huemac on account of his great virtues, considering him as just, saintly [holy], and good, teaching them by deeds and words the path of virtue and forbidding them their vices and sins, giving laws and good doctrine. And in order to refrain them from their pleasures and dishonesties, he instituted [established] fasting for them and [He was] the first who worshipped and placed the cross which they called *Quiahuiteotlchicahualizteotl* and others *Tonacaquahuitl,* which means: God of rains and of health and tree of sustenance or of life. (Hunter and Ferguson 203)

Quetzalcoatl, the Messiah of Mexico, is identified with the Tree of Life.

> They cast their eyes up again towards heaven; and behold, they saw a Man descending out of heaven; and he was clothed in a white robe; and he came down and stood in the midst of them; . . . And it came to pass that he stretched forth his hand and spake unto the people, saying: Behold, I am Jesus Christ, whom the prophets testified shall come into the world." (3 Ne. 11:8-10)

# NOTES TO CHAPTER ONE

### Name of God

Goetz and Morley add the following observation:

> The great civilizer was worshipped as a divinity by the ancient
> Mexicans, who gave him different names. They called him
> *Ehecatl,* or God of the Wind; *Yolcuat,* or the Rattle Snake;
> *Quetzalcoatl,* or Serpent Covered with Green Feathers. The last
> meaning corresponds also to the Maya name *Kukulcan,* and to the
> Quiche, *Gucumatz.*

Still another Guatemalan name for this god was Nacxit
Quetzalcoatl, mentioned several times in the Cronica Mexicana of
Alvarado Tezozomoc as the Founder of the throne on which the Aztec
emperors sat during their coronation ceremonies.

### 1. Names of the Messiah

About fifty of the Israelite-Jewish names of the Messiah were
applied to the New-World Messiah. In Mesoamerica, as in the Near
East, He was the God of the Sky and Earth, God of Abraham and
Jacob, Great Lord, Yohualli, Sovereign Lord, Father of Life, God of
Rains, Lord of the Green Earth, Creator, Son of God, the Wonderful
King. The virgin-born and crucified Man-God, Itzamna-Quetzalcoatl,
was symbolized by the cross, the serpent, the quetzal bird, the Tree of
Life, fire, the hand, the shepherd's staff, Venus—the Morning Star—
and other appropriate reminders of the Creator Life-God. These
symbols precede the earthly ministry of Jesus by many centuries, going
back to "the beginning."

In the following list, the Old World names are all from the Old and
New Testaments. The New World names are taken from the earliest
and most reliable sixteenth-century Mesoamerica documentary sources.
The letter in parentheses following each New World name for the
Messiah is the key to the source in each instance. The following
designations are used:

(H) Francisco Hernandez  (P) Popol Vuh
(I) Ixtlilxochitl  (S) Sahagun
(M) Maya Chronicles  (T) Totonicapan
(C) Juan de Cordoba

The names are grouped into obvious classifications.

| Old World Names from the Bible | New World Names from Mesoamerican Sources |
| --- | --- |
| Almighty | Conqueror (P) |
| Author of Eternal Salvation | Author of that which surrounds the heavens and the earth (T) |
| Creator | Creator and Maker (P) |
| Counselor | Wiseman (P) (I) |
| Everlasting Father | Grandfather (P) (I) |
| Father | Father (T) |
| Father of Heaven and Earth | Great Father (H) |
| Lord God of thy Fathers | God of the Sky and Earth (P) |
| | Heart of the Sky and Earth (P) |
| | Spirit of Heaven (P) |
| | Heart of Heaven (P) |
| God | God (I) (P) |
| Great Lord | Great Lord (P) |
| Great Spirit | Great God (T) |
| Heavenly Father | Spirit of Heaven (P) |
| Judge (Righteous Judge) (Eternal Judge) | The Only Judge (P) |
| King of Kings | Sovereign Lord (T) (P) |
| King of all the Earth | King (M) |
| King of Heaven | Monarch (M) |
| | Majesty (P) |
| Lamb of God | Tapir of the Dawn (P) |
| Light and Life of World | Light of the Sons (P) |
| | Splendor of the Lightning (P) |
| | Lord of the Eye of the Sun (M) |
| | Sun — Lord of the Day (M) |
| | Father of Life (P) |
| Lord | Lord (T) (M) |
| Lord God | Lord God (P) |
| Lord of Heaven and Earth | Lord of Heaven and Earth (I) |

| Old World Names from the Bible | New World Names from Mesoamerican Sources |
|---|---|
| Lord of the Vineyard | God of Maize (P) |
| Lord of the Harvest | Planting God (P) |
| Lord God of Hosts | God of Rains (I) (P) (M) |
| God of the Hills | Lord of the Green Earth (P) |
| Maker | Maker (P) |
|  | Former (P) |
|  | Builder (P) |
| Master | Giant Master (P) |
| Master of the Vineyard | Master of All Things (I) |
|  | Master Magician (P) |
|  | God of Rain (P) |
| Son of God | Son of God (H) |
| Son of Elohim | Son of Hunab Ku (M) |
| Supreme Creator God | Supreme Creator God (M) |
| The Only Lord God | The Only God (P) |
| The Word | The Word (P) |
| Wonderful | Wonderful King (P) |
| True and Living God | True and Living God (C) 41 |

## 2.    Attributes

The Messiah in Mesoamerica controlled certain fields of human experience and possessed certain powers in the natural world. The same powers were possessed by the Messiah of the Bible. The following list is one of attributes or powers common to the Messiah of both the Bible and Mesoamerica which suggest that he was one and the same divine Lord and God of all mankind.

**Attributes of the Messiah Common to Both the Old World and the New World:**

Creator and Lord of Nature
Lord of Heaven and Earth
Lord of Life
King, Prince, Monarch
Great High Priest

> God of the Sky
> Great Judge of Mankind
> Lord of the Winds
> Lord of Wisdom
> God of Health
> God of Rain and Agriculture
> God of Fertility
> Lord of the Resurrection
> Lord of Light

3. **Symbols**

The same symbols for the Messiah in Mesoamerica are also found in the Near East. They are symbols of the ancient Lord of Mexico and Guatemala, as well as for the ancient Israelites and early Christians:

**Symbols of the Messiah common to both the Old World and the New World**

| **Old World Symbols** | **New World Symbols** |
| --- | --- |
| Sun (symbol of light) | Sun (symbol of light) |
| Cross (symbol of the crucifixion and of the Messiah of Life) | Cross (symbol of the crucified God of Life — Quetzalcoatl) |
| Brazen Serpent (symbol of the river, of the sky, and water — source of life — and of Israel's Messiah) | Feathered Serpent (symbol of the river, of the sky, and water — source of life) |
| Tree of Life (symbol of the word of God — the way to happiness, law, order, and peace; opposite of death and evil) | Tree of Life (symbol of the word of God — the way to happiness, law, order, and peace; opposite of death and evil) |
| Bird (as in winged disk — symbol of the highest God — the Messiah — God of life) | Quetzal bird (and its long serpent-like tail feathers, symbol of the highest God — the Messiah — God of life) |

| Old World Symbols | New World Symbols |
|---|---|
| Fire (symbol of the mysterious power of God) | Fire (symbol of the mysterious power of God) |
| Hand (symbol of the powerful hand of God) | Hand (symbol of Itzamna — "he of the powerful hand") |
| Lion (symbol of the mysterious vitalism or life-force of God) | Jaguar (symbol of the mysterious vitalism or life-force of God) |
| Calf (or bull) (symbol of the mysterious vitalism or life-force of God) | Tapir (symbol of the mysterious vitalism or life-force of God) |
| Tall Staff (symbol of the divine royalty, majesty, power, and priesthood of God) | Tall Staff (symbol of the divine royalty, majesty, power, and priesthood of God) |
| Morning Star (symbol of the Messiah as the light of the world) | Morning Star (symbol of the Messiah as the light of the world) |
| All-Seeing Eye (symbol of the all-knowing Lord and God) | Divine Eye (symbol of the all-knowing Lord and God) |

### 4.   Baptism

Sahagun gives a full account of the baptismal ceremony as it was conducted by the late Toltec-Aztec people of conquest days in the central-mesa region of Mexico as follows:

> Concerning the baptism of the child, and all the ceremonies that were made of it, and of naming the child and the feast of the children, etc.

> At the time of baptizing the child they prepared the necessary things for the baptism. They made a little shield, a small bow and four small arrows, one arrow pointing to the east, one to the west, one to the south and the other to the north. . . .

> They also made food of *molli,* a dish with beans and toasted corn.

> And after having prepared everything that was necessary for the baptism, then all the relatives of the child, both old men and old women, would get together. Then they would call the

midwife, who was the one who would baptize the child that she helped to deliver. All would get together very early, before the sun was up, and when the sun was up, when it was somewhat high, the midwife called for a new pottery tub, filled with water. Then she would take the child in both hands and those who were present would take all the things that were ready for the baptism and place them in the middle of the patio of the house. To baptize the child the midwife would face the east and then she would begin to perform the ceremony by saying: "Oh eagle! Oh tiger! Oh brave, brave man — my grandchild — you have arrived in this world. Your father and mother, the great lord and the great lady have sent you. You were reared and engendered in your house, which is the place of the supreme Gods of the great Lord and the great Lady that are above the nine heavens; *Quetzalcoatl*, who art every-where, have mercy on our son."

After saying this she would then give him a taste of water, placing her wet fingers in its mouth, saying: "Take this [baptismal water], for upon it thou hast to live, to wax strong, and flourish — by it we obtain all necessary things — receive it." Then touching the child on the breast with her moistened fingers, she says: "Take the celestial water, try here the very pure water that washes and cleanses your heart — that takes away all uncleanliness — receive it. May it purify and cleanse your heart."

After this, she would put water on its head and say: "Oh my son, my grandchild receive and take the water of the Lord of the world, which is our life — it is to help our body to grow vigorous — it is to wash, to cleanse. I pray that this celestial light-blue water enter into your body and remain there. I beg that it destroy and deliver you from all evil and any adverse thing that was given you before the beginning of the world, because all of us are left in its care, because it is our mother *Chalchiuhtlicue* [Our Lady of the Turquoise Sky]."

After this, she would wash the entire body of the child and would say: "Evil, wheresoever thou art, be gone, depart — for the child *lives anew and is born again* — once more it is purified — again our mother *Chalchiuhtlicue* forms it and engenders it again."

Then lifting up the little one toward Heaven, she would say: "Behold, Oh Lord, your child, that you have sent to this place of sorrow, affliction and anguish which is this world. Give it, lord, your gifts and your inspirations, for thou art the great God, and also with thee [is] the great goddess." (Sahagun Book 6, Chapters 32, 37)

Chapter Two

# THE TIME OF THE MESSIAH'S APPEARANCE

*It is clear that 3 Nephi contains some of the most
moving and powerful passages in all scripture. It testifies of
Jesus Christ, His prophets, and the doctrines of salvation.
At this Easter time, what a blessing it would be if every
family would read together 3 Nephi, discuss its sacred
contents, and then determine how they can liken it unto
themselves and apply its teachings in their lives.*

*Third Nephi is a book that should be read and read
again. Its testimony of the resurrected Christ in America is
given in purity and beauty.*

President Ezra Taft Benson
General Conference, April 1987

(*Ensign*, May 1987, p. 6)
Used by permission

The appearance of the Messiah in Mesoamerica as recorded
in the Book of Mormon occurred soon after the crucifixion and
ascension of Jesus of Nazareth in the Old World. This date is
confirmed by one of the foremost experts on ancient Mexican
history, Don Carlos de Siguenza y Gongora (1645-1700).

On the basis of his life-long study of ancient Mexican
historical sources, Siguenza felt Quetzalcoatl appeared in Mexico
shortly after the crucifixion. In "coded" or disguised language he
tells us that Quetzalcoatl was the resurrected Messiah of the
Bible.

Siguenza believed that the "Olmecs" (people of the rubber-land of southern Veracruz and western Tabasco who were part of the Jaredite civilization) had come to Mexico from the Near East. He did not contend that all of the ancestry of the "Indians" came from the Near East, however. His book dealt with Mesoamerica.

Siguenza suspected that his lifetime work—his *Phoenix of the West*—would be suppressed. It was. It mysteriously disappeared at the time of his death and has never been found. This was the book which its author, the great Siguenza, believed would throw further light on the work of God. Siguenza's biographer, Irving Albert Leonard, reports as follows concerning Siguenza's attitude toward the book and his fears concerning it:

> It was his happy belief that in his Phoenix of the West he was throwing further light on the work of God. Thus, it was that he devoted the full measure of his intellectual resources to so noble a task. And this gratifying conviction moved him to be especially concerned regarding the ultimate fate of his work. Remarking somewhat dolefully that many of his works would probably die with him, Don Carlos exclaims: "May God our Lord grant that this may not be true of what I have ascertained about the preaching of the Apostle Saint Thomas in this land. . . ." But his devout prayer, seemingly, remained unanswered, for investigators, from shortly after the death of Siguenza up to the present, have sought diligently but vainly for it. (Leonard 98)

The very title of the book—*Phoenix of the West*—suggests that Siguenza believed that the resurrected Jesus of Nazareth was the Fair God of the Western Hemisphere.

*Phoenix* is a term from Egyptian mythology. It was a beautiful, lone bird which lived in the Arabian desert for 500 or 600 years and then consumed itself in fire, rising resurrected from the ashes to start another long life. It is used as a symbol of immortality. It was a subtle pseudonym for the resurrected Messiah of ancient Mexico and Central America.

Siguenza pretended to give the Apostle Saint Thomas credit for establishing Christianity in Mesoamerica "in the days of the apostles." But Jesus was referring to himself when he said, "and other sheep I have, which are not of this fold: them also I must bring, and they shall hear my voice: and there shall be one fold and one shepherd" (John 10:16). It was Jesus the Christ who was resurrected to immortality in the days of the apostles. It was he who appeared in Mesoamerica as a resurrected being.

Siguenza believed that *Phoenix of the West* would throw further light on the work of God. He must have known Quetzalcoatl was the true Shepherd. He apparently could not declare it openly, so he disguised his beliefs within the symbol of the phoenix. Siguenza obtained most of his data from the royal Ixtlilxochitl family of the Valley of Mexico. Ixtlilxochitl, it is recalled, reported darkness, earthquakes, and a breaking of rocks in Mexico at the very time of the crucifixion of Jesus in the Old World.

Ixtlilxochitl dates the appearance of the Messiah in Mexico in a more general way:

> He [Quetzalcoatl] having preached the said things in the majority of the cities of the Ulmecas and Xicalancas and in particular in that Cholula, where he most visited, and seeing the little fruit brought about by his doctrine, he returned through the same part from whence he had come, which was by the Orient disappearing through Coatzalcoalco. (Hunter and Ferguson 218)

Thus, when Ixtlilxochitl states that the Messiah visited Cholula of the "Ulmecas," he is dating the ministry of the Fair God to an early era many centuries before Aztec times. A whole series of communities were flourishing in Mesoamerica in the days of Jesus, and stone cities remain to prove it.

As previously mentioned, archaeologists working in Mesoamerica generally refer to the "Olmec" era as being included in the Preclassic period (2500 B.C.-250 A.D.). The "Olmec" era reached backward many centuries before 600 B.C.

John L. Sorenson, in a paper entitled "A Chronological Ordering of the Mesoamerican Pre-Classic," published in 1955 by the Middle American Research Institute at Tulane University, New Orleans, dates to about A.D. 50 the cultural remains known as Santa Clara (Guatemala), Chicanel (Guatemala), and Monte Alban II (Oaxaca, Mexico), observing:

> What now appears to be one of the most unprecedented religious events in Mesoamerica's long history can be detected in the late pre-Classic [time of Christ] in connection with indications of sharp, sudden change and other aspects of culture. The modification is evidenced most clearly by the widespread abandonment of the time-honored figurine cult. This drastic step occurred simultaneously over a wide area according to our studies. . . . This innovation can be seen to originate abruptly as Borhegyi has already tentatively pointed out, the figurine hiatus [a gap or break] corresponds in time to the abandonment of the long-traditional incense-burner forms of highland Guatemala (three pronged burners, scored covers and rim-head vessels), and presumably, the particular rituals associate those forms. . . . These suggestions of severity, austerity, or elegance in esthetics of the period might well be interpreted as appropriate indications of the puritanical religious spirit [of early and undefiled Christianity] which alone could account for the giving up of an old, established folk feature like figurines. (60)

Thus, shortly following the crucifixion of Jesus in the Old World, there occurred in Mesoamerica an abandonment of incense burning and idolatry—exactly as ordered by Jesus of Nazareth. Jesus said, in the Old World, with respect to the Israelite practices of incense burning and burnt offerings: "Think not that I am come to destroy the law, or the prophets: I am not come to destroy, but to fulfill" (Matt. 5:17).

The abandonment of figurine cult practices and the burning of incense, and their replacement with "indications of the puritanical religious spirit which alone could account for the giving up of an old established folk feature like figurines," took place simultaneously with the New-World appearance and ministry of the Messiah. Says Sorenson, "Santa Clara, Chicanel, Monte Alban II, Early Ticoman and contemporaries we place about A.D. 50" (60). This is rather close to 30 A.D., the date given by the original eyewitness record — soon to be introduced to the reader — for the New World appearance of the Light and Life of the World.

Further help on dating the appearance of the Messiah in Mexico comes from the Mexican scholar Jose Diaz-Bolio. In his book *La Serpiente Emplumada (The Feathered Serpent),* he states that the original Quetzalcoatl appeared in Olmec times (71). And he rightly says that the "cult" can be traced back entirely through the Old-Empire Maya period and to Olmec times (155). As has already been indicated, the serpent symbol of the Messiah accompanied to Mesoamerica the Israelite colonizers of the sixth century B.C. to Mesoamerica. The symbol dates to the time of Moses and Abraham and far beyond to the dawn of religion in the fourth millennium B.C. Diaz-Bolio also states that the time of Quetzalcoatl coincides with the end of the third age of the world of Mexican cosmogony (131), which is placed at the very time of the crucifixion of Christ, according to Ixtlixochitl. One of Diaz Bolio's primary themes is that we must distinguish the original Quetzalcoatl from the tenth-century Mexican hero who also bore the symbolic name "Quetzalcoatl." This tenth-century person, Topiltzin Quetzalcoatl, was a king and descendant of earlier Toltecs. He adopted the symbolic "bird-serpent" name of the Messiah as his own — just as many Mexicans today bear the name Jesus. But Topiltzin Quetzalcoatl followed the original Quetzalcoatl by almost 1000 years. The matter has been clarified to the point where very few now confuse the two personages.

Le comte H. de Charencey, in his book *Les Cites Votanides,* expresses his view that the first Quetzalcoatl appeared in southern Mexico to the serpent-men in A.D. 68 (57). If Jesus appeared in Mexico shortly after the crucifixion, Charencey is off in his dating by only 38 years.

Ixtlilxochitl and Siguenza date the appearance of the Messiah to the days of the apostles and the time of the crucifixion. He appeared in the days of the Zapotecs—whose culture dates to the time of Christ by carbon-14 determinations. The appearance of the Messiah in Mesoamerica was accompanied by an abrupt termination of idolatry—which reflects itself in archaeological sites by the absence of figurines shortly following the time of Christ.

## The Sixth Hour

Jesus was nailed to the cross at the third hour of the Jewish day. He died six hours later—at the ninth hour. At the sixth hour, three hours before his death, darkness fell over the land and continued during the three hours immediately preceding His death. Earthquakes occurred and rocks were rent. These details are highly important, because identical phenomena were experienced in southern Mexico.

Concerning these phenomena, the early Christian writers of the Old World stated:

> And it was the third hour, and they crucified him. And when the sixth hour was come, there was darkness over the whole land until the ninth hour. And at the ninth hour Jesus cried with a loud voice, Eloi, Eloi, lama sabachthani? which is, being interpreted, My God, my God, why hast thou forsaken me?
>
> And Jesus cried with a loud voice, and gave up the ghost. And the veil of the temple was rent in twain from the top to the bottom.
>
> And when the centurion, which stood over against him, saw that he so cried out, and gave up the ghost, he said, Truly this man was the Son of God. (Mark 15:25, 33-34, 37-39)
>
> Now from the sixth hour there was darkness over all the land unto the ninth hour.
>
> And about the ninth hour Jesus cried with a loud voice, saying, Eli, Eli, lama sabachtani? that is to say, My God, my God, why hast thou forsaken me?
>
> Jesus, when he had cried again with a loud voice,

yielded up the ghost.

And, behold, the veil of the temple was rent in twain from the top to the bottom: and the earth did quake, and the rocks rent. (Matt. 27:45-46, 50-51)

And it was about the sixth hour, and there was a darkness over all the earth until the ninth hour.

And the sun was darkened, and the veil of the temple was rent in the midst.

And when Jesus had cried with a loud voice, he said, Father, into thy hands I commend my spirit: and having said thus, he gave up the ghost.

Now when the centurion saw what was done, he glorified God, saying, Certainly this was a righteous man. (Luke 23:44-47)

Ixtlilxochitl, Mexico's sixteenth-century historian, working from records which preceded the coming of the Spaniards, describes and dates to the time of the crucifixion events as they occurred in southern Mexico. The darkness and the quaking and the rending of rocks at the very time of the crucifixion are described:

It was 166 years since they had adjusted their years and times with the equinox, and 270 since the ancient ones had been destroyed, when the sun and the moon eclipsed, and the earth trembled, and the rocks broke, and many other things and signs took place, although there was no calamity whatever toward men. This happened in the year of ce Calli, which, adjusting this count with ours, comes to be at the same time when Christ our Lord suffered, and they say it happened during the first days of the year. These and many other things the Tultecs comprehended, from the creation of the world up to our times. As I have said, in order to avoid prolixity all things they knew are not set out according as they appear in their histories and pictures, especially the original, I mean all the things which can be found in pictures and history, for everything is abridgment (contraction) in comparison with the histories that the first archbishop of Mexico ordered burned. (Hunter and Ferguson 190)

It is observed that Ixtlilxochitl was careful to state that this data came from the ancient histories of Mexico, and that, had not the archbishop destroyed many of the histories, more details would be available. He was not robbing the Christian scriptures brought to Mexico by the Spaniards, but accusing the Spaniards of robbing the Mexicans of their ancient records. Furthermore, the writings of Ixtlilxochitl, the elders of Totonicapan and the native reports recorded by the Spanish padres contain so many elements completely unique and foreign to the Spaniards as to leave little room for the argument that the native writers were "borrowing" from the scriptures brought by the Spaniards at the time of the conquest.

Is not the foregoing quotation from Ixtlilxochitl striking? Does it not suggest a special relationship between Jesus and ancient Mexico? Why else would Mexico experience the same astronomical and geological events visited upon Old-World Israel at the hour of the crucifixion?

Crucifixion was a method of capital punishment in ancient Mexico, as it was in ancient Palestine. The "refinement" of leg breaking as part of crucifixion procedure was practiced in both lands. Viscount Kingsborough, in Volume 8 of his monumental nine-volume work *Antiquities of Mexico,* states:

> The Mexicans were accustomed to break the legs of a crucified person on one of their most solemn festivals, and to leave him to die upon the cross. This curious fact is stated by Motolinia in the tenth chapter of the first part of his inedited treatise concerning the idolatry of the Indians of New Spain. (16)

Kingsborough's books, published between 1830 and 1848, include reproductions of most of the Aztec and Maya hieroglyphic and pictographic books written in Mexico before the discovery by Columbus. These books survived destruction at the hands of the Spaniards. One of the symbolic names of the Messiah in ancient Mexico was Quetzalcoatl. With respect to certain of the ancient Aztec paintings preserved by Kingsborough in Volume 2 of *Antiquities of Mexico,* he explains:

It is extremely singular that several Mexican paintings should represent Quetzalcoatl with his side pierced with a spear and water flowing from the wound. . . . The paintings which represent Quetzalcoatl pierced with a spear and water issuing from the wound, occur at the sixty-first page of the Borgian manuscript [Kingsborough's Volume 6] and at the ninth page of the Mexican painting preserved in the library of the Institute at Bologna. (Ferguson 1958:138)

After careful study and review of the evidence available in his lifetime, Lord Kingsborough was of the firm conviction that Quetzalcoatl was identical with Jesus of Nazareth and that he appeared to the ancient inhabitants of Mexico. In Volume 8, Kingsborough says:

In the tenth page of the manuscript of Bologna . . . in the lower compartment of the page is a mysterious image of the Sun transfixed by a spear, — symbolic, it is supposed, of Quetzalcoatl, who, like the Hebrew Messiah, was typified by the Sun. (21)

In the same volume he also says:

A slip of tiger skin was fastened by the Mexicans to the miter of Quetzalcoatl. . . . The Mexicans named Quetzalcoatl "Light," and believed that light was created before the sun. It hence appears that the tradition in the Pentateuch that light was created before the sun, was known in various parts of the New World very remote from each other. (34)

Referring to another of the manuscripts of the Aztecs, Kingsborough notes:

The seventy-fifth page of the Borgian manuscript [reproduced by Kingsborough] is very remarkable for the representation which it contains of Quetzalcoatl in the attitude of a crucified person, with the impressions of the nails visible in his hands and feet. (Ferguson 1958:139)

In 1541 Francisco Hernandez arrived in Yucatan as chaplain to the Spanish governor, Montejo II. Four years later, in 1545, Bartolome de las Casas, benevolent friend of the natives, took his post as second Bishop of Chiapas (which included Yucatan). By then Francisco Hernandez had learned the Maya language. He was able to serve efficiently as an aide to Las Casas. The latter sent Francisco Hernandez to the interior to preach to the native Mayas. About a year later Francisco Hernandez wrote to Las Casas concerning the religious beliefs of the Mayas of the interior. Las Casas reported the entire matter. He was strongly of the opinion that Christianity and the crucifixion of the Messiah were known in the region many centuries before the coming of the Spaniards to the region. With respect to Mexico's Messiah, Las Casas wrote:

> After a certain number of months (I believe it was one year) he [Francisco Hernandez] wrote me that on his trip he had met a principal lord or chief, and that on inquiring of him concerning his faith, and the ancient belief all over his realm, he answered him that they knew and believed in God who was in Heaven; that God was the Father, the Son, and the Holy Ghost.
>
> That the Father is called by them *Itzamna* and that he created man and all things. The Son's name was *Bacab*, who was born from a maiden who had ever remained a virgin, whose name was *Chiribirias,* and who is in heaven with God. The Holy Ghost they called *Echuac*. They say *Itzamna* means "the Great Father. . . ." About *Bacab*, who is the Son, they say that he was killed and lashed and a crown of thorns put on him, and that he was placed on a timber with his arms stretched out. They did not understand that he was nailed, but rather they thought he had been tied, and there he died. And he was dead for three days, and on the third day he came to life and went up to heaven, and that he is there with his Father.
>
> And after this, then came *Echvah* who is the Holy Spirit, and filled the earth to overflowing with all the things that were needed.
>
> Asked also how they had knowledge of these things, he

answered that the lords (chiefs) taught it to their children, and that this doctrine descended from generation to generation. They affirmed that in ancient times twenty men came to this land, and their leader was called Cozas, and that the leaders commanded the people to confess and fast. For this reason, some [of the Mayas] fasted on the day that corresponds to Friday since they say that Bacab [the Son of God] had died on that day. (I: 426- 27)

After ending his quotation from the letter of Francisco Hernandez, Bishop Las Casas went on to comment, "If these things are true, it seems that our holy faith was known in that land. . . . Finally, these are secrets that only God knows" (Ch. CCXXXV). Since he was one of the first Catholic priests to reach Mesoamerica, and since he was a brilliant and honorable man, his opinion that Christianity was known in Mesoamerica before he and his Spanish colleagues arrived there must be taken very seriously. Someone—and why not Jesus himself? (see John 10)—made it from the Mediterranean world to Mesoamerica with Christianity before Columbus.

It would seem that Hernandez and Las Casas were close enough to the picture, and arrived on the Mesoamerican scene close enough on the heels of Columbus, not to have been taken in by any false and fraudulent claims of native informants. The native informants, whether from Yucatan, Guatemala, or Mexico City, are entirely consistent with each other.

The events of "the sixth hour" were well known to the ancient colonizers of Mesoamerica.

## Destructions in Mesoamerica at the Time of the Crucifixion

There is particularly clear and abundant archaeological evidence of widespread destruction in Mesoamerica dating from the period of Christ's crucifixion. The New Testament relates that at the moment of Christ's death, "the veil of the temple was rent in twain from the top to the bottom; and the earth did quake, and the rocks rent; and the graves were opened; and many

bodies of the saints which slept arose, and came out of the graves
. . . and went into the holy city, and appeared unto many" (Matt.
27:51-53).

The very nature of earthquake and volcanic activity typical
of the Mesoamerican area is consistent with this whole set of
phenomena. Also, the range of nineteenth- and twentieth-century
activity gives us helpful analogues which we can project backward to reconstruct the seismic activity of the past.

Although earthquakes and volcanoes are certainly not
unknown in either North or South America, we think it is
significant, for example, that there is no historical record of
volcanoes or earthquakes in the Andes from the time of the
European arrivals until quite recently in our own century; and it
was not until 1983 that an archaeologist discovered an
archaeological site north of the general Andean region which had
been covered by volcanic material. However, since this eruption
occurred about 600 B.C., it is not of great interest to this study.

Mesoamerica, on the other hand, is known for its seismic
activity. One text on the archaeology of Mesoamerica is called
*The Sons of the Shaking Earth,* taking its title from a common
characteristic of the whole area.

An interesting and quite typical site is Tres Zapotes in
southern Veracruz, in the Tuxtla Mountains just south of the
mouth of the River Papaloapan where it empties into the Gulf of
Mexico. In the late 1930s, Matthew W. Sterling and Philip
Drucker did exploration and testing at this site, discovering at a
certain level a cap of volcanic ash which covered the
archaeological materials. Then later there was evidence that the
site had been reinhabited. They published their finds, including
profiles showing the excavations, ash layers, and pottery
examples. Because pottery dating forty years ago was less exact
than it is now, we know from more recent work that the volcanic
layer occurred at the time of Christ and covered materials that
dated back several centuries before the time of Christ.

No one had reported any recent work in southern Veracruz,
except John E. Clark, a former Brigham Young University student, who is now finishing his Ph.D. in anthropology at Michigan.

He wrote on 12 February 1983, of Matacapan, a site about twenty miles from Tres Zapotes and midway between San Andres Tuxtla and Lake Catemaco. He recently found that Robert Santley has discovered a Middle Preclassic (1500 B.C.-600 B.C.) site there (letter written to John L. Sorenson). Santley, an archaeologist from the University of New Mexico, worked earlier on the Teotihuacan project in the Valley of Mexico. Clark says, "These deposits were capped with 10 cm or more [about four inches] of volcanic ash from the Volcano San Martin"—the same volcano whose eruptions covered Tres Zapotes. The site was apparently abandoned at this time and reoccupied in the Classic period (A.D. 250 - A.D. 900) when the visible mounds were built containing the Teotihuacan architecture. What nobody knew was that below these mounds was this long sequence of late, middle, and early Preclassic materials capped with a volcanic ash layer.

Santley believes that the 1982 test pits were in an ancient corn field and that the eruption, by inference from the size of corn plants in the ash, took place in the spring of the year.

Apparently the same volcano put a layer of ash over the site of Tres Zapotes that we have known for about forty years, but we are just now discovering the extent of the area it covered. At Tres Zapotes, the ash layer varied between forty and seventy-one centimeters thick (between fifteen and twenty-seven inches). San Martin, the volcano in question, is northeast of both sites, but much closer to Tres Zapotes. Meteorologists tell us that by April or May the wind would be blowing west-southwest. Thus, Tres Zapotes would receive more ash than Matacapan.

Additional insight comes from a graduate paper prepared in 1981 by James E. Chase of the University of Colorado about the San Martin volcanic eruption and its effect on the Olmec at Tres Zapotes, Veracruz. He found that the archaeological site of Cerro de las Mesas, which is west-northwest from San Martin—the opposite direction from Tres Zapotes—has no ash layer. Thus, only Tres Zapotes and Matacapan, which are much closer to San Martin and within the path of the prevailing spring wind, show an ash layer. This suggests that sites south and west of this volcano would probably show evidence of ash, a hypothesis that could be easily tested by excavating a series of test pits to see how large an area is affected by that eruption. Of course, the blackening of the sky from airborne ash would be much larger than the ground area which received it. A useful field project would be an intensive survey of the fifty square miles around San Martin. Practically every site tested would likely show a similar ash layer, with some very exciting prospects for Preclassic occupation below the ash layer.

Chase's paper catalogues some interesting effects of a volcanic eruption. When the ash begins to fall back toward the earth, it is accompanied by many gases, including hydrochloric acid, hydrofluoric acid, carbonic acid, carbon dioxide and ammonia. If the ash fall is heavy, people will naturally suffocate, not only from the ash content itself but from these gases, which are lethal in large quantities. Animal, plant, and aquatic life would also succumb.

At Tres Zapotes, the ash fall was so thick that unquestionably nothing could have survived. It would have taken about eighty or ninety years for the soil to rebuild itself enough so that crops could profitably be grown. Survivors from nearby areas would have had to leave the areas. All drinking water would have been contaminated.

As an interesting parallel, a 1964 volcanic eruption in Nicaragua created such huge quantities of ash that the area experienced ninety mud flows in a single year. Because mud flows are deep deposits of ash, they are highly unstable. The impact of any significant amount of rain makes the ash flow down slopes, seeking a lower resting bed. Speeds of these mud flows can vary from twenty to thirty miles an hour and one flow was clocked at fifty-nine miles an hour. According to the records, the distances a single mud flow has moved can range from five miles (the average is between five and ten miles) up to the record-holder: ninety-nine miles. Chase notes the presence of about six feet of soil just above the ash layer that seems to have come suddenly at Tres Zapotes, thus paralleling the mud flows described for Nicaragua.

Even though much of Mesoamerica receives heavy seasonal rains, the situation would be further complicated by the volcano itself. The heat it injects locally into the atmosphere would trigger torrential rains as a side effect as this heated material contacted the stratosphere's colder wet air. Furthermore, if there is any weakness in the underlying rock strata, earthquakes would be triggered by volcanic action. Near the coast, this seismic activity would create tidal waves of huge heights and immense power. A common Mesoamerican pattern is for an erupting volcano to trigger an earthquake. In some cases, an earthquake can also cause a volcano. The noise, needless to say, would be deafening: lightning, thunder, great cracks where rock strata are giving way, and the noises of the eruption itself.

El Salvador has been an excellent site to study the archaeological effects of volcanoes until the recent intensification of the Civil War. Payson Sheets, an archaeologist from the University of Colorado at Boulder, investigated the volcano Ilopango, which had produced a layer of ash between seventeen and thirty-five inches thick. Again, because of the young corn plants in the ash, he was able to determine that the volcano had erupted in the spring. The layer that he investigated was dated at approximately A.D. 250 and included excellent preservation: homes where dishes were still on the tables, highly reminiscent of Pompeii.

Interestingly, he found evidence of at least four different volcanic eruptions. He dated the particular layer he was working on at A.D. 250, but test pits show that volcanic activity can be dated as early as the time of Christ. Not far away near the border of Guatemala is the site of Chalchuapa, a large Preclassic site that was occupied into Classic times. A layer of volcanic ash between the archaeological strata has been dated by radiocarbon processes to A.D. 30, a date that provides a correlation with the crucifixion of Christ. Although Sheets' work was interrupted by the war, it might be hypothesized that these active volcanoes over much of the Mesoamerican area would have erupted periodically, with perhaps a mega-event occurring near the time of Christ.

Another area in El Salvador near San Salvador has archaeological sites buried under thick ash layers about the time of Christ. A 1955 article by Muriel Porter, written while she was attending the University of California at Berkeley, reports her study of a site covered by ash ranging from thirty to sixty-five feet deep. Clearly nothing could survive that kind of density.

Cummings studied the site of Cuicuilco, near the National University in Mexico City. Another site about five miles away, Copilco, has a lava flow thirty feet thick, covering architecture, burials, and pottery vessels. This layer of lava dates from the time of Christ. Further confirmation of the dating is that Cuicuilco and Copilco are on the west side of the Valley of Mexico where the volcano Xitle is located; and about thirty miles northeast is the huge site of Teotihuacan. Between two architecture levels at Teotihuacan appears a layer of volcanic ash probably blown in from that eruption. By radiocarbon dating, that eruption dates to A.D. 30.

In short, then, from the Valley of Mexico on the north to El Salvador on the south, we have a pattern of major volcanic eruptions. The north saw lava flows over thirty feet thick; the south saw ash layers of up to sixty-five feet deep. Between these points is the volcano San Martin in the Tuxtla Mountains, which covered at least two sites at the same time. This new information will probably reinforce, not modify, this pattern of distribution of volcanic eruptions throughout Mesoamerica.

We have mentioned to this point only volcanic activity and mud flows. In highland Guatemala to the west of Guatemala City lies a large inland lake, Lake Atitlan (probably the Waters of Mormon; see maps). During a period of low water in the 1930s, ruins were detected in the water, and Samuel Lothrop, then with Harvard, was able to recover some ceramics which had the same style and pattern as the Miraflores ceramics from nearby Kaminaljuyu and dated from about the time of Christ, as did the ash layer immediately beneath the Ilopango volcano in El Salvador. It is reasonable to hypothesize that this city in the lake was Preclassic, was occupied near the time of Christ, and was covered subsequently by the lake waters. There are, interestingly, several volcanoes in the mountains surrounding the lake.

In a 1973 report of the New World Archaeological Foundation, Gareth Lowe, then Field Director, mentioned discovering an Olmec monument on the coast of Chiapas which had been broken and displaced by a shift in the earth at some point *after* it was carved, about 500 B.C. Of course, there are other evidences of earthquakes as well.

Another event, which can only be regarded as a footnote, is Mound 5 in Chiapas de Corzo in the Mexican state of Chiapas, which shows that the roof burned and fell in on a collection of 830 whole vessels sitting on the floors. Radiocarbon dating of the main roof beam supplies a date of about A.D. 30. However, there is no evidence of more widespread burning in the same site, and we cannot generalize that the city itself experienced a fire at the time.

We think it is well to remember that our study of volcanic and seismic activity in Mesoamerica is far from complete and that modern studies continue to revise our picture of what volcanoes do and don't do. For example, the 1982 eruption of El Chichon in Chiapas, Mexico, turned the site of Palenque gray from the ash fallout, well over a hundred miles away. John L. Sorenson quotes the report of a 1793 eruption in the Tuxtla Mountains which has some interesting parallels: "Don Joseph Mozino reports that it all started with a buildup of towering clouds over the mountains and great grand thunderclaps but underground, that sounded like all the artillery in Veracruz going off" (322). The account estimates the number of these thunderclaps at 400, says they could be heard hundreds of miles away, and concludes, "No doubt the thunder was of two kinds. One resulted from exceptionally violent storms caused by the heat and dust and the other from the fracturing of the strata underground" (322).

We think we must also be cautious about the size of the area we include in the destruction zone. John L. Sorenson has pointed out that in the centuries immediately following Christ, figurines seem to disappear from Teotihuacan and southeastern Mesoamerica in general (60). This is a general pattern, not a universal pattern; if you keep looking in more distant areas, the figurines reappear. And of course in more recent layers, we also find them in widespread use.

The evidences are striking of huge volcanic eruptions, mud

slides, and destructions in several areas in Mesoamerica which date to about A.D. 30. These archaeological discoveries parallel the natural destruction described in the Book of Mormon at the time of the crucifixion of the Savior:

> And now it came to pass that according to our record, and we know our record to be true, for behold, it was a just man who did keep the record—for he truly did many miracles in the name of Jesus; and there was not any man who could do a miracle in the name of Jesus save he were cleansed every whit from his iniquity—
>
> And now it came to pass, if there was no mistake made by this man in the reckoning of our time, the thirty and third year had passed away;
>
> And the people began to look with great earnestness for the sign which had been given by the prophet Samuel, the Lamanite, yea, for the time that there should be darkness for the space of three days over the face of the land.
>
> And there began to be great doubtings and disputations among the people, notwithstanding so many signs had been given.
>
> And it came to pass in the thirty and fourth year, in the first month, on the fourth day of the month, there arose a great storm, such an one as never had been known in all the land.
>
> And there was also a great and terrible tempest; and there was terrible thunder, insomuch that it did shake the whole earth as if it was about to divide asunder.
>
> And there were exceeding sharp lightnings, such as never had been known in all the land.
>
> And the city of Zarahemla did take fire.
>
> And the city of Moroni did sink into the depths of the sea, and the inhabitants thereof were drowned.
>
> And the earth was carried up upon the city of Moronihah, that in the place of the city there became a great mountain.
>
> And there was a great and terrible destruction in the land southward.
>
> But behold, there was a more great and terrible

destruction in the land northward; for behold, the whole face of the land was changed, because of the tempest and the whirlwinds, and the thunderings and lightnings, and the exceeding great quaking of the whole earth;

And the highways were broken up, and the level roads were spoiled, and many smooth places became rough.

And many great and notable cities were sunk, and many were burned, and many were shaken till the buildings thereof had fallen to the earth, and the inhabitants thereof were slain, and the places were left desolate.

And there were some cities which remained; but the damage thereof was exceeding great, and there were many of them who were slain.

And there were some who were carried away in the whirlwind; and whither they went no man knoweth, save they know that they were carried away.

And thus the face of the whole earth became deformed, because of the tempests, and the thunderings, and the lightnings, and the quaking of the earth.

And behold, the rocks were rent in twain; they were broken up upon the face of the whole earth, insomuch that they were found in broken fragments, and in seams and in cracks, upon all the face of the land.

And it came to pass that when the thunderings, and the lightnings, and the storm, and the tempest, and the quakings of the earth did cease—for behold, they did last for about the space of three hours; and it was said by some that the time was greater; nevertheless, all these great and terrible things were done in about the space of three hours—and then behold, there was darkness upon the face of the land.

And it came to pass that there was thick darkness upon all the face of the land, insomuch that the inhabitants thereof who had not fallen could feel the vapor of darkness;

And there could be no light, because of the darkness, neither candles, neither torches; neither could there be fire kindled with their fine and exceedingly dry wood, so that there could not be any light at all;

And there was not any light seen, neither fire, nor glimmer, neither the sun, nor the moon, nor the stars, for so great were the mists of darkness which were upon the face of the land.

And it came to pass that it did last for the space of three days that there was no light seen; and there was great mourning and howling and weeping among all the people continually; yea, great were the groanings of the people, because of the darkness and the great destruction which had come upon them.

And in one place they were heard to cry, saying: O that we had repented before this great and terrible day, and then would our brethren have been spared, and they would not have been burned in that great city Zarahemla.

And in another place they were heard to cry and mourn, saying: O that we had repented before this great and terrible day, and had not killed and stoned the prophets, and cast them out; then would our mothers and our fair daughters, and our children have been spared, and not have been buried up in that great city Moronihah. And thus were the howlings of the people great and terrible. (3 Nephi 8)

# NOTES TO CHAPTER TWO

1.  Siguenza's biographer, Irving Albert Leonard, says of this great scholar:

    He was unfortunate enough to live in a time and environment when chiefly those writings which glorified the Church and its servants were thought worthy of the press. The rigorous censorship imposed by the Inquisition too often precluded the publication of other works of a more secular nature.

    In 1668, at the age of 23, Siguenza began his studies of the ancient glories of the aborigines of New Spain. . . . While this was not the first time that this had been done in New Spain, Don Carlos undoubtedly brought together, hampered as he was by his many other duties and limited resources, the most complete aggregation of original books, manuscripts, maps, and paintings related to native life before the arrival of the Spaniards, that had ever been assembled before his time. He was aided in this laudable enterprise by his association with the De Alva Ixtilxochitl family from whom, no doubt, he received much instruction in the Mexican languages which he mastered.

    Some of the Indians, particularly those belonging to noble families, had hidden certain of them [ancient historical documents] and, through fear of their new masters, did not dare to reveal their knowledge of them. Thus, it was not only through the most painstaking efforts of Don Carlos and the wide cultivation of friendships with the natives that he was able to bring forth these manuscripts and paintings from their hiding-places and submit them to the scrutiny of his curious eye.

    At his [Don Carlos'] death, it seems as if a "surprise attack" upon his papers had been sounded and everyone got possession of what he could. Siguenza's abiding interest in all matters pertaining to the Indians together with his intimacy with the De Alva Ixtilxochitl family, drew him like a magnet to the nearby pyramids of Teotihuacan, of which region this illustrious Indian family were the overlords. These structures claimed his close attention and afforded him much food for cogitation.

    If it cannot be said that he extended human knowledge in the field of mathematics, astronomy, and kindred sciences, he showed far more understanding and enlightenment on these subjects than did the vast majority of his contemporaries on either side of the Atlantic. What can be stated with confidence is that the diversity of his interests, and the high degree of attainment reached in all of them, and his prolific literary activity mark him as one of the greatest scholars of the seventeenth century in the Western Hemisphere—including the English colonies—and a figure whom no true historian of the early cultural history of the New World can properly neglect.

He was a poet, a philosopher, a mathematician, an astronomer, an antiquarian, and a historian . . . and in nearly all of them he excelled. . . . Don Carlos was a thinker. . . . With tireless zeal, despite limited financial resources, he collected a museum of Mexican antiquities and other material pertaining to the early history of New Spain--a collection which excited the admiration of later scholars though they had access to but a small part of it. Becoming proficient in the languages of the aborigines through his studies and his daily contacts with the Indians, he was able to decipher many of the early monuments and interpret Indian events in terms of the Christian calendar (1-2).

## Chapter Three
# SACRED BOOKS OF MESOAMERICA

---

*There is a book we need to study daily, both as individuals and as families, namely the Book of Mormon. I love that book. It is the book that will get a person nearer to God by abiding by its precepts than any other book. President Romney recommended studying it half an hour each day. I commend that practice to you. I've always enjoyed reading the scriptures and do so on a daily basis individually and with my beloved wife.*

President Ezra Taft Benson
General Conference, April 1986

(*Ensign*, May 1986, p. 78)
Used by permission

The prophet Lehi was warned by the Lord, "that he should take his family and depart into the wilderness" (1 Ne. 2:2). Lehi obeyed and fled from Jerusalem before its pending destruction. The armies of Babylonia, under Nebuchadnezzar, marched into Jerusalem in 587 B.C. Zedekiah, King of Judah, was taken captive. His sons were killed before his eyes, and then his eyes were put out. The leadership of Israel was marched off in captivity to Babylonia (2 Kings 24:17 and 2 Chron. 36).

Following this great destruction of Jerusalem, Ezekiel, the prophet, went to the Lord and inquired concerning the destiny of fallen Israel. The Lord told Ezekiel that captive and scattered Israel was like a valley of dry bones — desolate and without hope. But the Lord went on to promise Ezekiel that the people of Israel ultimately would be gathered back to their own land.

The Lord assured Ezekiel that with the gathering to the

homeland He would again be the God of Israel, and even the
heathen would come to know that He, the Lord, did sanctify
Israel. The Lord promised not only to eventually gather Israel
back from among the nations and restore the people to their own
land, but also to breathe His Spirit back into Israel.

Intricately involved in Ezekiel's prediction of a restoration of
the tribes of Israel was the book referred to as the "stick of
Joseph." The book was to be in the hand of God, together with
the "stick of Judah," which is the book of the Jews, or the Bible.
The ancient Jewish books were scrolls. Each was rolled about a
stick, like the Torah.

In 1953, M. E. L. Mallowan discovered two sets of wax
coated writing tablets at the bottom of a well at the
archaeological site of Nimrud in Iraq. The phrase *is le'u shinpiri*
was inscribed on the cover-board. *Is le'u* means "wooden tablet"
and *shin piri* "ivory." The Hebrew word in Ezekiel 37 that is
translated as stick or wood is *'es*, which means wood or board.
Mallowan's writing board, dated to 707 B.C., provides an
important confirmation that the two "sticks" in Ezekiel 37 refer
to two written records (Meservy 26).

The Joseph in the phrase "stick of Joseph" that Ezekiel
referred to was the Joseph in the Old Testament. He received the
coat of many colors from his father, Jacob, and then was sold
into slavery in Egypt by his jealous brothers. He became a high
official in Egypt and was patriarchal father of one the Twelve
Tribes of Israel. He lived about 1,650 years before Christ, and
about 400 years before Moses.

Jacob, whose name was changed by God to Israel, blessed
each of his sons as the head of one of the Twelve Tribes of Israel.
When it was Joseph's turn, Jacob gave him a special and more
lengthy blessing than the others:

> Joseph is a fruitful bough, even a fruitful bough by a
> well; whose branches run over the wall: The archers have
> sorely grieved him, and shot at him, and hated him: But his
> bow abode in strength, and the arms of his hands were made
> strong by the hands of the mighty God of Jacob; (from

thence is the shepherd, the stone of Israel): Even by the God of thy father, who shall help thee; and by the Almighty, who shall bless thee with blessings of heaven above, blessings of the deep that lieth under, blessings of the breasts, and of the womb.

The blessings of thy father have prevailed above the blessings of my progenitors unto the utmost bound of the everlasting hills: they shall be on the head of Joseph, and on the crown of the head of him that was separate from his brethren. (Gen. 49:22-26)

The statement that Joseph is a "fruitful bough" means that he would have numerous descendants. That his branches would "run over the wall" appears to mean that his descendants would migrate beyond the borders and boundaries of Palestine. The blessings which Israel pronounces upon Joseph are to be greater than those received by Israel's forebears and are to reach to "the utmost bound of the everlasting hills: they shall be on the head of Joseph." The American continent is the only place in the world where the mountains run continuously the length of the continent. They emerge from the sea in Alaska and run as if everlastingly until they enter the sea at the southern tip of South America.

There is nothing to suggest that Joseph himself wrote a scroll or a book. The "stick of Joseph" was written by his descendants who went "over the wall" and beyond the vineyard unto the "utmost bound of the everlasting hills." It was written by the ancients of the New World who claimed to be descendants of Jacob.

## Ixtlilxochitl

The knowledge of the existence—in earlier times—of the Sacred Books in ancient Mesoamerica was fairly widespread in Mexico and Central America when the first Europeans arrived after the discovery of America by Columbus. Ixtlilxochitl, a native prince who lived near Mexico City, knew that there had been such books in Mesoamerica in very early times.

He tells of the compilation of a divine book by one Huematzin — who lived in the fourth century after Christ:

> And before going on I want to make an account of Huematzin the astrologer. . . . Before dying he [Huematzin] gathered together all the histories the Tultecas had, from the creation of the world up to that time [A.D. 450] and had them pictured in a very large book, where were pictured all their persecutions and hardships, prosperities and good happenings, kings and lords, laws and good government of their ancestors, old sayings and good examples, temples, idols, sacrifices, rites, and ceremonies that they had, astrology, philosophy, architecture, and the other arts, good as well as bad, and a resume of all things of science, knowledge, prosperous and adverse battles, and many other things; and he entitled this book calling it *Teoamoxtli,* which well interpreted means Various things of God and divine book: the natives now call the Holy Scriptures *Teoamoxtli,* because it is almost the same, principally in the persecutions and hardships of men. (Hunter and Ferguson 337-38)

The "divine book" to which Ixtlilxochitl refers dealt with the creation of the world and the history of some of the New World colonizers. The complete consistency between Ixtlilxochitl's statement that these colonizers possessed histories and the story of the creation of the world and the declaration of the Catholic father Dionisio Jose Chonay is significant. In the preamble to the Totonicapan account, which he translated from the Maya into Spanish in 1834, Chonay explains:

> His said manuscript consists of thirty-one quarto pages; but the translation of the first pages is omitted because they are on the creation of the world, of Adam, the early paradise in which Eve was deceived, not by a serpent, but by Lucifer himself, as an angel of light. (Recinos and Goetz 166-67)

Genesis creation data of the ancient colonizers was still in the possession of the Mayas in Guatemala when the Totonicapan account was written in 1554. Both Ixtlilxochitl and the Lords of Totonicapan credit the early colonizers with possession of the creation account. They therefore corroborate each other.

Huematzin lived in the fourth and fifth centuries A.D. and was a great religious leader and prophet. Ixtlilxochitl dates one particular event in his lifetime to the very year — 400 after the true birth date of Christ. Huematzin's divine book covered the period from the creation of the world up to his time — the fourth century A.D. In that time period it would encompass the personal New World appearance of the Messiah and should contain the details of his appearance and ministry.

## Popol Vuh

From the people of Chichicastenango in the beautiful highlands of Guatemala, neighbors of the nobles of Totonicapan, comes another independent testimony of a sacred book in ancient Mesoamerica. The Quiche-Maya were the most powerful nation of the Guatemalan highlands in immediate pre-Conquest times, and a branch of the ancient Maya. Before the conquest they painted the Popol Vuh in hieroglyphics. It was first transcribed in the Quiche language in the middle of the sixteenth century by highly literate Quiche-Maya natives (Tedlock 28, 59-61):

> This we shall write now [16th century alphabetic text] under the Law of God and Christianity; we shall bring it to light because now the hieroglyphic Popol Vuh, as it is called, cannot be seen any more, in which was clearly seen the coming from the other side of the sea and the narration of our obscurity, and our life was clearly seen. The original book, written long ago, existed, but its sight is hidden to the searcher and to the thinker. Great were the descriptions and the account of how all the sky and earth were formed, how it was formed and divided into four parts; how it was

partitioned, and how the sky was divided; and the measuring cord was brought, and it was stretched in the sky and over the earth, on the four angles, on the four corners, as was told by the Creator and the Maker, the Mother and the Father of Life, of all created things, he who gives breath and thought, she who gives birth to the children, he who watches over the happiness of the people, the happiness of the human race, the wise man, he who meditates on the goodness of all that exists in the sky, on the earth, in the lakes and in the sea. (Tedlock 71-72)

The same source makes another reference to the sacred book of ancient Mesoamerica:

Great lords and wonderful men were the marvelous kings Gucumatz and Cotuha, the marvelous kings Quicab and Cavizimah. They knew if there would be war, and everything was clear before their eyes; they saw if there would be death and hunger, if there would be strife. They well knew that there was a place where it could be seen, that there was a book which they called the Popol Vuh. (219)

At the very end of the sixteenth century *Popol Vuh,* the author explains again that he had to write it because the original sacred ancient book had disappeared long ago. He was providing the best substitution that he could for the original. "And this was the life of the Quiche, because no longer can be seen the book of the *Popol Vuh* which the kings had in olden times, for it has disappeared" (227).

## The Stick of Joseph

Shortly after 600 B.C. a group of two families left Jerusalem before the children of Israel were carried away to captivity into Babylon. They were descendants of the tribe of Joseph that was sold into Egypt. They kept a record on plates of gold of the sacred instructions they received from God on how they were to make their way across the ocean to Mesoamerica. The descendants of these two families continued to keep the record for over 1,000 years until the people were destroyed in civil war. The many volumes were abridged into one record by the prophet-historian Mormon, before he was killed in the civil war. The sacred record was given to his son, Moroni, who completed it and hid the gold plates in the earth in A.D. 410.

The earth held its treasure for over 14 centuries while the ruins of a once mighty civilization were covered with dust. Finally, on the night of 21 September 1823, in the frontier village of Palmyra, New York, this same Moroni who had buried the plates returned as a resurrected being to a young man named Joseph Smith. Moroni showed him where the sacred record was hidden. By the power of God, Joseph Smith translated the ancient record and published it in 1830 as the Book of Mormon.

## The Book of Mormon

The Book of Mormon is a fourth-century record from ancient Mesoamerica. It is a unique witness that Jesus is the Christ. It is a personal family record passed on, in most instances, from father to son. It is a witness over many generations of what happens when people choose to obey or disobey the gospel of Jesus Christ.

It is a story of fathers trying to teach their children about the Savior that someday was to be born in Jerusalem:

> Yea, even six hundred years from the time that my father left Jerusalem, a prophet would the Lord God raise up among the Jews—even a Messiah, or in other words, a Savior of the world. (1 Ne. 10:4)
>
> And I, Nephi, saw that he was lifted up upon the cross and slain for the sins of the world. (1 Ne. 11:33)
>
> And after Christ shall have risen from the dead he shall show himself unto you, my children, and my beloved brethren; and the words which he shall speak unto you shall be the law which ye shall do. (2 Ne. 26:1)

It is a story of fathers and leaders trying to teach their people who their ancestors were and who they really are:

> Behold, we are a remnant of the seed of Jacob; yea, we are a remnant of the seed of Joseph, whose coat was rent by his brethren into many pieces; yea, and now behold, let us remember to keep the commandments of God, or our garments shall be rent by our brethren, and we be cast into prison, or be sold, or be slain. (Alma 46:23)

The Book of Mormon is also a story of ancient American prophets trying to warn their people what will happen if they do not follow the Savior. The decaying ruins of Mesoamerica are solemn sentinels of their prophecies:

> And now, we can behold the decrees of God concerning this land, that it is a land of promise; and whatsoever nation shall possess it shall serve God, or they shall be swept off when the fulness of his wrath shall come upon them.
> For behold, this is a land which is choice above all other lands; wherefore he that doth possess it shall serve God or shall be swept off; for it is the everlasting decree of God. And it is not until the fulness of iniquity among the children of the land, that they are swept off. (Ether 9:9-10)

## Time of The Appearance

Chapter 2 discussed the time of the appearance of the Messiah in Mesoamerica. It may be recalled that Ixtlilxochitl stated:

> The sun and the moon eclipsed, and the earth trembled, and the rocks broke, and many other things and signs took place. . . . This happened . . . at the same time when Christ our Lord suffered, and they say it happened during the first days of the year. (Hunter and Ferguson 190)

The Book of Mormon provides an eyewitness account of

what happened in Mesoamerica during the "sixth hour" when the crucifixion took place in Jerusalem:

> In the thirty and fourth year, in the first month, on the fourth day of the month [from the time of the sign of the birth of Christ], there arose a great storm, such as one as never had been known in all the land. And there was also a great and terrible tempest; and there was terrible thunder, insomuch that it did shake the whole earth as if it was about to divide asunder. And there were exceeding sharp lightnings, such as never had been known in all the land. . . .
>
> And there was a great and terrible destruction in the land southward.
>
> But behold, there was a more great and terrible destruction in the land northward; . . . And there was not any light seen, neither fire, nor glimmer, neither the sun, nor the moon, nor the stars, for so great were the mists of darkness which were upon the face of the land. . . . And it did last for the space of three days that there was no light seen; and there was great mourning and howling and weeping among all the people . . . because of the darkness and the great destruction which had come upon them. (3 Ne. 8:5-23)

Ixtlilxochitl indicates that the events which accompanied the crucifixion ocurred in "the first days of the year." The Book of Mormon states that the events occurred "in the first month, on the fourth day of the month." Ixtlilxochitl says, "And the earth trembled and the rocks broke." The Book of Mormon says:

> It did shake the whole earth as if it were about to divide asunder . . . and behold, the rocks were rent in twain, they were broken upon the face of the whole earth. (3. Ne. 8:6, 18)

Ixtlilxochitl states, "The sun and the moon eclipsed." The Book of Mormon states, "And there was not any light seen, neither . . . the sun, nor the moon, nor the stars" (3 Nephi 8:22).

**Christ's Appearance in Mesoamerica**

The visit of Jesus of Nazareth to Mesoamerica after his crucifixion is described in detail in thirty-four pages in the Book of Mormon. The eyewitness account of his appearance is recorded as follows:

> There were a great multitude gathered together . . . round about the temple which was in the land Bountiful; and they were marveling and wondering one with another, and were showing one to another the great and marvelous change which had taken place. And they were also conversing about this Jesus Christ, of whom the sign had been given concerning his death.
>
> And . . . while they were thus conversing one with another, they heard a voice as if it came out of heaven . . . [saying]:
>
> Behold my Beloved Son, in whom I am well pleased, in whom I have glorified my name — hear ye him. . . .
>
> And as they understood they cast their eyes up again towards heaven; and behold, they saw a Man descending out of heaven; and he was clothed in a white robe; and he came down and stood in the midst of them; and the eyes of the whole multitude were turned upon him, and they durst not open their mouths, even one to another, and wist not what it meant, for they thought it was an angel that had appeared unto them.
>
> And . . . he stretched forth his hand and spake unto the people, saying: Behold, I am Jesus Christ, whom the prophets testified shall come into the world. And behold, I am the light and the life of the world; and I have drunk out of that bitter cup which the Father hath given me, and have glorified the Father in taking upon me the sins of the world, in the which I have suffered the will of the Father in all things from the beginning. (3 Ne. 11:1, 3, 7-11)

## Jesus' Ministry in Mesoamerica

Following are a few examples of what Jesus taught and did during his brief ministry in Mesoamerica:

> And now . . . when Jesus had ended these sayings he cast his eyes round about on the multitude, and said unto them: Behold, ye have heard the things which I taught before I ascended to my Father [He had just repeated to them the Sermon on the Mount]; therefore, whoso remembereth these sayings of mine and doeth them, him will I raise up at the last day. . . .
>
> Behold, I say unto you that the law is fulfilled that was given unto Moses. Behold, I am he that gave the law, and I am he who covenanted with my people Israel; therefore, the law in me is fulfilled, for I have come to fulfill the law; therefore it hath an end. Behold, I do not destroy the prophets, for as many as have not been fulfilled in me, verily I say unto you, shall all be fulfilled. . . .
>
> And . . . now when Jesus had spoken these words, he said unto those twelve whom he had chosen: Ye are my disciples; and ye are a light unto this people, who are a remnant of the house of Joseph. And behold, this is the land of your inheritance; and the Father hath given it unto you. And not at any time hath the Father given me commandment that I should tell it unto your brethren at Jerusalem.
>
> Neither at any time hath the Father given me commandment that I should tell unto them concerning the other tribes of the house of Israel, whom the Father hath led away out of the land. This much did the Father command me, that I should tell unto them: That other sheep I have which are not of this fold; them also I must bring, and they shall hear my voice; and there shall be one fold, and one shepherd. (3 Ne. 15:1, 4-6, 11-17)
>
> Behold, verily, verily, I say unto you, ye must watch and pray always lest ye enter into temptation; for Satan desireth to have you, that he may sift you as wheat. Therefore ye must always pray unto the Father in my name; And whatsoever ye shall ask the Father in my name, which is

right, believing that ye shall receive, behold it shall be given unto you. Pray in your families unto the Father, always in my name, that your wives and your children may be blessed. And behold, ye shall meet together oft; and ye shall not forbid any man from coming unto you when ye shall meet together, but suffer them that they may come unto you and forbid them not; But ye shall pray for them, and shall not cast them out; and if it so be that they come unto you oft ye shall pray for them unto the Father, in my name. Therefore, hold up your light that it may shine unto the world. Behold, I am the light which ye shall hold up — that which ye have seen me do. Behold ye see that I have prayed unto the Father, and ye all have witnessed. (3 Ne. 18:18-24)

And it came to pass that Jesus commanded that it should be written; therefore it was written according as he commanded. And now it came to pass that when Jesus had expounded all the scriptures in one, which they had written, he commanded them that they should teach the things which he had expounded unto them. (3 Ne. 23:13-14)

## And It Came to Pass

The phrase "and it came to pass" occurs frequently throughout the Book of Mormon. It has a fascinating parallel in Mayan hieroglyphs. J. Eric Thompson, probably the leading Maya scholar until his death in the early 1970s, discussed what he called posterior and anterior date indicators in Classic Maya Hieroglyphs. He discovered that the posterior date indicators meant "to count forward to"; the anterior date indicators meant "to count backward to." When he wrote this in 1950, he did not know of an equivalent phrase in contemporary Yucatec or other Mayan dialects (162-64).

Proto-Cholan is now considered to be the main Mayan dialect used in the Classic period hieroglyphs. In 1984 David Stuart gave a Proto-Cholan reading of *uht* as "to finish, come to pass," or Chontal *ut* with the same meaning (5). Schele, a professor of anthropology at the University of Texas, considered one of the leading scholars of ancient Maya hieroglyphs, also translated this Maya hieroglyph as "then it came to pass" (21-25).

Some posterior phrases from the Maya hieroglyphs are "count forward to," "count until," "until it came to pass," and "then it came to pass," etc. Schele also lists some phrases for the anterior indicators as "count back to," "count since," "since it had come to pass," etc. A couple of hieroglyphic examples of this usage can be found on the Palace Tablets at Palenque, Chiapas, Mexico (Schele 68-69). (See photo opposite title page.)

In 1982, Schele illustrated with Maya glyphs and verbal descriptions four types of directional count indicators: posterior date indicators, posterior event indicators, anterior date indicators, and anterior event indicators (*Maya Glyphs: The Verbs* 22).

Many examples of several types of these directional count indicators can be found in the Book of Mormon:

### Posterior Date Indicator
"And it came to pass that thus passed away the ninety and fifth years also" (3 Ne. 2:1)

### Posterior Event Indicator
"And it came to pass that the people began to wax strong in wickedness and abominations" (3 Ne. 2:3)

### Posterior Date and Event Indicator
"And it came to pass in the thirteenth year there began to be wars and contentions throughout the land" (3 Ne. 2:11)

### Anterior Date Indicator
"And thus did pass away the ninety and sixth year" (3 Ne. 2:4)

### Anterior Event Indicator
"And it had come to pass, yea, all things, every whit, according to the words of the prophets." (3 Ne. 1:20)

### Combined Anterior Date and Event Indicator
"And six hundred and nine years had passed away since Lehi left Jerusalem." (3 Ne. 2:6)

The combined forms of directional count indicators in the Book of Mormon have not yet been detected in hieroglyphic studies. Perhaps Mesoamerican linguists should be encouraged to search for similiar phrases in Mayan dialects and other Mesoamerican Indian languages. It might lead to some startling discoveries.

## Dating the Resurrection

The Mixtec Indians of Oaxaca in southern Mexico are noted for their beautiful painted books. Two of these painted books are the Codex Vienna and the Codex Nuttall. Both were painted in A.D. 1350, one hundred and fifty years before Cortes came to Mesoamerica in 1519. Page 4 of the Codex Nuttall shows two deities in death bundles (Figure 14). Their descent into the underworld and then their emergence from the underworld are also depicted. Scenes of death and resurrection are not unknown in other Mesoamerican codices. But what makes this scene compelling is the identity of the god—Quetzalcoatl—and the calendar date for the event—A.D. 30.

The Codex Nuttall is a Mixtec codex from ancient Mexico, one of two codices sent by Cortes in 1519 back to Charles V of Spain. It was sent from Veracruz before Cortes marched into Mexico on the only ship which Cortes did not burn off the coast of Veracruz. Actually two codices (the Nuttall and the Vienna/Vindobonensis) arrived in Spain before the time that Cortes arrived in Tenochtitlan in the valley of Mexico.

The base date of the Codex Nuttall is A.D. 11, the year 13 Reed. It has a different base date than many of the other codices from Oaxaca and central and southern Mexico. Some other codices which have the 3114 B.C. base date, like the Vienna, were probably not Mixtec, but rather Tulteca, as Ixtlilxochitl refers to

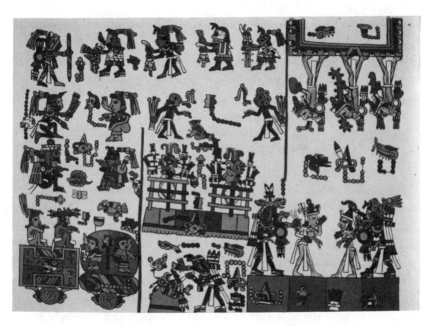

**Figure 14: A death and resurrecton scene from Codex A.D. 30. The central column shows two dead gods in death bundles and the left column shows the same two gods resurrected.**

these people; or they are probably from the language group of the Chocho-Popoloca people, who live in northern Oaxaca and southern Puebla, Mexico.

On page 4 of Nuttall there is a date of 6 Rabbit, which Jill Leslie Furst determined from her studies of the Codex Vienna was a Quetzalcoatl date. This 6 Rabbit year was A.D. 30. The codex depicts two deities in death bundles. One deity is Four Earthquake; the other is Seven Flower. Four Earthquake is a calendar date of a deity representing a descent into the underworld and death. The other deity, Seven Flower, represents an ascent out of the underworld, like the sun or Venus in the east.

In the fixed calendar of 260 days, the date Four Earthquake would be the 6th of April. The date Seven Flower would be three days later, or the 9th of April. The birthdate of Quetzalcoatl from other codical sources is Nine Wind, just two days later than Seven Flower, or April 11th.

Seven Flower is associated with the sunrise or the rise of the planet Venus as the morning star. Birth and rebirth are also symbolic of Seven Flower. So what is shown in the codex is that on April 6, A.D. 30 a deity shown first as dead and descending into the underworld leaves the underworld and comes back to life or is resurrected (reborn) three days later.

The codex symbolically shows Quetzalcoatl's death dated 6 April A.D. 30 and his resurrection three days later, 9 April A.D. 30. The codices provide the world with some convincing external evidences of the Savior's birth, death, and resurrection.

Many more such discoveries are likely to occur in the near future. Much study is still needed of numerous other codices which have not been sufficiently researched and evaluated. One reason for the lack of attention to the codices is that only a handful of scholars in the world are attempting to decipher and read the codices. Much new knowledge has come from the codices in just the last few years, and much more is surely yet to come. It is expected that some of this new information will shed additional light on the Book of Mormon.

## Birth of Jesus

The Book of Mormon and information from recently published Babylonian tablets and from the Maya calendar system now make it possible to fix the birth of Jesus Christ.

Nephi, the Book of Mormon prophet who left Jerusalem with his father Lehi in the "commencement of the first year of the reign of Zedekiah, king of Judah" (1 Ne. 1:1), wrote, "he [the Messiah] cometh, according to the words of the angel, in six hundred years from the time my father left Jerusalem" (1 Ne. 19:8). Thus, we can ascertain the true date of Christ's birth if we can ascertain the date of the first year of the reign of Zedekiah. This birth was to have been 600 years after Lehi left Jerusalem.

Biblical scholars have lately completed the translation and

publication of Babylonian tablets and chronicles for the years 626 B.C.-556 B.C. They are of great interest and importance. These Babylonian records establish that Nebuchadnezzar, king of Babylon, captured Jerusalem 16 March 597 B.C. This date is set forth in one of the newly published tablets. King Jehoiachim of Judah went down with the fall of Jerusalem, his reign ending the day of the fall, 16 March 597 B.C. Zedekiah was appointed by the Babylonian king to succeed Jehoiachim. "Zedekiah's first regnal year began the following month, April 597 B.C." (Freedman XII.100).

Since Lehi departed from Jerusalem "in the commencement of the first year of the reign of Zedekiah, king of Judah" (1 Ne. 1:4), we now know that he left in December 597 B.C.

Six hundred years following the departure of Lehi from Jerusalem a Book of Mormon historian recorded:

> it was six hundred years from the time that Lehi left Jerusalem . . . in the commencement of the . . . year; . . . and it came to pass that there was no darkness in all that night, but it was as light as though it was mid-day. And it came to pass that the sun did rise in the morning again, according to its proper order; and they knew [in Mesoamerica] that it was the day that the Lord should be born, because of the sign which had been given. (3 Ne. 1:1, 4, 19)

If Lehi and his companions left Jerusalem in 597 B.C., and 600 years later the Savior was born in Bethlehem, then the Savior's birth should be in A.D. 2 or 3. However, the Savior was born while Herod the Great was still alive. Herod died in 4 B.C. At first glance it appears there is an error in the Book of Mormon, when it states that 600 years are involved from the first year of King Zedekiah to the birth of Christ. Jay H. Huber, in his article "Lehi's 600 Year Prophecy and the Birth of Christ," demonstrates that the Nephite years were 360 days in length and not 365.2422 days. Huber initiated his research from a suggestion from Dr. John L. Sorenson that a Nephite year could have been a *tun* year in the Maya Long Count Calendar. A *tun* year consists of 360 days. Huber concludes that the Savior was probably born on 11 April 4 B.C.

According to the Nephite record, the Nephites used the birth of Christ as a new and additional zero point from which to count the years in ancient Mesoamerica:

> And nine years had passed away from the time when the sign was given, which was spoken by the prophets, that Christ should come into the world. Now the Nephites began [in A.D. 6] to reckon their time from this period when the sign was given, or from the coming of Christ; therefore, nine years had passed away. (3 Ne. 2:7-8)

The Mesoamericans adjusted their calendar in A.D. 6 when a mass planetary conjunction occurred. A mass planetary conjunction occurs when the five visible (to the human eye) planets arise on the eastern horizon at the same time: Mercury, Venus, Mars, Jupiter, and Saturn. This phenomenon occurs every 179-180 years. Nine years back from A.D. 6 is 4 B.C., the year suggested as the birth of Christ.

## Birth Trees

The Vienna Codex depicts a "birth tree" from which nine deities were born (Figure 15). One of these deities is Nine Wind Quetzalcoatl. The dates for this birth tree are 3075 and 3072 B.C. The codex also shows the birth tree as a goddess with the calendar name of Nine Reed (Figure 16). She is giving birth to approximately 47 deities. The God Quetzalcoatl is supervising this episode. These births take place between 7 B.C. and A.D. 46.

The Codex Gomez de Orozco from northern Oaxaca shows a picture of Quetzalcoatl descending from the heavens (Figure 17) in the year A.D. 46 The significance of the calendar date A.D. 46 being mentioned twice must be explained. It involves the famous Maya Long-count calendar.

The unique feature of the Long-count calendar is that it counts days from a fixed event in the distant past. The date of this fixed "flood" date is 13 August 3114 B.C. All events in

Fig. 15: Birth tree of nine deities associated with a calendar of 3072 B.C., from page 50 of the Codex Vienna.

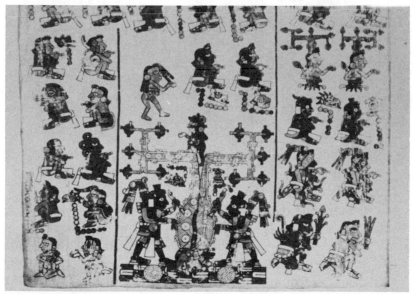

Figure 16: Birth tree at Apoala (Cerro de las Mesas? in south central Veracruz) about 46 A.D., from the Codex Vienna page 37.

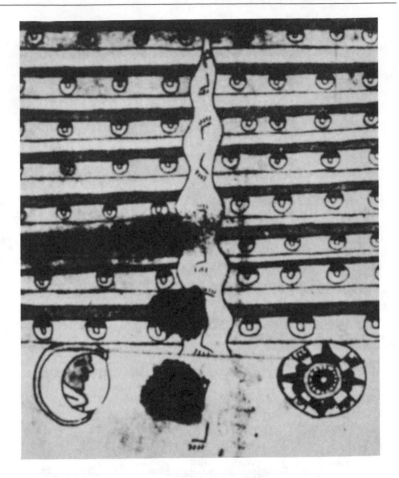

**Figure 17: Damaged scene of a descent of Quetzalcoatl from the heavens in the first century A.D. The source of this scene is the Codex Gomez de Orozco from the Coixtlahuaca region of northern Oaxaca, Mexico.**

Mesoamerica dated with the Long-count calendar were set by counting the days from this base date.

Since the Long-count calendar does not keep track of leap years, it loses one day every four years. Every 1507 years there would be a slippage of one complete year because of this leap year problem. Fortunately, the beginning of one of these 1507 year cycles occurred on 26 July 1553. It was recorded with the Maya Calendar Round date of 10 Ik and 0 Pop, New Year's day in the Maya Long-count calendar. One 1507 year cycle earlier would place the beginning of the original New Year's day on 26 July A.D. 46, 10 Ik O Pop (8.0.4.17.2).

The shifting of the New Year's beginning date to 26 July from on or near the spring equinox has something to do with the "birth tree" and the birth of the gods at the beginning of the first century A.D.

### Izapa Stela 5

In 1943 the Smithsonian Institution of the Bureau of American Ethnology published its Bulletin 138, entitled "Stone Monuments of Southern Mexico," by Matthew W. Stirling. Plate 52 in Bulletin 138 is a photograph of a cast of a large ancient stone monument discovered at the ancient ruin of Izapa near the present town of Tapachula in the state of Chiapas, Mexico. Izapa is near the border of Guatemala and not far from the Pacific Ocean.

Izapa Stela 5 is possibly one of the most important graphic depictions of the tree of life (Figure 18). It is a stone carving that weighs 15 tons and is 255 centimeters high. Dated to the late Preclassic Guillen phase, about 300-50 B.C, it is the earliest Mesoamerican depiction of the tree of life discovered so far.

The most recent study of this stela is by V. Garth Norman, who recently summarized the significance of Stela 5:

> What makes the monument so interesting . . . is its possible connection to the Book of Mormon. In the 1950s and early 1960s, studies by Dr. M. Wells Jakeman of the Brigham Young University Department of Archaeology indicated that certain features of the monument seem to correspond to features of Lehi's vision of the Tree of Life. [See also 1 Nephi 8 and 11.] The most obvious of the parallels is a fruit-bearing tree in the center with a stream running by. A pathway extends from the river's head to the tree, and a broad grooved line paralleling the path lines suggests the rod of iron. Two cherubim-like beings attend the tree, and seated around it are six people who, it was

**Fig. 18: Izapa Stela 5 Tree of Life dating from between 300 to 1 B.C. Izapa is located in southwestern Chiapas, Mexico near the Pacific ocean and a few miles from the Guatemalan border.**

suggested, could represent Lehi's family in the attitudes they assume in Lehi's vision. Attaching their names to the figures, we see Lehi, on the left and attended by Sariah, facing Laman, and on the right Nephi, attended by Sam, facing Lemuel. In fact, Dr. Jakeman deciphered possible name hieroglyphs above the heads of two of these figures as "Lehi" and "Nephi." . . .

The years of research since Dr. Jakeman's first study have neither proved nor disproved his thesis. As yet, published data has been inconclusive, and will continue to be until we have a more complete picture of Izapan culture.

In the 1970s I published an interpretive study of Izapa monuments, including Stela 5, in a large work entitled "Izapa Sculpture." The study shows that Stela 5 occupies a central position, conceptually speaking, in relation to the other carvings discovered in Izapa, which display, among other concepts, the following: (1) There is an anthropomorphic god whose prime symbol is the sun and who dwells in the heavens and on mountains. (2) He is god of the Tree of Life, which relates to life after death. (3) At death, the human spirit rises into heaven from the body. (4) A physical resurrection is implied. (5) Worship involves sacrifice and divine sacrificial atonement. And (6) the spirit of an unborn child originates in the heavens. . . .

Some of the new details do more than support previous interpretations; they strengthen those interpretations in deeper and more meaningful ways. For example, there is a glyph beyond the head of the river where the path line originates, decipherable as "dark mists," in its relationship to Maya hieroglyphics. In the Lehi vision context this glyph could express the duality of the spiritual journey from darkness into the full gospel light achieved at the Tree of Life. (See 1 Ne. 8:4-8, 22-24.) It is located at the far right center of the carving, where the creation life-cycle begins in which rain bands or "mist" cover the eyes and ear of a human head. Other concepts now recognizable are that immortality is connected with eating the fruit of the tree, and that the two cherubim mentioned earlier are male and female, as was the case in the ancient Israelitish temple, and function together in behalf of man in bringing him to the Tree of Life.

My current research involves astronomical orientations and calendar significance of the monuments at Izapa. This study could provide a key to help unlock the meaning of the monuments as a whole, integrated unit supporting the Izapa temple center function. Also, Old World comparative studies are under way to help trace the roots of Izapan culture and evaluate its role in the rise of Mesoamerican civilization. (54-55)

The tree (l), the river (2), the path (3), and the rod of iron (4) are clearly portrayed on the stone. Cherubim typical of Mesopotamian and Egyptian scenes are shown on each side of the tree. They face the tree and are in human form but have bird heads. Bird heads, and sometimes only wings on the human form, characterize the guardians in Assyrian and Egyptian art.

The Book of Mormon also gives the meaning and interpretation of the symbols carved on the stone. The river represents the barrier of evil between people and happiness. The rod of iron represents the word of God, which, if followed, leads one to the tree of eternal life and happiness. The tree symbolizes the love of God—and if one loves God he will keep His commandments, and this leads to the fruits of the tree—happiness and eternal life. It is an entire philosophy of life, set out succinctly on 15 tons of stone.

The Book of Mormon description of the scene is found in 1 Nephi 8:

> I beheld a tree, whose fruit was desirable to make one happy. . . . I knew that it was desirable above all other fruit. And as I cast my eyes round about, that perhaps I might discover my family also, I beheld a river of water; and it ran along, and it was near the tree of which I was partaking the fruit. . . . And I beheld a straight and narrow path, which came along by the rod of iron, even to the tree by which I stood; and it also led by the head of the fountain. . . .

Chapter Four
# THE TREE OF LIFE

*Success in righteousness, the power to avoid deception
and resist temptation, guidance in our daily lives, healing of
the soul—these are but a few of the promises the Lord has
given to those who will come to His word. . . . However
diligent we may be in other areas, certain blessings are to be
found only in the scriptures, only in coming to the word of
the Lord and holding fast to it as we make our way through
the mists of darkness to the tree of life.*

President Ezra Taft Benson
General Conference, October 1986

(*Ensign*, May 1986, p. 82)
Used by permission

The Tree of Life is one of the oldest and most prevalent
symbols in the Near East and Mesoamerica. This sacred symbol
is discussed in the Bible and the Book of Mormon. The prophet
Nephi stated:

I beheld that the rod of iron, which my father had seen,
was the word of God, which led to the fountain of living
waters, or to the tree of life; which waters are a representation of the love of God; and I also beheld that the tree of life
was a representation of the love of God" (1 Ne. 11:25).

The cross representing the tree of life was one of the ancient
symbols of the Messiah of Mexico. Figure 1 (see page 4), from
an ancient Aztec codex, shows the cross on the cloak of
Quetzalcoatl. Ixtlilxochitl (a sixteenth-century native prince from
Texcoco, a city in the Valley of Mexico) wrote that Quetzalcoatl
was "the first who worshipped and placed the cross [among them]
which they called *Quiahuiteotlchicahualizteotl,* . . . which means:
God of rains and of health and tree of sustenance or life." The
cross and the tree of life, both related to the highest God—the
God of Life—were regarded in ancient Mesoamerica as identical.

In early Christian tradition the tree of life was considered the prototype and the equivalent of the cross of the crucifixion. Alan W. Watts makes this point clear in his book *Myth and Ritual in Christianity:*

> The clear identity of the Cross with this central tree of Eden is shown, not only in the legends of the Holy Rood which assert that the Cross of Christ was made from the wood of that Tree, but also in the famous Great Cross of the Lateran, a mosaic dating, perhaps from the time of Constantine. (159)

Watts describes crucifixion scenes in early Christian art in which the various elements of the ancient tree-of-life symbol (as shown in Figures 19, 20, and 21), including the bird above the cross-tree and the skull (monster) beneath are "contrasting figures of life and death."

The tree of life from the temple of the cross at Palenque, Mexico, which dates from A.D. 692, is in the form of a cross and includes all the other elements—the bird above, the monster beneath, and the guardians on each side of the tree-cross. The cross tree of life is shown with the Quetzal bird on top in Figure 22 (items 6 and 7) hereafter. Thus, Ixtlilxochitl's claim that the Biblical tree of life was known in ancient Mesoamerica has been confirmed in stone by surviving physical evidence.

From Yucatan comes direct confirmation of the claim of Ixtlilxochitl that the cross was associated with the Tree of Life in ancient Mesoamerica.

*Chilam* was revered by the Maya of Yucatan as a prophet who lived in the town of Mani in northern Yucatan during the closing decades of the fifteenth century and the early part of the sixteenth century. His book is described by Ralph L. Roys as having been:

> written in the Maya language but in the European script which the early missionaries [from Spain] adapted to express such sounds as were not found in Spanish. Many passages were no doubt originally transcribed from older hieroglyphic manuscripts, some of which were still in

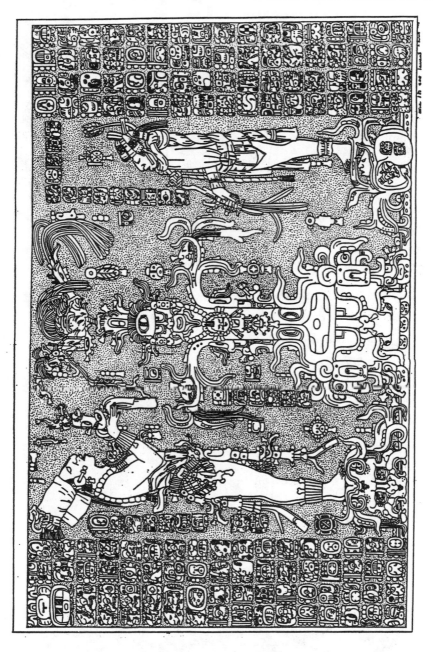

**Fig. 19: Tablet of the Foliated Cross from Palenque, Chiapas, Mexico. The carving dates from A.D. 692. Note the human heads in the leaves of the maize tree representing birth. (Courtesy of Linda Schele.)**

Fig. 20:  Assyrian Tree of Life scene from Nineveh in the eighth century B.C.

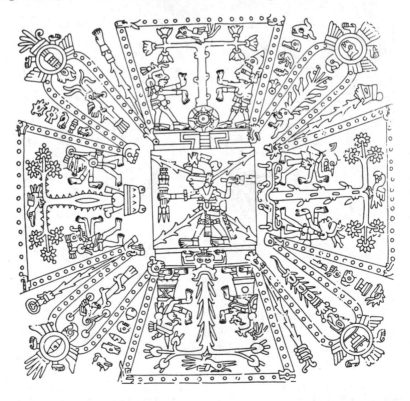

Fig. 21a:  Directional trees from page 1 of the fourteenth century A.D. Codex Fejervary-Mayer from central Mexico.

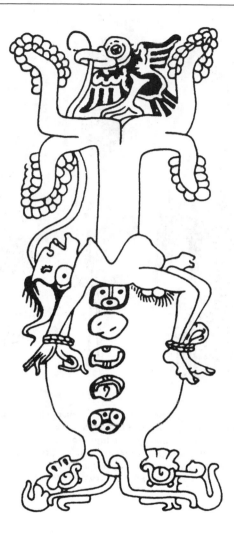

**Fig. 21b: Tree of Life growing from a human heart (the Maya Codex Dresden page 3 dating from between A.D. 1000 to 1200).**

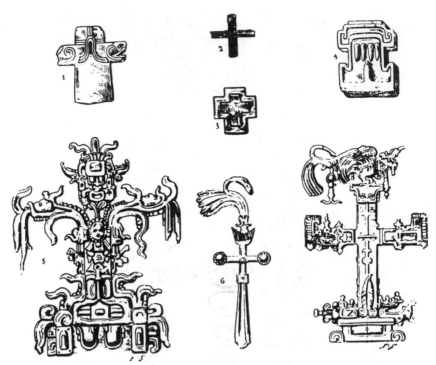

*Ancient Cities of the New World* (Charnay), page 86.

**Fig. 22: Ancient Mesoamerican crosses: No. 1 is a Serpent Cross; No. 2, Cross shown on Quetzalcoatl's tunic; No. 3, Cross from Mayapan, Yucatan; No. 4, Cross of Teotihuacan (near Mexio City) with Life symbol at the top; No. 5, Cross from the tablet of the Foliated Cross temple at Palenque, Chiapas; No. 6, Cross and Tree of Life from Yaxchilan, Guatemala, with serpent-like tail feathers extending from the tail of the bird at the top of the cross; No. 7, Tree and cross from the tablet of the Cross at Palenque, Chiapas.**

existence in northern Yucatan as late as the close of the seventeenth century. (3, 10) Shortly before the arrival of the Spaniards in the New World, *Chilam* prophesied the return of *Itzamna-Quetzalcoatl,* the bearded, white-robed, white-skinned Messiah of his ancient ancestry. When the Spaniards arrived, the Mayas of Yucatan believed at first, as did Moctezuma's people of central Mexico, that the "Fair God" had finally returned as promised (Roys 187). His people thereafter regarded *Chilam Balam* as a great prophet. Actually, he had merely repeated the ancient prophecy of the Fair God himself who had announced anciently that someday he would return. The prophet *Chilam* said a number of interesting and important things about *Itzamna,* the ancient prophecy of *Itzamna's* return, and *Hunab-ku,* father of *Itzamna.*

There is the sign of *Hunab-ku* on high. The raised wooden standard [the cross] shall come. You see the mutbird surmounting the raised wooden standard. Good indeed is the word of God that comes to us. The day of our regeneration comes. You do not fear the world, Lord, you are the only God who created us. It is sufficient, then, that the word of God is good, Lord. [He is] the guardian of our souls. He who receives him, who has truly believed, he will go to heaven with him.

Let us exalt his sign on high. . . . The First Tree of the World [the tree of life] is restored; it is displayed to the world. This is the sign of *Hunab-ku* on high. You shall be converted to the word of *Hunab-ku*, Lord; it came from heaven. Oh it is he who speaks to you! (Roys 167-69)

The raised wooden standard surmounted by the bird is an obvious reference to the Tree of Life, illustrated in Figures 20, 22, and 23. It is also observed that it is referred to as the "First Tree of the World." This may show the direct influence of the book of Genesis of ancient Israel upon the Mayas many centuries before the time of Columbus. The Tree of Life found in 1952 by

**Fig. 23: Tree of Life scenes in the form of crosses from Aztec codex, after Kingsborough.**

Alberto Ruz on the sarcophagus lid of the pyramid tomb at Palenque, Mexico, dates about 800 years before Columbus. Chilam's reference to the Tree of Life as a thing known to his own people has been verified in stone. The Tree of Life is mentioned, of course, in the book of Genesis. Archaeologists have found representations of it in the Near East and in Mexico (Parrot 359). The Itza people were the followers of *Itzamna*—that is, they may have been Christians of ancient Yucatan and Chiapas, Mexico.

Peter Martyr D'Anghera, an Italian geographer and historian who wrote in 1516 on the discovery of the Yucatan and the Mayas, observed,

> They worship idols, and some of them, but not all, are circumcised. They have laws, and are extremely honest in trading, which they carry on without money. Crosses have been seen amongst them; and when they were asked, through interpreters, the meaning of that emblem, some of them answered that a very beautiful man had once lived amongst them, who had left them this symbol as a remembrance of him; others said that a man more radiant than the sun had died upon the cross. (MacNutt 7-8)

J. Eric S. Thompson, Maya scholar of the Carnegie Institution, writes in The *Rise and Fall of the Maya Civilization* that at the time of the Spanish conquest, the Maya people associated the Christian cross with their own ancient Tree of Life, "conventionalized in art as a cross, decked with vegetation, on which the Quetzal bird perched" (142). Thus we see that the Quetzal bird, itself symbol of the Mesoamerica Messiah, or highest God, was associated with the ancient American cross.

Figures 24 and 25 are photographs taken by Rafael Girard of Guatemala City. Girard has worked many years among the present-day Mayas and particularly among the Chortis, a subdivision of the Mayan people, in Guatemala. The Chortis have held tenaciously to the religion and general way of life of their ancient ancestors. The ancients, for many centuries before the coming of the Spaniards, used the cross in their religious

**Fig. 24: Cross, symbol of Quetzalcoatl-Gucumatz. Photograph by Rafael Girard in the Maya temple of Chiquimula, Guatemala, 1956.**

ceremonies, covering it with green vegetation as they continue to do today—as illustrated in Figures 24 and 25.

The New World Christians of old emphasized the resurrection and the hope of eternal life—life after death—rather than upon the agony of Calvary. In keeping with their symbolism of the cross, "The Maya believed in the immortality of the soul and a life hereafter which the soul enjoyed when it left its earthly body" (Morley 221).

In his discussion of Mexico's Messiah, Morley points out that *Itzamna* stood at the head of the Maya pantheon with the father, *Hunab-Ku,* the Creator, "who does not appear to have

**Fig. 25: Cross, photographed in the native present-day Chorti Maya temple of Cayur, Guatemala by Rafael Girard in 1956.**

played an important part in the life of the common people" (222-25). In Christianity it is the Son who deals directly with man. Morley tells us that the glyph or day-sign for *Itzamna* was a benevolent deity, always the friend of man. He was the God of Life — the Light and the Life of the World — the Resurrection and the Life.

The ancient Mayas prayed to the Messiah for good crops of corn. Their society depended upon corn for its very existence. The Messiah thus became associated with maize and was sometimes referred to as the "God of Maize." As such, his primary symbols were still the serpent, the cross, and the Tree of Life, basic symbols of the Messiah of Israel. When the Spaniards came with their medieval European version of Christianity, the Mayas immediately recognized this Messiah in the Spanish doctrines and identified "Jesus, as the Bread of Life, with the maize God" (Thompson 237). The Mayas knew that the Christ of Cortes was identical to the God of Light and Life of their own New World ancestors, and that they themselves were a branch of the Old World fold of the Messiah.

The basic concept of the ancient religious ideas of both Palestine and Mexico is illustrated by the Tree of Life symbol. Opposites exist in all things. The death monster stands in opposition to the life forces — life in opposition to death, light in opposition to darkness, good to evil, sweet to bitter, kind to cruel, noble to base, morality to immorality, knowledge to ignorance, mature to immature.

Man is given intelligence to make choices. If there were no opposites, man would have no choices to make, for there would be nothing upon which to exercise his intelligence and choice. The joy of living is in making selections. To interfere with the freedom of exercising preferences is to interfere with the plan of God. For man to exercise freedom, the things to be acted upon must not be all of one kind. There must be an opposition or there is no freedom. If there were no opposition, life would be homogeneous, like gelatin — uniform, simple, and of no consequence. To know life, we must know death. To appreciate harmony, we must know discord. To know good, one must understand evil. God provided us with a world that was not prefabricated and predetermined for us. Were it not so, there would be no growth, no progress, and no maturing. With opposites and opposition in all things, man has infinite possibilities for eternal progress, everlasting growth, and endless maturing. Man can go on from achievement to achievement, in eternal progression.

The key to real success and happiness, according to the Tree of Life symbolism, is to make those choices in harmony with the word of God. God reveals the way but does not compel man to follow it. The opposite way, which leads to death and sorrow, is permitted for good reason.

The concept of a conflict between two great forces, good and evil, dominated the religious thinking of the ancients of Mexico. Miguel Covarrubias has stated the Mexican idea concisely:

> The legends of the struggle between Quetzalcoatl and Tezcatlipoca [the devil] are probably a Toltec rationalization to correlate historical events with an older myth, the eternal war between good and evil, black and white, war and peace, darkness and light, which is the basic undercurrent in Mexican religious philosophy. An old Indian legend claims that the feud dated back to the beginning of the world, when Tezcatlipoca ruled over the earth as the sun that lit and fed an incipient world. (136)

## Symbol of Good and Evil

Two sacred trees are related to the concept of Hamlet's Mill and the movements of the planets and constellations. (Hamlet's Mill is a northern European concept of the universe in the shape of an hour glass. The earth is in the middle and all the planets, stars, and constellations revolve around a spindle that passes from the top of the universe [north] to its bottom [south].) One is a Tree of Life; the other is a Tree of Enlightenment or Truth. In Old Testament terminology this latter would be the Tree of the

Knowledge of Good and Evil. The illustrations from the Near East for the Tree of Knowledge of Good and Evil are represented by the two serpents intertwined to form a caduceus (in modern times the symbol of the medical profession). This Tree of Knowledge of Good and Evil as well as the Tree of Life in the ancient mythologies involved in Hamlet's Mill concept are cosmic trees. They have their setting in the night-time sky. They also have connections with the Milky Way, particularly the Tree of Life. Several examples of clay cylinder seals from the ancient Near East show different examples of both the Tree of Life and the Tree of Knowledge of Good and Evil.

In India and the Far East as well as parts of Europe, often the symbolism of the two trees is combined in the same tree so that the symbolism of the Tree of Enlightenment or the Tree of Knowledge of Good and Evil as well as the Tree of Life symbols are shared in the same scenes. In the Near East and in ancient Mesoamerica we see illustrations of the two trees separately.

We see a Classic Maya illustration equivalent to the Tree of Knowledge and Enlightenment at Palenque in the Tablet from the Temple of the Cross. Here the tree in the form of a cross is coming out of the head of a monster at its base. The head of the monster has a band of seven planetary signs representing the sun, moon, Mercury, Venus, Mars, Jupiter, and Saturn (Figure 26). Obviously, this is a cosmic tree. The other tree, the Tree of Life, in the Near East was depicted by the ancient Sumerians as a god by the name of Dumuzi. He is considered the son of the Abyss, referring to the waters of the Underworld and Lord of the Tree of Life, the ever-dying, ever-resurrected Sumerian god (Campbell 14).

Dumuzi, known to the Hebrews as Tammuz, is referred to in the book of Ezekiel (8:14) in the Old Testament.

In Mesoamerica, the early Spanish historian of the sixteenth century Diego de Landa says this of the Tree of Life: "The Tree of Life was a symbol of good as opposed to evil, since it is said to have been created with great virtue against the evil spirit" (Tozzer 43).

A good example of the Tree of Life from Mesoamerica is

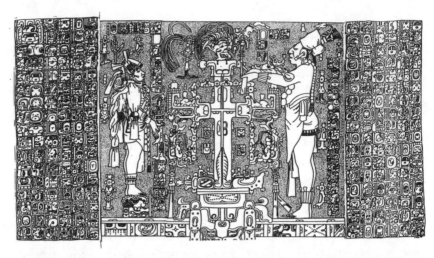

**Fig. 26: Tablet of the Cross from the Temple of the Cross at Palenque, Chiapas about A.D. 692 This tablet gives much mythological and legendary ancestry for the Maya rulers Pacal and Chan-Bahlum who lived in the seventh century A.D. However, the earliest mythological ancestry dates back into the third millennium B.C. (Courtesy of Linda Schele.)**

from the tablet of the Temple of the Foliated Cross at Palenque, which illustrates the Tree of Life as a corn plant and depicts the resurrection or rebirth of plants as well as humans (Fig. 19). It is associated with the daytime sky, whereas the Tree of Knowledge of Good and Evil or the World Tree is shown associated with the night-time sky and the planets and not in the context of rebirth or resurrection. Related to this scene of the Tree of Life as a corn plant among the Classic Maya of ancient Mesoamerica is a similar idea used by the Hopi Indians of the southwestern United States. The sacred corn plant symbolizes life to the Hopi.

In Mesoamerica we can associate the two trees with two different concepts of paradise. One is the Paradise of Tamoanchan, which refers to the 13th or highest heaven. It was the connecting link between mankind and the gods in the heavens until a fall took place in which the trunk of the tree was split and broken. The second tree is associated with the earthly Paradise of Tlalocan, and the Rain God Tlaloc. It is located in the east in the land of rain and is generally considered to be the gulf coast area of Mesoamerica. Tlaloc is also considered the god of rain and the god of mountains. An important Tlaloc ceremony in

Mesoamerica involved a large tree that was erected in the ceremonial center for rituals. Surrounding this large central tree were four smaller trees representing the four directions associated with the tlaloques, who were helpers of the rain god. As we mentioned earlier, the rain god Tlaloc in Mesoamerica is associated with the planet Mercury. In the Near East the god of this Tree of Knowledge or the World Tree is also associated with the planet Mercury.

What we have is a mythology involving Hamlet's Mill and the structure of the universe, with the movements of the constellations and the planets all being part of this mythology, and particularly seven planets, these planets being the moon and the sun, plus the five planets visible to the unaided eye: Mercury, Venus, Mars, Jupiter, and Saturn. But we find in this mythology that two other positions often represent eclipses. These eclipse dragons have two heads. The seven planets and these two eclipse phenomenon bring the total number of positions in this model to nine.

In Table 1, we have charted the nine positions for Greece, Egypt, Syria, Mesopotamia, India, and Mesoamerica. What is very intriguing is the possibility that these nine astronomical positions may be in the Old Testament. This will be dealt with later.

The two eclipse phenomena that are emphasized in the Ennead refer to powers in mythology that are greater or higher than the planets, even the sun, because the two trees were above and beyond the sun. They could even darken the earth or eclipse the sun. But they were not visible (just a section is visible to the observer here on earth), so therefore they are represented in mythology as dragons with double heads—a creature that no one has ever seen on earth. Associated with these two-headed dragons are the stars or constellations known as Polaris or the North Star; and Sirius, representing the equivalent of the South Polar region of the universe. In Egypt, Mesopotamia, India, and Mesoamerica we find a good deal of mythological information and a certain amount of art work depicting these two-headed eclipse demons. But in ancient Israel we have an artifact that represents seven of

# Table I

## ENNEAD (NINE) COMPARISONS

| Greece | Egypt | Syria | Mesopotamia | India | Mesoamerica |
|---|---|---|---|---|---|
| Uranus, sky | Horus/Min Khem/Nut sky | Baal Leviathan | Anu, *above*, sky. Ecliptic pole star. Tiamat. | Visvakarma | Tlaloc/Chac, Tapir-like nose. G8, Chac Xib Chac. Hunahpu, 9 Wind, TI, rear-head of the eclipse dragon. Kin sign, God B, God H (headband twin). |
| Dionysus, leader of the fire breathing start (pleiades) Sirius. | Shu, air, Af, night sun. | Adonis (Youth, no king). Crete (Zageus-Dionysus). | Bel-Enlil/ Kaksidi/ Dumunzi/ Tammuz. Equator pole star, Sirius (night sun). | Ganapati: head, ascending node (head of the clipse dragon cut off from his body). | Cinteotl, I Flower, G3, TII. Front head of the eclipse dragon, kan sign. White Tezcatlipoca, God E. Hun Hunaphu. *Tah*, obsidian mirror, God K, Bolon Dzacab, Flare God, Manikin Scepter. |
| Helius | Re/Atun Shagreel | Sipish, Masc. Shapash, fem. | Utu/Shamash | Agni | Piltzintecuhtli, 7 Flower, G2. |
| Constell: | Constell: | Constell: | Constell: | Constell: | Constell: |
| Planet: Sun | Planet: Sun | Planet: Sun | Planet: Sun | Planet: Sun | Planet: Sun |
| Selene | Tefenet, | Tanit-phane-balos | Nanna/Sin | Vyana | Chalchihuitlicue, 8 Ahau, Twins, G5. |
| Constell: | Constell: | Constell: | Constell: | Constell: | Constell: |
| Planet: Moon | Planet: Moon | Planet: Moon | Planet: Moon | Planet: Moon | Planet: Moon |

| Greece | Egypt | Syria | Mesopotamia | India | Mesoamerica |
|---|---|---|---|---|---|
| Ares/Typhon/Herekles | Seth, long legged type of boar. | Resheph/Hauron, Melcarth, Mot, Ullikummi. | Nergal, Imdugud-bird. Ningirsu. | Kalmasha | Xiuhtecuhtli, G9. Blue Tezcatlipoca/ Vucub Cakish, God L, I Death (Hiutzilopochtli, Gr. Bear, *Burland*, p. 106 79 & *Dutting*, p. 139 |
| Constell: | Constell: Great Bear | Constell: | Constell: Great Bear | Constell: | Constell: Great Bear |
| Planet: Mars | Planet: Mars | Planet: Mars | Planet: Mars | Planet: Mars | Planet: Mars |
| Hermes (crane-ibis) | Thoth/ Nephthys (ibis mask) | Humbaba | Nabu/ Ningishzida. | Vishnu | Mictlantecuhtli, G4. God N; Cabracan, pillar or spindle. Red Tezcatlipoca. |
| Constell: | Constell: | Constell: | Constell: | Constell: | Constell: |
| Planet: Mercury | Planet: Mercury | Planet: Mercury | Planet: Mercury | Planet: Mercury | Planet: Mercury |
| Zeus/Jove | Osiris, dead in the under-world, no return. | Assur*/Baal-Shamem | Bel-Merodach, Ninurta/ Nibiru. | Sukra | Itzlli, 7 Crocodile, GI. Black Tezcatlipoca, Mixcoatl, 7 Cimi, Zipacna or Itzamna, God C & D, blood and sacredness. *Burland*, p. 106. Head of Osiris on a Croc. *Jairazbhoy*, 70. |
| Constell: | Constell: Orion | Constell: | Constell: Orion | Constell: | Constell: Orion |
| Planet: Jupiter | Planet: Jupiter | Planet: Jupiter | Planet: Jupiter | Planet: Jupiter | Planet: Jupiter |

| Greece | Egypt | Syria | Mesopotamia | India | Mesoamerica |
|--------|-------|-------|-------------|-------|-------------|
| | | *s r<br>Osiris<br>Assur<br>Asaru (epithet<br>of Marduk). | | | |
| Aphrodite,<br>Hera | Hathor/Isis | Astarte/<br>Anath,<br>'Ashtar,<br>masc.,<br>Chemosh (M.<br>star) | Inanna/Ishtar,<br>Beltis/Nidaba,<br>Nasaba?<br>Ninhursag | Guart | Tlazolteotl, I<br>Caban, G6.<br>God I. |
| Constell: | Constell:<br>Virgo | Constell:<br>Virgo | Constell: | Constell: | Constell: |
| Planet:<br>Venus | Planet:<br>Venus | Planet:<br>Venus | Planet:<br>Venus | Planet:<br>Venus | Planet:<br>Venus |
| Kronos, fish<br>god, stag. | Geb, earth.<br>Ptah, stag?<br>Khepri. | Kumarbi,<br>Hittite.<br>El/Koshar/<br>Baal<br>Hadad/Dagan,<br>fish. | Enki, earth.<br>Ea/Ninib/<br>Apsu, *below*,<br>Abzu, watery<br>abyss. | Prajapati,<br>deer shape. | Tepeyollotl, 8<br>Jaguar, 13<br>Death, G7.<br>Ixbalanque, TIII,<br>Xib-balam &<br>Xib-bolon. Deer. |
| Constell: | Constell: | Constell: | Constell: | Constell: | Constell: |
| Planet:<br>Saturn | Planet:<br>Saturn | Planet:<br>Saturn | Planet:<br>Saturn | Planet:<br>Saturn | Planet:<br>Saturn |

these deities correlated with planets and constellations. This is the Menorah, the golden seven-lamp candlestick described by Moses when he came down from Mt. Sinai (Exo. 25:31-40 and 37:12-24). Carol L. Meyers explains:

> In Hebraic tradition the Tree of Life represented scripturally goes back to Adam and Eve in the Garden of Eden wherein two trees played a symbolic role, the Tree of Knowledge of Good and Evil and the Tree of Life. The Tree of Life ritualistically symbolizes this tradition as found throughout other parts of the Near East or the ancient Hebrews, but the Hebrews expanded the cosmic symbolism by transferring the plant motif from god to the people of Israel, resulting in a perpetual point of contact with the Divine sphere, [so that the] conception of Israel as the Tree on God's mountain can be seen as the ultimate challenge to the pagan fertility and immortality themes. . . . [Thus] the people of Israel . . . achieve collective immortality existing forever on their inherited land, and in this sense share the eternal attributes of the tree deity. (156)

Bonnie E. Percival writes:

> The most well known ritualistic symbol of the stylized Tree of Life in Hebraic traditions is the seven branched lampstand called the Menorah. The Menorah, like the Tree of Life in the cella [inner part] of Mesopotamian temples, has been an integral part of the Jewish temples since the Tabernacle of Moses in the wilderness. (8)

Meyers suggests that the Menorah is "a symbol of the cosmic tree within the tabernacle precinct to contribute toward securing the reality of God's presence" (180). Meyers also points out that the "ornamentation [of the Menorah] is the combination of three elements, cup, knob, and flower, repeated three times on each of the branches and four times on the main stem stand" (22). The Menorah represents the almond tree in full bloom. Indeed the word Menorah means "made like almonds" or "almond blossoms."

However, the Menorah deals with only seven of the nine elements of our model. All nine elements are brought together in the fourth chapter of the Old Testament book of Zechariah. In this chapter an angel of the Lord appears to the Prophet Zechariah (about 537 B.C.) as the Jewish people are coming out of captivity in Babylon and going back to Jerusalem. The angel shows the Prophet Zechariah a candlestick of gold with a bowl on top of it. The candlestick has seven lamps, and there are two olive trees, one upon the right side of the bowl and the other on the left side. The angel asks Zechariah if he knows what all of this means, and when he says he does not, the angel explains, referring to the seven candlestick lamps:

> . . . they are the eyes of the Lord, which run to and fro through the whole earth. Then answered I, and said unto him, What are these two olive trees upon the right side of the candlestick and upon the left side thereof? And I answered again, and said unto him, What be these two olive branches which through the two golden pipes empty the golden oil out of themselves? And he answered me and said, Knowest thou not what these be? And I said, No, my Lord. Then said he, These are the two anointed ones, that stand by the Lord of the whole earth. (Zech. 4:10-14)

These two anointed ones are the two witnesses of the book of Revelation who in the last days prophesy in the streets of Jerusalem, are killed and then three days later taken up into the Heavens before the eyes of all the people of Jerusalem. (A more complete discussion of the two witnesses is found in the eleventh chapter of the book of Revelation.) In our Ennead model, the two anointed ones take the position of the two heads of the eclipse dragon.

Zechariah 4 and related Biblical scriptures indicate that we may have the equivalent of nine astronomical elements (the seven planets and the two witnesses or eclipse events) in the Old Testament story that we find in Near Eastern mythology and the mythology of other parts of the world.

## The Stepped Fret

The art and culture of Mesoamerica were primarily religious. One great characteristic of a religion is its tendency to preserve forms with the meaning accumulating around them. Out of all the motifs and symbols of Mesoamerica, possibly none is more important than the stepped fret, which absolutely dominates its art. Hermann Beyer documented approximately 250 variations in his study cited in Paul Westheim's *The Art of Ancient Mexico*. Despite its prevalence and its importance, scholars express no consensus on what the stepped fret means.

It remained for Darrell J. Stoddard, an appreciator of Mesoamerican art and a former Brigham Young University student of archaeology, to connect this potent Mesoamerican symbol to the most widespread symbol of the Old World — the tree of life. Much of what follows is based on his research.

The tree of life is a near-universal symbol. As Willets has noted,

> The notion of a Tree of Life, growing in a paradise inaccessible to ordinary mortals, and bearing fruit capable of rejuvenating, reanimating, or prolonging life when eaten, is part of the stock of world myth. Sometimes associated with a Well or Fountain of Life-giving water, and varying in species according to its geographical setting, it crops up in Egyptian, Sumerian, Babylonian, Phoenician, Norse, and Gaelic Folk-lore [sic], and no doubt in that of many other cultures as well. . . .
>
> The *motif* traveled widely. Like the myth behind it, it is known in almost every ancient culture of the Old World, including Assyria and Babylonia, Palestine, Egypt, Mycenae, and India. The Arabs carried it to Spain, Sicily, and western Europe, while under Byzantine auspices it reached Russia and Italy.
>
> All versions have the same heraldic air — a highly stylized, geometrical tree flanked by two figures. At Mohenjo-daro, these are bulls; at Suza, lions; on Sumerian seals, mountains; on Sassanian silks, duck or the Holy Ibis; from Assyria, figures with eagles' heads; from Cyprus, goats eating; from Crete, snakes. (159-60)

Count Goblet D'Alviella's classic work *The Migration of Symbols,* after more than eighty years still one of the best sources on symbols, notes that the first type—the tree between facing animals—first appears in southern Mesopotamia at the time of Sargon I, "some four thousand years before our era." He traces its route to the Phoenicians, who abstracted it into "an interlacing of spirals and strap-like curves," some of which bear winged sphinxes. They transmitted it to "the whole of Western Asia," but its introduction in Greece may have predated even the Phoenician influence. Moving in the other direction, the Persians adopted it after the fall of Babylon and transmitted it eastward into India immediately before Alexander's invasion. Thus it appears among Buddhist sculptures at Bharhut (122-124).

A second variation, according to D'Alviella, is the image of the tree between two human or semi-human personages facing each other. As might be expected with two variants so closely related, there are many combinations of beast-headed humans and human-headed animals. This variant followed the same route and appears in China as well as India. He continues:

> From the Indian Archipelago—or from Eastern Asia—it may have even reached the New World, if we are to judge from the resemblance of the scene depicted on the Javanese medals to certain images found in manuscripts connected with the ancient civilization of Central America.
>
> We have seen that the Cross was used, in the symbolism of the ancient inhabitants of America, to represent the winds which bring the rain. These crosses sometimes assume a tree-like form, and are then composed of a stem bearing two horizontal branches, with a bird perched on the fork, as in the famous panel of Palenque. Moreover, this tree is sometimes placed between two personages facing one another, with a sort of wreath of feathers on their heads, who cannot but recall the monstrous aspect of the beings depicted on both sides of the Tree upon the medals of Javanese temples. . . . We have here certainly fresh evidence in favor of the theory which already relies upon so many symbolical and ornamental similarities in order to discover,

in the pre-Columbia civilization of America, the traces of
intercourse with Japan, China, or the Indian Archipelago.
(12)

Other characteristics of the great mythic trees are that they
emit a fluid or substance which bestows or sustains life; they may
be the home of a deity or a manifestation of a deity; and they
may also through their stems, flowers, and fruits represent
symbols of fertility.

For those in the more modern Judeo-Christian tradition, the
mention of the tree of life and associated fountains begins with
the description of "the tree of life also in the midst of the [Garden
of Eden]. And a river went out of Eden to water the garden; and
from thence it was parted, and became into four heads" (Gen.
2:9-10). In the Slavonic version of the apocryphal book of Enoch
II, "the tree is the source of the four rivers which flow to the
earthly Eden," and as such "they had the power of the tree of life"
(Goodenough 7:126, 128).

The most direct connection of the tree of life and the
fountain of water appears in Revelation 22:1-2:

> And he shewed me a pure river of water of life, clear as
> crystal, proceeding out of the throne of God and of the
> Lamb.
> In the midst of the street of it, and on either side of the
> river, was there the tree of life, which bear twelve manner of
> fruits, and yielded her fruit every month: and the leaves of
> the tree were for the healing of the nations.

Thus we see a vivid manifestation of the Old World tradition
linking tree and fountain in the first century A.D., long after the
New World inhabitants had established their own forms of the
symbols. (See also Gen. 3:22,24; Prov. 3:18, 11:30, 13:12, 15:4;
Rev. 2:7.)

Thanks to the biblical record, there is a literary tradition of
the tree of life, but although "many other elements of symbolism
were clearly connected with the tree cults of the ancient world,
the oldest and most persistent is the mystic notion that the tree

represents, symbolizes, the deity and is, or represents the source of life" (Goodenough 7:91). In both Mesopotamia and Egypt, the tree (usually the date palm or the sycamore) represented the powers of fertility of the god or goddess assigned to that tree with the power to confer immortality and fertility on the worshipper, usually by the medium of a life-giving fluid (Goodenough 7:94-96). He finds the same pattern present in Greece as well.

It is in Greece, however, that one of the most interesting aspects of the tree of life develops through a process of representation and abstraction that strips it to its essential form. As D'Alviella notes:

> A representation . . . does not aim at being a reproduction. A reproduction implies if not identity with at least similitude to, the original; but a symbol only requires that it shall have certain features in common with the object represented, so that, by its presence alone, it may evoke the conception of the latter, as is the case with a missile weapon and lightning, a sickle and harvest-time, a ring and marriage, a pair of scales and the idea of justice, kneeling and the sentiment of submission, and so forth. (1)

Stoddard comments:

> It is, I believe, a universal trait of human nature to create artistic symbols just as it is to create words which are in themselves symbols; but with pictorial symbols as with words, we cannot understand those of a foreign civilization without some common ground from which to view the symbol or understand the word. . . .
>
> The process through which a work of art is reduced to an abstract symbol is something which may take several hundred years, or as I have observed in the art of children (who readily create and interpret their visual world through symbols much the same as primitive peoples) may take just a few minutes. It is a process which may be compared to the origin of folk poetry which evolves through being passed by word of mouth through numerous generations with each generation eliminating that which is insignificant.

> . . . In the graphic or visual arts, the end product may
> be unintelligible — and usually is — to those who do not know
> of the process through which it evolved and the portentous
> meanings which it may hold, but to those who comprehend
> its significance it is all the more meaningful because the
> imagination is set free. (8-9)

In the case of the tree of life, Greek architecture was heavily
influenced by Egypt and "the territories of other nations with
which she maintained commercial relations, the Canaanites and
Hittites, so that we have to take into account the remains in
Palestine, Phoenicia, Cyprus, and Anatolia" (Dinsmoor 58). In
all of these regions, a "sacred tree" design was popular. It has
been traced back from the thirteenth or fourteenth century
Anatolian cylinder seals to the throne room of Nebuchadnezzar
in the sixth century. In all cases, we see some form of the spiral or
volute. Since Greeks actually served in these latter courts, the
influence could have been direct as well as indirect in creating the
Ionic column which has become the hallmark of Greek
architecture the world over.

Dinsmoor observes clear "arboreal" elements in the Proto-
Ionic capitals, but by the sixth century B.C. the column had
evolved into its classic form. Gone are the leaves, to be replaced
by the "egg-and-dart ovolo, which thereupon becomes the
characteristic lower member and likewise, because of its Oriental
origins, the most typical Ionic moulding" (Dinsmoor 62).
Frequently accompanying the Ionic column is a decorative frieze
or capital motif — the palmette. Dinsmoor calls it "a floral
decoration of Mesopotamian origin related to the 'sacred tree,' at
first imitated faithfully by the Greeks and later varied with
pointed or even flame-shaped petals" (393). The palmette is also a
stylized tree of life.

The spiral volutes which so distinctively mark the Ionic
capital are, Stoddard argues, a representation of the fountain of
living water. Some examples show the column rising between
paired volutes, which puzzles scholars, who know that leaves
should be on the top of the trees. In Mesopotamian art, however,
"whorls symbolize water. . . . These are traditional motifs and the

artist makes no attempt to free himself from them" (Moscati 97-98). These whorls are simple spirals, just as parallel zigzags represent water in Egyptian mural art, and the letter M in Greek is drawn from the symbol for "sea." The association of life-giving liquid with the tree and the placement of volutes at the base of the tree becomes clear.

Nor is it confusing when the volutes are moved to the top of the tree. As Stoddard explains, "They were originally at the bottom of the tree and then were moved to the top as an architectural necessity to reduce the length of the lintel required to span the distance between columns" (12). Another insight Stoddard contributes which no other scholar has noticed is that the "Greek fret which consists of a running band of spirals in various forms as a decorative motif is almost certainly a variation of the tree of life volute. It is often in an interlocking pattern and is used on the interior as well as the exterior and may be either circular or rectangular. . . . I have observed that in nearly every culture which uses the spiral as a design, the modification of the spiral into a rectilinear form also is used with the same meaning" (13).

If Stoddard's perception is correct and the tree of life symbol with an associated fountain of water has shaped the distinctive forms of Greek architecture, then the possible links between this powerful Old World image and the universally prevalent but mysterious stepped fret of ancient Mesoamerica becomes very intriguing. (See photo of stepped fret opposite title page.)

In Paul Westheim's chapter on the stepped fret, he points out that:

> Together with the plumed serpent, the stepped fret (Xicalcoliuhqui) is the most typical ornamental form of the Valley of Mexico, territory of the Nahua tribes. It is as characteristic of Nahua culture as the stylized lotus flower of Egyptian art, the rosette of Assyrian art, the palmette and meander of Greek art, and the ornament of lacery or plaits, an ornament steeped in exaltation of the Celto-Irish. We find the stepped fret as far north as Arizona (Pueblo

Indians, Casas Grandes), passing through Yucatan, to as far south as Peru, where it is of predominant importance in ornaments. (92-123)

Its meaning, however, has puzzled scholars. Herman Beyer, whose documentation of the form Westheim cites, found it a purely decorative formal element. Westheim disagrees. Even while he acknowledges that the lack of written sources and the antiquity of the form may prevent a final interpretation, he argues:

> The art of ancient Mexico is markedly religious art, an art of suprasensible contents of knowledge. What determines the creative will is not the esthetic experience but the religious. . . . It is difficult for us to believe that one of the essential ornaments of the world of ancient Mexico was no more than a decorative element. In the first place, the great frequency of the stepped fret and the fact that it was used for centuries oppose this thesis. As we can observe from some of the "dying" European styles, any exclusively ornamental form would have spent itself in the course of time, lost its attraction, and been superseded by new formal creations with new fascination and suggestive force. The stepped fret was not replaced by new ornaments because the Nahua people saw in it a psychic or magic value beyond that of the esthetic. The stepped fret is no more a purely decorative form than is the cross. (100-101)

Westheim, noting that the symbol is never associated with death, suggests that "it constitutes a sign of magic protection against death" and agrees with other Mexicanists that it is a stylized representation of the serpent and the water—both of which are closely associated. He himself argues more specifically that the stepped fret may be derived from the zigzag form of lightning, an attribute of the rain god, Tlaloc. "It proves nothing that our eyes cannot at first glance distinguish in the stepped fret the serpentine form from which it probably is derived. Rather, it shows that since time immemorial the Nahua people were so familiar with this sign that the stylization could be limited to a mnemotechnical [memory aid] insinuation" (105).

Observing that the stepped fret is "totally asymmetrical," Westheim argues that it represents a religious world view of "tension":

> The dynamic rhythm of the stepped fret springs from the clash of antagonistic formal elements and from the violent interruptions that are produced again and again in its drawing. The stairway is a vehement ascent; the hook breaks this movement, twists it, destroys it with identical vehemence. It is as though a demoniacal force had committed itself to annihilating all the energy inherent in the stairway. In the next figure we see the same ascent, the same interruption. Each time that the stairway breaks away, it is prevented from achieving a free, unhampered development; its destiny is always to come upon the counterforce that destroys it, pushes it back down to the level it started from. There is a near harmonious flow. There is a struggle of elements, an interruption of the course of the movement, a brusque change of direction, a new advance, a new defeat, birth, and death. A rhythm that rests in the constant repetition of the motif and in an energetic contrast among the different elements [sic]. (108)

This exciting aesthetic definition provides an alternative reading to the symmetrical shapes of such typical Old World forms as the lotus, the palmette, the rosette, and the Greek meander:

> The spiral form exists in all cultures. It has one almost identical basic form with many variations, but the value of the essence is, in each case, entirely different. The Celtic spiral is ecstatic longing for redemption; the Greek meander is neutrality, euphony, esthetic harmony; the oriental tapestry of ornaments is a passive submersal in the consciousness of the infinite. And the stepped fret expresses the vital tension of forces subject to a rhythm. (112-113)

Westheim agrees with Beyer that the typical forms of the stepped fret are the stairsteps, the spiral, and the hook. Sometimes the spiral will be on the inside of the steps and sometimes on the outside. It can be curved or rectangular. In appraising photographs of hundreds of manifestations of the stepped fret, Stoddard felt an insight emerging as he studied a temple portrayed in one of the pre-Hispanic codices which had two volutes on top of a stepped temple. The parallelism matched that of the volutes on an Ionic column, and the bisected temple, complete with volute, formed a stepped fret.

The association of the tree of life, the water of life, and the feathered serpent — the Mesoamerican deity most closely associated with the Christ figure — makes a rich and powerful combination of symbols with obvious links to their counterparts in the Old World. Placing the fret atop a temple where the altar is located and where a priest would go to commune with deity is also appropriate, particularly since the stepped temples have traditionally been thought to represent sacred mountains, or places of communication with deity.

One version of what may be a stepped fret is the wind-jewel symbol (Figure 27) used to identify Quetzalcoatl. The only form of the stepped fret found in nature, it is derived from making a transverse cut of a voluted brachiopod or conch shell. Such a cut produced a stepped effect around the outside of a spiral, a unique combination of shapes. Furthermore, the wind-jewel symbol, like the stepped fret, is never found in association with the god or the cult of the dead in Mesoamerica, but instead is related to water, wind, and fire — also symbols of Quetzalcoatl.

In yet another interesting parallel, the wind-jewel is also associated with birth. Another birth symbol is the snail or the sea shell. Many Mesoamerican deities are depicted as being born out of sea shells, while human reproductive organs are frequently portrayed in the form of snails or sea shells (Westheim 115-19). Not unexpectedly, representations of Quetzalcoatl often depict him wearing a necklace of snails.

Before the meridian of time, the stepped fret symbolically represented the stepped temple and tree of life or fountain of

**Fig. 27: Wind-jewel on the chest of Quetzalcoatl from the codex Magliabecchiano (Late Postclassic period of central Mexico).**

living waters. After the visit of Jesus Christ to the Western Hemisphere, it becomes his symbol. Interestingly, the same symbols (temple, tree of life, and fountain of living water) are also identified with Christ in Christian (Eastern Hemisphere) art and theology.

## Hopi Indians

The stepped fret in Mesoamerica today is found primarily in ornamental objects (Kubler 17, 29). The stepped fret, however, found as a living cultural element among the Hopis of the American Southwest, probably constitutes the single most popular design element in Hopi jewelry, pottery, and weavings. Darrell Stoddard, who made many trips to the Hopi Reservation, interviewed dozens of Hopis at First Mesa, Second Mesa, and Third Mesa, Arizona. Initially reluctant to discuss the stepped fret with him, they eventually divulged that the spiral of the stepped fret was a symbol of eternal life, sacred water, and the serpent. They did not mention the tree of life, would not tell him any meaning attached to the stepped portion of the figure, and remained clearly reluctant to talk about it at all, saying that "much of the meaning of the stepped fret was too sacred to discuss" (Hopi informants).

Figure 28 shows a stalk of corn topped by a stepped fret, an appropriate conjunction, since corn is the most important food crop among the Hopis, as it also was among the Indians of Mesoamerica.

Another typical variation, as seen in Figure 29, is the stepped fret with an attached curve which the Hopis claim represents a water bird. This representation is extremely interesting for two reasons. In both Mesopotamian art, as we have seen, as well as in depictions of Mesoamerican art, there is nearly always a bird above the tree. The Fejervary-Mayer Codex alone has four tree of life forms, each with the spiral symbol, life symbol, a bird at the top, and figures facing the tree (Westheim cover, 13). The fact that it is a water bird is particularly significant for a desert people and makes the link stronger between the "fountain" and the tree.

**Fig. 28: Hopi silver jewelry showing a corn stalk capped by a stepped fret.**

**Fig. 29: Hopi silver jewelry depicting the stepped fret and a detached curve that represents a water bird.**

## Pueblo Indians

The Rio Grande Pueblo Indians use the stepped fret, a combination of the serpent symbol and the stepped temple. The two symbols are always associated to form the stepped fret. The Zuni Indians, whose territory is adjacent to that of both the Rio Grande Pueblos and the Hopis, also use the stepped fret. The area of cultural influence of this symbol is further evidence of its power in Mesoamerica. The stepped fret is never seen among northern Indians or Eastern Indians. The Navajos, who arrived in Hopi territory in the seventeenth century, use the fret a great deal in their rugs, but they never put them together in the stepped fret form.

The fleur-de-lis, a stylized form that appears often in Mesoamerican art, also has elements that suggest the flowing vase. Its outside curves represent the two streams flowing from the center, while the inverted V in the middle represents a plant budding from the life-giving waters. Thus it may represent an artistic experiment that is an alternative to the stepped fret representation of the tree of life.

## Jade Bird

A bird reposing on top of the Tree of Life was a symbol of the God of Life. This was true in both Palestine and Mesoamerica, as is illustrated in Exhibit l6 (Ferguson 1958:85). The bird, like the serpent, was a symbol of the highest God, the God of Life. In Egypt the sun disc was given wings. The winged disc—the solar bird—represented the highest God, the God of Life. Respecting the Egyptian symbol, Count Goblet D'Alviella tells us "that the Winged Globe is the Egyptian symbol *par excellence.* According to the inscription at Edfu, it was Thoth himself who caused it to be placed above the entrances to all the temples in order to commemorate the victory won by Horus over Seth, i.e., by the principle of light and good over that of darkness and evil" (205). It symbolized the God of Light, the Egyptian hope of life after death. Goblet D'Alviella goes on to say:

> The Winged Globe of the Phoenicians is found wherever their art was introduced, in Carthage, Cyprus, Sardinia, Sicily, and among different peoples of Palestine. It has even been pointed out on Israelitish seals of the oldest epoch, and nothing prevents us from supposing that—like the serpent, the golden bull or calf, and the idolatrous images denounced by the prophets—*it served, perhaps, to furnish a figured representation of Yahweh.* (Ferguson 1958:127)

In ancient Israel, then, the bird (or Winged Globe) placed above the Tree of Life symbolized Yahweh, Jehovah, the Messiah.

In Mesoamerica the bird was also used in conjunction with the serpent and with the Tree-of-Life symbol. The bird most often used in Guatemala and southern Mexico was the lovely quetzal bird. As has been said, one of the primary symbolic names of the Messiah of ancient Mexico was Quetzalcoatl. In the name itself we have a bird symbol and the serpent associated together, as in Palestine. We have seen that the personal and anthropomorphic Quetzalcoatl possessed all of the attributes of the Messiah as the Light and the Life of the World. In view of the

Milky Way serpent symbolism, it is not difficult to understand why the quetzal bird was chosen in southern Mexico and Guatemala as the sacred bird of that region, where it lived and is still to be found.

A look at Figure 30, a representation of the quetzal bird, will be helpful. The long, undulating tail feathers of the quetzal bird call to mind the undulating serpent—most ancient of the Milky Way, Life-God symbols. That the ancients of Mesoamerica used the quetzal feathers as an emblem of the ancient Mesopotamian Milky Way symbolism is clear. In the June 1937 issue of the Mexican archaeological journal *El Mexico Antiguo,* the then-editor of that journal, Dr. B. P. Reko, wrote: "The quetzal-bird . . . because of its long tail-feathers symbolized the bifurcated galaxy [the Milky Way]." Further, the tail feathers of the quetzal bird are green—the color green itself being symbolic of life and the Creator Life God. As Dr. Ackerman has pointed out in connection with the concept of vitalism of the ancients of Palestine, the evergreen tree was a manifestation of the vital life force. Also, the deciduous plants, "dead" in the winter, "revivified" in the spring, bursting into green foliage, were manifestations of life and the resurrection. Rain came from the Creator Sky-God, and from rain developed the green plants. The ancient Mesopotamians, and after them others throughout Palestine, believed that the green grass, grains, and plants were given birth each year through divine power. (See *Intellectual Adventure of Ancient Man* 145.) The same idea prevailed in ancient Mesoamerica. There, jade, native to the region, green and precious, was likewise a symbol of the Messiah, God of Life—Quetzalcoatl.

Covarrubias tells us that jade was linked to rain, vegetation, life, godliness, water, maize, and to the sky (109). These are aspects or symbolisms of the ancient Jehovah—Creator-God of Palestine manifest in the Milky Way serpent symbolism of Mesopotamia, Palestine, and Egypt.

*Gucumatz* (Maya equivalent of Quetzalcoatl) was described as "a serpent covered with green feathers, the name having been derived from the Quiche word *guc* (*kuk* in Yucatan Maya) "green

**Figure 30: Lacandon Maya holding the sacred quetzal bird. Photo by Thomas Stuart Ferguson of a stained glass window in Hotel Los Lagos, Comitan, Chiapas, Mexico, May 1956.**

feathers" (particularly those of the quetzal), and *Cumatz,* "serpent." In the *Popol Vuh,* the Messiah is referred to in Maya as *Ah Raxa Lac,* meaning "Lord of the Green Plate or the earth," *Ah Taxa Tzel,* meaning "Lord of the Green Gourd, or the blue bowl—the sky" (Goetz and Recinos 78).

In a book devoted exclusively to the serpent-bird symbolism of ancient Mexico, *La Serpiente Emplumada,* Jose Diaz-Bolio makes it clear that Quetzalcoatl, God of Life, was symbolized by jade in his role as God of Water and Life. The authors refer to the Messiah of Mexico as the God "Man-bird" (81). The beautiful green Quetzal bird was one of the major symbols of this anthropomorphic God. In the same paragraph Diaz-Bolio refers to the solar-serpent symbolism of Quetzalcoatl.

Thus it is demonstrated that the Quetzal bird — with its long, green, serpent-like undulating tail feathers — in association with the serpent, and as the primary symbol of life and vitalism, was a common representation of the Messiah in ancient Mesoamerica. J. Eric S. Thompson adds that to the ancient Maya the symbol for water was a jade bead, because water and jade were both precious and green (166). It is interesting and consistent that the serpent, jade, and the Milky Way each represent water, the source of life. The basis for the symbolism is in the oldest religious tradition of the world's oldest civilization.

Jade has been found in connection with the highly sophisticated Preclassic culture of the Valley of Mexico, which culture has been radio-carbon dated to 1700 B.C. Mexican and Central American jades are pure and native. In 1952 Robert Leslie found a boulder of jade measuring eleven inches in diameter in a freshly-plowed field on the north bank of the Motagua River of Guatemala. Alfred Kidder, Jessie Jennings, and Edwin Shook found a jade boulder at Kaminaljuyu near Guatemala City in 1946 during archeological efforts conducted for the Carnegie Institution.

In Genesis, Chapter 49, Verse 24, the Messiah of Israel is referred to as "the shepherd, the *stone* of Israel."

The sixteenth-century Maya prophet Chilam Balam refers to jade as a symbol of the Messiah, calling it "the first precious stone of grace." He puts into an allegory the birth, crucifixion, and resurrection or "coming forth" of Jesus. His allegorical reference to Christ is so apparent in this connection that J. Eric S. Thompson, distinguished Carnegie Maya scholar, asserts, with reference to it, "Christian ideas have led to the identification of Jesus, as the bread of life, with the maize god. (237)" The ancient book of Chilam Balam of Chumayel has been translated from the Maya tongue into English by Ralph Roys:

Three, seven, eight thousand was the creation of the
world, when he who was hidden within the stone, hidden
within the night was born, and occurred the birth of the first
precious stone of grace, the first infinite grace. . . . Not yet
had he received his divine rank. Then he remained alone
within the grace. Then it was pulverized [crushing of green
jade stone = crucifixion]. There were his long locks of hair .
. . ; his divinity was assumed when he came forth [the
resurrection].

Thompson explains the allegory:

The precious stone of grace is jade, which in the
Mexican allegorical writing is the ear of corn, before it
ripens. The passage states that the green corn, like precious
jade, is hidden within the rock. Then the rock is smashed
asunder, and the maize is born and becomes divine. The
maize god always has long hair, perhaps derived from the
beard of the maize in its husk. Hence the reference to the
long locks. (237)

Chilam Balam believed that the Messiah of early Mexico was
Jesus of Nazareth. The first Spanish padres to arrive in
Mesoamerica held the same opinions, and they, too, were careful
in how they put their views on paper. The native nobles of
Guatemala also held to the view that Naxcit-Gucumatz, their
Messiah, was identical with the Messiah of Israel.

The Spirit of the Lord asked the prophet Nephi:

Knowest thou the meaning of the tree which thy father
saw? And I answered him, saying: Yea, it is the love of God,
which sheddeth itself abroad in the hearts of the children of
men; wherefore, it is the most desirable above all things. . . .
Yea, and the most joyous to the soul." (1 Ne. 11:21-23)

# Chapter Five
# KNOWLEDGE OF THE OLD TESTAMENT

---

*And more than anywhere else, we see in the Book of Mormon the dangers of materialism and setting our hearts on the things of the world. Can anyone doubt that this book was meant for us and that in it we find great power, great comfort, and great protection? . . .*

*There is a power in the book which will begin to flow into your lives the moment you begin a serious study of the book. .*

*When you begin to hunger and thirst after those words, you will find life in greater and greater abundance. . . .*

President Ezra Taft Benson
General Conference, October 1986

(*Ensign*, November 1986, p. 7)
Used by permission

The Indians of ancient Mesoamerica preserved histories of the creation, their lineages and their beliefs in various historical records. Some of these ancient records have recently been discovered. They shed light on the many fascinating parallels between the Old Testament and the Book of Mormon.

At 5,000 feet above sea level, the Pan-American Highway passes through the ancient Guatemalan town of Totonicapan. In 1554, the leading native nobles of the town wrote a document that told the origin of their ancestors. The original compilers signed it and certified its authenticity before the local Spanish magistrate. It was translated into Spanish in 1834 by Padre Dionisio Jose Chonay, a priest at Sacapulas, Guatemala. It was first published in 1885 in both Spanish and French. Its history and contents are a fascinating view of the sixteenth-century Quiche, the Indian people of Guatemala who were the descendants of the Maya.

Robert M. Carmack, an ethnohistorian from Albany

University, describes his dramatic rediscovery of the original Totonicapan document whose whereabouts had been unknown for more than four hundred years:

> As part of our ethnological and archaeological survey [in the summer of 1973], we went to Totonicapan. We were primarily interested in locating the pre-Hispanic settlement of Totonicapan, which was unreported at that time. As I had visited the community many previous times in search of ancient documents, we were well received by the native officials, who gave us their full collaboration. With the help of a guide assigned to us, we located the pre-Hispanic settlement. . . . More importantly, the indigenous alcalde was so excited about our work that he allowed me to do what I previously had been trying to do for 10 years; to personally examine the large stack of ancient titulos, which they kept in the alcadia. I was disappointed to find, however, that the original Titulo Totonicapan was not one of the documents in their possession; even though I had previously been told that it was. In fact, the only document which seemed to refer to the pre-Hispanic cultures was the translation into Spanish of a tiny part of some document with which I was unacquainted. The document had been instigated as a land title by the parcialidad Yax, which I knew to be the most influential clan of the community.
>
> It so happened that our guide was from the Yax parcialidad, and with his help, I was able to meet with the leaders of that group. I explained my interest in their history and culture, and showed them my book as an example of the kind of studies I made of ancient documents.
>
> As we conversed in Quiche, I tried to communicate understanding of and interest in their clan organization. The approach worked because they soon sent for the keeper of the documents. Inside were several modern land titles and other legal documents, as well as a large, leather-bound ancient book, written in the Quiche language.
>
> It did not take long to realize the importance of this book. I saw  immediately that it contained the original Quiche text of the *Titulo Totonicapan,* and other chronicles

I had never seen before. As calmly as I could speak, for I was *very* excited, I asked permission to have the book copied. I offered several services in return: to make a type-written copy of the documents and a translation of them into Spanish for their grandchildren; to provide them with their own photocopy of the documents, which were disintegrating; to donate money to their clan.

They agreed, and together we marched to the photocopying machine in the town center. They personally cut the binding holding the book together, and handed over and received in turn each page as it was copied. Unfortunately, the machine was not a very good one, and the pages became more faded as time went on (to my great anguish). Finally, after about three hours of photocopying, the work was completed. I took them all to dinner, and we parted. Later, as I returned to my pension [boarding house] with my precious treasure, I remember how paranoid I felt about losing the copies. I have since returned to Totonicapan to take photographs of certain parts of the documents, and to check my transcriptions with the original texts. The Yax have remained friendly and cooperative, and I have visited them several times since the 1973 discoveries. (84-86)

The Yax book which Carmack photocopied has been translated and published in Spanish (Carmack and Mondlach 1983). It actually contained six documents: a land title of the Yax Clan, three land titles for the Tamub clan, a document produced by the Ilocab clan, and the *Titulo Totonicapan* itself. The document concludes:

> Now on the 28th of September of 1554 we sign this attestation in which we have written that which by tradition our ancestors told us, who came from the other part of the sea, from Civan-Tulan, bordering on Babylonia. (Recinos and Goetz 194)

The first part of the text had never before been translated. It gave, in Carmack's words, "an account which is similar to that of the Old Testament, from the Creation to the Babylonia captivity. While it is true that this part of the narration follows the Bible much more closely than does the *Popol Vuh,* it nevertheless diverges in subtle and interesting ways. I recommend it highly as one of the first attempts by native Guatemalans to synchronize their historical tradition with the Christian one" (87).

The sixteen authors of the *Titulo* used biblical names and references (derived from the manuscript of the Dominican Friar Domingo de Vico titled *Theological Indorum* written in 1553) to describe their peoples' origins (Carmack and Mondlach 1983:13):

> The three wise men, the Nahuales, the chiefs and leaders of three great peoples and of others who joined them, called U Mamae [the ancients], extending their sight over the four parts of the world and over all that is beneath the sky, and finding no obstacle, came from the other part of the ocean, from where the sun rises, from a place called [in Mayan] Pa Tulan, Pa Civan.
>
> The principal chiefs were four. . . . Together these tribes came from the other part of the sea, from the East, from Pa Tulan, Pa Civan. These, then, were the three nations of Quiches, and they came from where the sun rises, descendants of Israel, of the same language and same customs.
>
> When they left Pa Tulan, Pa Civan, the first leader was Balam-Quitze, by unanimous vote, and then the great father Nacxit [God] gave them a present called Giron-Gagal. When they arrived at the edge of the sea, Balam-Quitze touched it [the sacred director] with his staff and at once a passage opened, which then closed up again, for thus the great God wished it to be done, because they were the sons of Abraham and Jacob. (Recinos and Goetz 169-70)

Significantly, the same group of sixteen nobles who wrote the *Titulo Totonicapan* produced a second document, the famous *Popol Vuh,* about two to four years later. This work, the single most extensive account of Quiche history, does not use any biblical names, but it begins with the creation of heaven, earth, human beings, and animals; contains long sections of myths and legends; reports migrations, wars, settlements, and councils; and also gives the genealogies of the leaders. It was written in Santa Cruz Quiche, another important city in highland Guatemala, in Quiche about 1554-58 and although the location of the original manuscript is unknown, it was translated into Spanish by Fray Francisco Ximenez (1666-1729) in Chichicastenango about 1702.

The sacred book of the Quiche-Maya people of ancient Guatemala, the *Popol Vuh,* has been referred to as the "Genesis" of Central America. It was written in the Maya tongue from older records and traditions going back centuries before the time of Columbus. This ancient sacred book has been translated into English by Dennis Tedlock. The lovely Maya creation account states in the preamble:

> This is the beginning of the ancient word, here in this place called Quiche. Here we shall inscribe, we shall implant the Ancient Word, the potential and source for everything done in the citadel of Quiche, in the nation of the Quiche people.
> And here we shall take up the demonstration, revelation, and account of how things were put in shadow and brought to light . . . by the gods. The account of the creation follows:
> Now it still ripples, now it still murmurs, ripples, it still sighs, still hums, and it is empty under the sky.

Here follow the first words, the first eloquence:

> There is not yet one person, one animal, bird, fish, crab, tree, rock, hollow, canyon, meadow, forest. Only the sky alone is there; the face of the earth is not clear. Only the sea alone is pooled under all the sky; there is nothing whatever gathered together. It is at rest; not a single thing stirs. It is held back, kept at rest under the sky.
> And then came his word, he came here to the Sovereign Plumed Serpent, here in the blackness, in the early dawn. He spoke with the Sovereign Plumed Serpent, and they talked, then they thought, then they worried. They agreed with each other, they joined their words, their thoughts.

Then it was clear, then they reached accord in the light, and then humanity was clear, when they conceived the growth, the generation of trees, of bushes, and the growth of life, of humankind, in the blackness, in the early dawn, all because of the Heart of Sky, named Hurricane.

And then the earth arose because of them, it was simply their word that brought it forth. For the forming of the earth they said, "Earth." It arose suddenly, just like a cloud, like a mist, now forming, unfolding. Then the mountains were separated from the water, all at once the great mountains came forth. By their genius alone, by their cutting edge alone they carried out the conception of the mountain-plain, whose face grew instant groves of cypress and pine.

Such was the formation of the earth when it was brought forth by the Heart of the Sky, Heart of the Earth, as they are called, since they were the first to think of it. The sky was set apart, and the earth was set apart in the midst of the waters. Such was their plan when they thought, when they worried about the completion of their work. (72-75)

A third Mayan source of related stories and legends has recently been reported for the Lacandon Maya Indians of Chiapas, located about 180 miles northwest of the Quiche Maya Indians of highland Guatemala. These Lacandon Maya number less than 200 and live in a very remote area of southern Mexico. They had little European cultural influence until after World War II, so their stories and legends are relatively free of any European and Christian influences. These stories and legends are similar to those in the Titulo de Totonicapan and the Popol Vuh. They contain themes of the creation, the fall, and the crossing of the sea, but they have no biblical names or terminology (Bruce 77).

Evidently, what we are seeing in the sixteenth century *Titulo de Totonicapan* is one of the earliest attempts by native Quiche Maya priests to synthesize their native beliefs and legends with the teachings of the Spanish friars concerning the Bible and Christianity.

Apart from the Lacandon Maya traditions, these native

records, produced by people who had grown up under Spanish rule but whose memories included pre-Conquest legends, are a very important body of modern literature and history about Mesoamerica for modern researchers.

Although it would be natural for the Spanish priests to read biblical parallels into native legends of migration, redemption gods, creations, and ceremonies, they were still so impressed at what seemed to be Israelite and Near-Eastern customs found among the Mayas that they commented on the puzzle and stated that a knowledge of Near-Eastern traditions existed in Central America long before the discovery of the New World by Columbus.

Ixtlilxochitl (pronounced Eesh-tleel-sho-cheetl) was part Spanish but on his mother's side descended from the pre-Conquest rulers of Texcoco, one of the three cities in the Aztec Triple Alliance, and thus spoke Aztec. His mother owned the site of Teotihuacan, and it had been in the family ever since the beginning of the Late Postclassic period (the time span between A.D. 1250-1530). Perhaps for this reason, Ixtlilxochitl wished to link his ancestors back to Tula, probably Teotihuacan.

His history is the earliest and most important of Mexico after European contact, incorporating as it does earlier historical sources. He wrote *Relaciones* and the *Historia Chichimeca.* The *Relaciones* consists of a multi-part and somewhat repetitious history of the Acolhua Chichimecs from the time of Xolotl (13th century A.D.) into that of Nezahualcoyotl (his descendant and king of Texcoco) and up through the Spanish conquest.

The *Historia Chichimeca,* also known as the *Historia General de la Nueva Espana*, consists of ninety-five consecutive chapters and treats Toltec, Acolhua, Chichimec, Tepanec, and Tenochca history from the creation of the world up through the Spanish conquest, but it was not finished. He apparently had access to a large library of native records — he calls them "paintings" — for he mentions several that have disappeared.

His manuscripts seem to have been completed between 1600 and 1625, when they came into the hands of Siguenza y Gongora (1645-1700, an antiquarian living in Mexico City) and from him to the Jesuit College Library of San Pedro y San Pablo in the Valley of Mexico.

Ixtlilxochitl's history was organized around the four world-age system, a period lasting 1716 years and consisting of a water age, a wind age, an earth age (see Table II), and a fire age. Because it is linked directly to the Long Count calendar (this calendar system counts days from a base date of August 13th 3114 B.C.) of the Maya, it is possible to assign dates with considerable accuracy.

Thus, the Water Age, which begins with the creation in 4829 B.C., lasts until the great flood in 3113 B.C. After his brief account of these events, Ixtlilxochitl introduces the second world age:

> And how afterwards men, multiplying made a very tall and strong *Zacualli,* which means the very high tower, in order to shelter themselves in it when the second world should be destroyed.
>
> When things were at their best, their languages were changed and, not understanding each other, they went to different parts of the world, and the *Tultecas,* who were as many as seven companions and their wives, who understood their language among themselves, came to these parts, having first crossed large lands and seas, living in caves and undergoing great hardships, until they came to this land which they found good and fertile for their habitation.
>
> And they say that they traveled for 104 years through different parts of the world until they arrived at *Huehue Tlapallan,* their country, which happened in *Ce Tecpatl,* for it had been 520 years since the Deluge had taken place, which are five ages. (12)

These details resemble the Book of Mormon account of the journey of the Jaredites to the New World:

> Which Jared came forth with his brother and their families, with some others and their families, from the great tower, at the time the Lord confounded the language of the people, and swore in his wrath that they should be scattered

# TABLE II: TULTEC FOUR-SOLAR AGE SYSTEM

**I. WATER SUN:**   Beginning of Age to the Flood.   1 Flint, 4829 B.C. to 1 Flint, 3113 B.C.
Age Destruction: 0.0.0.1.19
4 Cauac 2 Uo, 21 Sep 3114 B.C.

**II. EARTH SUN:**   Flood to Earth destruction.   1 Flint, 3113 B.C. to 1 Flint, 1397 B.C.
Age Destruction: 4.7.1.10.17
4 Caban 15 Mac, 21 Mar 1397 B.C.
    A.   Zacualli episode, 1 Flint: 2697 B.C.
    B.   Arrival of Seven Tulteca leaders to *Huehuetlapallan.* 1 Flint: 2593 B.C.

**III. WIND SUN:**   Earth destruction to Wind destruction. 1 Flint, 1397 B.C. to 1 Flint, A.D. 320
Age Destruction: 8.14.2.6.2 4 Ik 15 Zac, A.D. 22 Dec 319.
    A.   Quiname or Huixtoti migration. 1 Flint: 929 B.C., Ixtill.Tomo 11:23,n.1.
        1.   Astronomical convention at *Huehuetlapallan* at the end of the 9th calendar round of the Third or Wind Sun Age in which the concept of four Sun Ages was tied to the four natural elements (Veytia, Chapter 4).
           5.10.16.7.10 13 Oc 3 Pop, 21 Mar 929 B.C.
    B.   *Huehuetlapallan* conference: leap-year and equinox adjustment.
      1 Flint:  97 B.C.
    C.   Quetzalcoatl Huematzin's flight from the Cholula area to the general region of Coatzacoalcos. 1 Reed: A.D. 307.

**IV. FIRE SUN:**   Wind destruction to Fire destruction.
1 Flint, A.D. 320 to 1 Flint, A.D. 2036.
Age Destruction: 13.1.4.15.4 4 Kan 2 Tzec, A.D. 21 June 2037.
    A.   Tulteca flight from the area of *Hueytlapallan.* 1 Flint: A.D. 320

## TULTEC FOUR-SOLAR AGE SYSTEM (Continued)

B. First king and queen at Tula
(Coixtlahuaca region of northern
Oaxaca).
7 Reed: A.D. 447

- - - - - - - - - - - - - - - - - - - - - - - - -

**Equinoctial Precession:** 25,740 year period in Mesoamerica, but
modern astronomers say the period is 25,692
years.

| Summer Soltice | Spring and Fall Equinoxes | Winter Soltice |
|---|---|---|
| 24° | | 24° |

One degree of a 360 degree circle equals 71.5 years in the equinoctial
precession cycle. Twenty-four degrees of a solstice to equinox cycle
equals 1716 years. Fifteen 1716 year periods equal the full equinoctial
precession cycle of 25,740 years.

upon all the face of the earth; and according to the word of
the Lord the people were scattered.

And the brother of Jared being a large and mighty man,
and a man highly favored of the Lord, Jared, his brother,
said unto him: Cry unto the Lord, that he will not confound
us that we may not understand our words.

And it came to pass that the brother of Jared did cry
unto the Lord, and the Lord had compassion upon Jared;
therefore he did not confound the language of Jared; and
Jared and his brother were not confounded.

Then Jared said unto his brother: Cry again unto the
Lord, and it may be that he will turn away his anger from
them who are our friends, that he confound not their
language.

And it came to pass that the brother of Jared did cry
unto the Lord, and the Lord had compassion upon their
friends and their families also, that they were not
confounded.

> And it came to pass that Jared spake again unto his
> brother, saying: Go and inquire of the Lord whether he will
> drive us out of the land, and if he will drive us out of the
> land, cry unto him whither we shall go. And who knoweth
> but the Lord will carry us forth into a land which is choice
> above all the earth? And if it so be, let us be faithful unto
> the Lord, that we may receive it for our inheritance. (Ether
> 1:33-38)

Thus the ancestral group consisting of as many as seven men
and their wives left the Old World 416 years after the Deluge
(2697 B.C.), traveled 104 years, and settled in southern Mexico at
a place called *Huehuetlapallan* (2593 B.C.). A parallel Book of
Mormon event states:

> And when Corihor was thirty and two years old he
> rebelled against his father, and went over and dwelt in the
> land of Nehor; and he begat sons and daughters, and they
> became exceedingly fair; wherefore Corihor drew away
> many people after him. (Ether 7:4)

There is general agreement among Mesoamerican scholars that
this land of Huehuetlapallan is located in southern Veracruz
(Jimenez Moreno 1094). See Table II for a chronology of Ixtilxo-
chitl's event sequences.

Ixtlilxochitl relates an important council of the colony's
intellectual leaders which, in our calendar system, took place in
97 B.C.:

> All the land of this New World being in peace, all the
> Tulteca wisemen, the astrologers as well as men of other
> arts, got together in Huehuetlapallen, seat of the kingdom,
> where they discussed many things, happenings and
> calamities that they had, and movements of the heavens
> since the creation of the world, as well as many other things
> which, because their histories were burned [by Spaniards],
> have not been able to be known nor understood more than
> what has here been written. Among other things, they added
> the leap year in order to make the solar year agree with the

equinox, and many other curiosities, as will be seen in their
tables and rules for their years, months, weeks, and days,
signs, and planets, according as they understood them, and
many other curiosities. (Hunter and Ferguson 147)

Thus, by 97 B.C., the descendants of the original colonizers
had become a real kingdom, with enough differentiation of labor
to support a leisure class of learned artisans and scholars. They
had an important capital city, "Ancient Place of the
Red" — Huehue meaning "ancient" and Tlapallan meaning "place
of the red."

Ixtlilxochitl describes their kings as "high of stature, and
white, and bearded like the Spaniards." He also reports that as
late as the tenth century A.D., white blond children were born to
the descendants of these early Tultecas.

The third type of records consists of written accounts
*(relaciones)* and histories *(historias)* left by sixteenth and
seventeenth century Spanish priests who found themselves in the
position of receiving and preserving native records. Many of
these educated men produced their own versions of native
histories.

Ixtlilxochitl related the following about the ancients of
Guatemala and Mexico:

> The Tultecas understood and knew of the creation of
> the world and how God created it, and the other things that
> are in it, such as planets, mountains, animals, etc., and in
> the same manner they knew how God created a man and a
> woman from whom men descended and multiplied.
>
> And they say that the world was created in the year of
> the *ce Tecpatl*, and this epoch up to the deluge they called
> Atonatiuh, which means, *age of the sun of water*, because
> the world was destroyed by the deluge; and it is found in the
> Tulteca histories that this age and first world, as they called
> it, lasted 1,716 years; that men were destroyed by very great
> storms and lightnings from heaven, and the whole world
> without a thing remaining, and the highest mountains  . . .
> were covered with water; and how men began to multiply

from a few that escaped this destruction within a *Toplipetlacalli,* which . . . means closed ark.

On this topic, Father Torquemada relates:

> These Tultecs occupied these provinces [Mexico and Guatemala] as lords and proprietors of them. They say of them that they had knowledge of the creation of the world, and how the people of it were destroyed by the Deluge, and many other things which they had in painting and in history.
> . . . and they also say that they had knowledge of how the world is to end again, by consummation, by fire. (I:36)

Bishop Landa, writing in 1556, stated that the Mayas of Yucatan believed "the world was destroyed by a deluge." The Maya word for "flood" is *haiyokocab,* meaning "water over the earth."

The *Popol Vuh* speaks of the knowledge found in the records and books of the early colonizers:

> There is the original book and ancient writing, but he who reads and ponders it hides his face. It takes a long performance and account to complete the emergence of all the sky-earth: the fourfold siding, fourfold cornering, measuring, fourfold staking, halving the cord, stretching the cord in the sky, on the earth, the four sides, the four corners, as it is said, by the Maker, Modeler, mother-father of life, of humankind, giver of breath, giver of heart, bearer, upbringer in the light that lasts of those born in the light, begotten in the light; worrier, knower of everything, whatever there is: sky-earth, lake-sea. (Tedlock 71-72)

The *Popol Vuh* contains the Quiche-Maya version of the creation story as it survived down through the ages to the sixteenth century:

> This is the account of how all was in suspense, all calm in silence; all motionless, still, and the expanse of the sky was empty.

This is the first account, the first narrative. There was neither man, nor animal, birds, fishes, crabs, trees, stones, caves, ravines, grasses, nor forest; there was only the sky.

The surface of the earth had not appeared. There was only the calm sea and the great expanse of sky.

There was nothing brought together, nothing which could make a noise, or tremble, or could make noise in the sky.

There was nothing standing; only the calm water, the placid sea, alone and tranquil. Nothing existed.

There was only immobility and silence in the darkness, in the night.   Only the Creator, the Maker, *Tepeu, Gucumatz* [the Fair God, Quetzacoatl, the Messiah], the Forefathers, were in the water surrounded with light. They were hidden under green and blue feathers, and were therefore called Gucumatz.

By nature they were great sages and thinkers. In this manner the sky existed and also the Heart of Heaven, which is the name of God and thus He is called.

Then came the word. *Tepeu* [God] and *Gucumatz* came together in the darkness, in the night, and *Tepeu* and *Gucumatz* talked together. They talked then, discussing and deliberating; they agreed, they united their words and their thoughts.

Then while they meditated, it became clear to them that when Dawn would break, man must appear. Then they planned the creation, and the growth of the trees and the thickets and the birth of life and the creation of man. Thus it was arranged in the darkness and in the night by the Heart of Heaven who is called *Huracan.*

The first is called *Caculha Huracan.* The second is *Chipi-Caculha.* The third is *Raxa-Caculha.* And these three are the Heart of Heaven [Godhead].

Then Tepeu and Gucumatz came together; then they conferred about life and light, what they would do so that there would be light and dawn, who it would be who would provide food and sustenance. Thus let it be done! Let the emptiness be filled! Let the water recede and make a void, let the earth appear and become solid; let it be done.

Thus they spoke. Let there be light, let there be dawn in

the sky and on the earth! There shall be neither glory nor grandeur in our creation and formation until the human being is made, man is formed. So they spoke.

Then the earth was created by them. So it was, in truth, that they created the earth. Earth! they said, and instantly it was made.

Like the mist, like a cloud, and like a cloud of dust was the creation, when the mountains appeared from the water; and instantly the mountains grew. Only by a miracle, only by magic art were the mountains and valleys formed; and instantly the groves of cypresses and pines put forth shoots together on the surface of the earth.

And thus *Gucumatz* was filled with joy, and exclaimed: "Your coming has been fruitful, Heart of Heaven; and you, *Huracan,* and you, *Chipi-Caculha, Raxa Caculha!*"

"Our work, our creation shall be finished," they answered.

First, the earth was formed, the mountains and the valleys; the currents of water were divided, the rivulets were running freely between the hills, and the water was separated when the high mountains appeared.

Thus was the earth created, when it was formed by the Heart of Heaven, the Heart of Earth, as they are called who first made it fruitful, when the sky was in suspense, and the earth was submerged in the water.

So it was that they made perfect the work, when they did it after thinking and meditating upon it. (Goetz and Morley 57; trans. 141)

A similar record was had among the Jaredites and Nephites:

And now I, Moroni, proceed to give an account of those ancient inhabitants who were destroyed by the hand of the Lord upon the face of this north country.

And I take mine account from the twenty and four plates which were found by the people of Limhi, which is called the Book of Ether.

And as I suppose that the first part of this record, which speaks concerning the creation of the world, and also of Adam, and an account from that time even to the great tower, and whatsoever things transpired among the children of men until that time, is had among the Jews —

Therefore I do not write those things which transpired from the days of Adam until that time; but they are had upon the plates; and whoso findeth them, the same will have power that he may get the full account.

But behold, I give not the full account, but a part of the account I give, from the tower down until they were destroyed. (Ether 1:1-5)

Gaspar Antonio Chi was born in Yucatan, Central America, in 1531. His mother was a Maya princess and his father a Maya nobleman of the Xiu family. For a number of years, he served as royal interpreter to the Spanish governors of Yucatan. He had a knowledge of Maya, Nahuatl (Mexican), Spanish, and Latin languages. Chi provided Bishop Landa with much of the data for Landa's book. And he supplied the Spanish civil authorities with material they needed for the purpose of replying to a questionnaire sent to them by the Spanish crown in 1579. The crown wanted to know, among other things, something about the ancient inhabitants. The original questionnaires and answers turned up in the archives of the Indies in Seville, Spain, during the latter part of the nineteenth century. In them we have the truth concerning the ancient colonizers as the Spanish authorities of the time accepted it:

They had letters. Each letter was a syllable, and with them they were understood. And they had a year consisting of three hundred and sixty-five days.

They had knowledge of a Creator of all things, of the creation of the sky and of the earth, and of the fall of Lucifer, and of the creation of man, and of the immortality of the soul, and of Heaven and Hell, and of the general Flood.

Those who anciently came to people this land of Yucatan . . . were very simple in their worship and did not worship idols or make any sacrifice. It is said that the first settlers of Chichen Itza were not idolaters. For a thousand years they did not worship idols, because the lords of Chichen Itza and their subjects wished it to be said that they were not idolaters. (Jakeman 95-102)

The date of the arrival of the colonizers at Chichen Itza is fixed at about the time of Christ's death and resurrection. If they did not have idolatry for "a thousand years," it must have been introduced about 1000 A.D. That leaves over five hundred years for religious beliefs and traditions to decay and change before the coming of the Spaniards.

Bernardino de Sahagun, a Catholic priest who lived in the Valley of Mexico from 1529 to 1590, compiled Nahuatl texts and had native informants write histories. Sahagun's work has been called "one of the most comprehensive and important collections of material for the study of the culture, ethnology, and history of the Aztecs" (Gibson and Glass 360).

His history also describes a migration to the Valley of Mexico. He describes their immediate descendants as "white and of good and well-proportioned faces and good features. . . . These lived in good breeding, because the men wore good clothes and mantles; they were [sic] shoes, jewels, and beads around the neck. They look at themselves in mirrors and their women put on painted and elegant skirts and blouses. They are polished and expert in everything" (Book 10:188).

Sahagun was apparently convinced that the people whose history he recorded had an authentic Old World origin:

> They never ceased to have their learned men, or prophets. . . . Before their [the prophets'] departure they discourse as follows: "Know that our God commands you to remain here in these lands of which He makes you masters and gives you possession. He [God] returns to the place whence He and we came but He will come back to visit you when it shall be time of the world to come to an end; in the meantime you will await Him in these lands, expectantly and possessing them and all contained in them, since for this [God's] purpose you came hither; remain therefore, for we go without God." (Book 1:190)

Another interesting seventeenth-century Spanish work is a three-volume history published in Spain by Juan de Torquemada, a Spanish priest who lived in Mexico. He recounts the legends of the Indians about their own origins:

> They were a very wise people, and skilled in ship-building and in working gold and silver, and they were very great artisans in whatsoever art you mention; they were great lapidaries and they were skilled in delicate things, and in other industries for human sustenance; and in tilling and plowing land; and they were strong people noted for their good government and great industries and skills, and they were men of great capacity. They were greatly esteemed and honored. (I:255)

Torquemada continues his summary by observing that the original colonizers wore "long robes of black linen, like Turks, the robes being like the cassocks of the clergy, open in front, and without capes, low-cut at the neck, and with short, wide sleeves which did not reach the elbow" (I:37). This garb would have resembled the loose-fitting robes of the ancient Holy Land. They also wore head coverings like short stocking caps and sandals, both of which were also articles of clothing in the ancient world.

Diego de Landa, the first bishop of Yucatan and a self-trained ethnologist, also wrote a history of the Mayas, called the *Relacion de las Cosas de Yucatan*. He also believed the Maya claims of a transoceanic origin:

> Some of the old people of Yucatan say that they have heard from their ancestors that this land was occupied by a race of people who came from the East and whom God had delivered by opening twelve paths through the sea. If this were true, it necessarily follows that all the inhabitants of the Indies [the New World] are descendants of the Jews. (16-17)

The sixteenth century Christian influence stemming from Spanish priests and converted native writers also had an impact.

However, the reports from native and Catholic sources all agree that the concepts were possessed by the original colonizers many centuries before the coming of the Spanish priests. The ancients of Guatemala and Mexico did have some knowledge of the Old Testament and of their Old World roots.

And it shall come to pass that the Jews shall have the words of the Nephites, and the Nephites shall have the words of the Jews; and the Nephites and the Jews shall have the words of the lost tribes of Israel; and the lost tribes of Israel shall have the words of the Nephites and the Jews. (2 Ne. 29:13)

# NOTES TO CHAPTER FIVE

1.  Bishop Landa gives us the details of the ancient Maya baptismal rite—which is obviously a mixture of the ancient Hebrew purification rite and the Christian baptism taught by Mexico's Messiah. The indisputable parallels are clearly seen when quotations from Leviticus are paralleled with those from Bishop Landa's description of the Maya ceremony:

**Hebrew Purification Rite**

And the Lord spake unto Moses, saying, This shall be the law of the leper in the day of his cleansing: He shall be brought unto the priest. (Lev. 14:1-2)

**Maya Baptismal Rite**

When there was anyone who wanted to have his child baptized, he went to priest and gave him notice of his intention. . . . For three days before the festival, the fathers of the children and the officials fasted, abstaining from intercourse with their wives. On the appointed day all assembled at the house of the man who gave the feast, and brought with them all the children who were to be baptized. They were placed in the patio or court of the house, which they had swept and spread with fresh leaves.

**Scapegoat**

And he shall take the two goats and present them before the Lord at the door of the tabernacle of the congregation. . . . And Aaron shall bring the goat upon which the Lord's lot fell, and offer him for a sin offering. But the goat, on which the lot fell to be the scapegoat, shall be presented alive before the Lord, to make an atonement with him, and to let him go for a scapegoat into the wilderness. (16:7, 9-10)

**Scapegoat**

And these censings being over, they took the brazier in which they made them, and the cord with which the *Chacs* had surrounded them, and they poured out a little wine into a vessel, and they gave the whole to an Indian to be carried out of town, enjoining upon him that he should not drink nor look behind him as he came back, and by this they said that the evil spirit had been driven away. (A close parallel in Hebrew rites is found in Num. 5:17-18.)

## The Sprinkling or Anointing

As for the living bird, he shall take it, and the cedar wood, and the scarlet, and the hyssop, and shall dip them and the living bird in the blood of the bird that was killed over the running water: And he shall sprinkle upon him that is to be cleansed from the leprosy seven times, and shall pronounce him clean, and shall let the living bird loose into the open field. (Lev. 14:6-7)

And the priest shall take some of the blood of the trespass offering, and the priest shall put it upon the tip of the right ear of him that is to be cleansed, and upon the thumb of his right hand, and upon the great toe of his right foot. (14:14)

## The Sprinkling or Anointing

Then the principal whom the fathers of the children had chosen for this festival, rose, and armed with a bone, which the priest had given him, he went over to the boys and threatened to strike each one in turn on the forehead with the bone nine times. Then he wet it in a vessel of a certain water which he carried in his hand, and anointed them on their foreheads and the features of their faces, as well as the spaces between the fingers and toes of all of them, without speaking a word. They made this water from certain flowers and of cacao pounded and dissolved in virgin water, which they called that brought from the hollows of the trees or of the rocks of the forest.

## Linen Garb

He [the priest] shall put on the holy linen coat, and he shall have the linen breeches upon his flesh, and shall be girded with a linen girdle, and with the linen mitre shall he be attired: these are holy garments; therefore shall he wash his flesh in water, and so put them on. (16:4)

## Linen Garb

After this anointment, the priests arose and took off from their heads the white linen which had been put upon them, as well as others [white linens] which linen had hanging from their shoulders.

2.   The presence of so much of the Jewish purification rite in Mesoamerica does not suggest that all of the Mayas of the conquest days were of Israelite descent. Many Mayas could qualify as Jews in appearance, but others look very much like Mongoloids. Certainly the Mongoloids had joined the ranks in Mesoamerica long before 600 B.C.

The previous information suggests that a knowledge of the ancient Israelite religious practices as found in the Old Testament did find their way into Mesoamerica. That knowledge remained intact because there were few forces present in Mesoamerica to diminish it. Most of the converts to Christianity in the

Mediterranean world were Gentiles, and Jewish tradition and customs were easily discarded. Jewish tradition was simply stronger in Mesoamerica, so Jewish rites were carried over into Christianity in Mesoamerica.

Chapter Six
# THE STARS IN HEAVEN

---

*My beloved brethren and sisters, today I would like to speak about one of the most significant gifts given to the world in modern times. The gift I am thinking of is more important than any of the inventions that have come out of the industrial and technological revolutions. This is a gift of greater value to mankind than even the many wonderful advances we have seen in modern medicine. It is of greater worth to mankind than the development of flight or space travel. I speak of the gift of the Book of Mormon.*

President Ezra Taft Benson
General Conference, October 1986

(*Ensign*, November 1986, p. 4)
Used by permission

When Abraham was a very old man, God told him that He would make Abraham a great nation (Gen. 12:1-3). Abraham then asked the Lord how that could possibly be, since his wife, Sarai, was barren and well stricken in age. God answered Abraham:

Look now toward heaven, and tell [count] the stars, if thou be able to number them: and he said unto him, So shall thy seed be. (Gen. 15:5)

And I will establish my covenant between me and thee and thy seed after thee in their generations for an everlasting covenant, to be a God unto thee, and to thy seed after thee. (Gen. 17:7)

And I will make of thee a great nation, and I will bless thee above measure, and make thy name great among all nations, and thou shalt be a blessing unto thy seed after thee, that in their hands they shall bear this ministry and Priesthood unto all nations;

And I will bless them that bless thee, and curse them that curse thee; and in thee (that is, in thy Priesthood) and in thy seed (that is, thy Priesthood), for I give unto thee a promise that this right shall continue in thee, and in thy seed after thee (that is to say, the literal seed, or the seed of the body) shall all the families of the earth be blessed, even with the blessings of the Gospel, which are the blessings of salvation, even of life eternal. (Abr. 2:9, 11)

And after that ye were blessed then fulfilleth the Father the covenant which he made with Abraham, saying: In thy seed shall all the kindreds of the earth be blessed — unto the pouring out of the Holy Ghost through me upon the Gentiles, which blessing upon the Gentiles shall make them mighty above all, unto the scattering of my people, O house of Israel. (3 Ne. 20:27)

Down through the ages, the stars in heaven have been associated with divine promises of fertility. From the basically rural vantage point of the ancient cultures, the ever-present heavens were a vivid reminder of their relationship with God. To Abraham's descendants in particular, the stars, especially the Milky Way, may have been a visible reminder of God's covenant with the House of Israel. To the Nephites the stars were a source for analogies and signs of the times (1 Ne. 1:10; 2 Ne. 24:13; Isa. 14:13; Hel. 14:5, 20; 3 Ne. 1:21; and 3 Ne. 8:22).

### Serpent and Milky Way

The serpent was a symbol of the Creator-God-of-Life at the very dawn of religion in Mesopotamia and Egypt. The ideas behind the symbol have been explained recently as a result of discoveries in Mesopotamian and Egyptian archaeology and inscriptions. The identical significance and meaning were attached to the serpent symbol in ancient Mesoamerica.

The body of a living serpent is never straight. It curves and undulates, as do all rivers and streams. The serpent was a logical likeness and symbol of the river. The river was the very basis of civilization in both Mesopotamia and Egypt, the very source of life. Water for the rivers came from the sky in the form of rain. And there was a great river in the sky — the source of rain — which could be seen at night, the wonderful and beautiful Milky Way. It was observed to curve and undulate across the sky as the Euphrates and the Nile curved through the river valleys. From the Milky Way came the source of life — rain water, for the rivers of the earth. The Milky Way came from the Creator-God, and the stars were regarded as the creative water or seed of God, the source of life.

The thinking of the ancients took them from the serpent back to the Creator in a series of logical symbolic steps. The serpent = the river = the Milky Way = the source of water = source of life = Creator. Thus the serpent equaled the Creator in the symbolism of the early Sumerians and Egyptians.

The serpent had been used as a life-creator symbol in Mesopotamia a thousand years before Abraham left his home at Ur. The serpent had been a life-creator symbol in Egypt for two thousand years before Moses lived there. It was one of the earliest symbols of deity used by civilized man, and was a part of the sacred symbolism of earliest Israel and the entire Near East.

In Mesopotamia the chief of all gods was *Apsu;* and his spouse, the mother goddess, was known as *Tiamat.* The latter was known as "Mother River," regarded as the "River of Heaven," the Milky Way. The serpent was regarded as a synonym for *Tiamat.* Exactly the same concepts existed in Egypt, having probably been transferred there from Mesopotamia. In Egypt, the sky goddess, *Nut,* is the exact same deity as *Tiamat.* She is symbolized by a band or river of stars representing the Milky Way. In one ancient Egyptian work of art the band of stars representing the Sky Goddess is shown undulating across the underside of a milk cow (Milky way), itself a symbol of life.

The top Babylonian creator deities, *Apsu* and his wife *Tiamat*, were the parents of twins, *Lahmu* and *Lahumu,* according to the traditions. Each of these twins was regarded as a god, and each was represented by a serpent. In the symbolism, a pair of serpents issued from the creator god and goddess. The Milky Way was deemed to issue from the creator god. There is a break or gap in the Milky Way, so it was regarded as twin rivers of the sky, going out from the Creator god. *Enki,* Babylonian "lord of the watery deep," is shown in the ancient art as holding a vase, out of which flows the Milky Way in the form of two undulating, serpent-like streams. This is shown in Figures 31-37. It is noted that the flowing vase is to be found in Mesoamerica.

Figure 5 shows a beautiful serpent symbol found at La Venta, Mexico in 1955. See also Figures 38 and 39 from La Venta, which have the earmarks of ancient Mesopotamia. In early Egyptian art, twin serpents undulate outwardly and down from the sun-disc (symbol of the creator god), just as the streams undulate downward from the flowing vases of Mexico and Mesopotamia.

The sacred serpent appeared on the front and center of the headdress or crown of the ancient Egyptian rulers. It was a symbol of the God of Life—a representation of the idea of life force and immortality. A beautiful, tall Maya crown dates to the sixth century A.D.; on the front and center of it is the head of a serpent, in exactly the position of the Egyptian Uraeus. The crown was found by the Mexican archaeologist Alberto Ruz, at Palenque in the state of Chiapas, Mexico in 1952. Thompson shows the crown in *The Rise and Fall of Maya Civilization* (252). In the same tomb was found the beautifully executed Tree of Life mentioned earlier (Figure 40).

Moses chose wisely when he selected the serpent with which to illustrate a main point in his speech to the Israelites when he was trying to inspire them during the hard days in the wilderness:

> And the people spake against God, and against Moses,
> Wherefore have ye brought us up out of Egypt to die in the

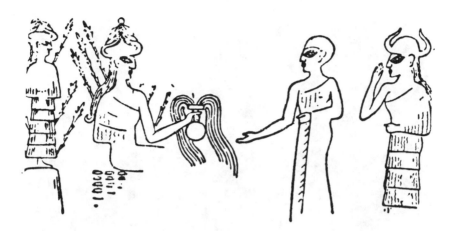

**Fig. 31: Flowing vase in the hands of a goddess from ancient Mesopotamia.**

wilderness? for there is no bread, neither is there any water; and our soul loatheth this light bread.

And the Lord sent fiery serpents among the people, and they bit the people; and much people of Israel died.

Therefore the people came to Moses, and said, We have sinned, for we have spoken against the Lord, and against thee; pray unto the Lord, that he take away the serpents from us. And Moses prayed for the people.

And the Lord said unto Moses, Make thee a fiery serpent, and set it upon a pole: and it shall come to pass, that every one that is bitten, when he looketh upon it, shall live.

And Moses made a serpent of brass, and put it upon a pole, and it came to pass, that if a serpent had bitten any man, when he beheld the serpent of bronze, he lived.

And the children of Israel set forward, and pitched in Oboth. (Num. 21:5-l0)

In the foregoing quotation from the Jewish record, the Lord himself is recorded as designating the serpent of bronze — symbol of the Giver of Life, symbol of the creator of the Life Force — as a symbol of the power of God to save mankind from death and

**Fig. 32:  Flowing vases in the hands of a king from Lagash, Iraq.**

destruction. It is obvious that the brass serpent had no real
intrinsic power. God was merely teaching Israel to look to Him
for life and protection and hope—hope for eternal life. The
people had but to have faith in the word of Moses—the word of
God—to live. They had but to believe him, as symbolized by the
serpent, and cast their eyes on the brass serpent which Moses
raised up before them as a symbol of the Life Power of God.
Doubtless many did not look because they did not believe that

**Fig. 33: Flowing vase in the hands of a goddess about 2400 B.C. from ancient Mesopotamia.**

**Fig. 34: Flowing vase from Ur in ancient Mesopotamia about 2000 B.C.**

**Fig. 35: King Gudea holding the symbolic flowing vase (about 2100 B.C.).**

they would be healed according to the promise of Moses. They perished.

That the serpent symbol of Moses represented the Creator-Messiah is borne out by curious language in the Babylonian *Enuma elish* of 2000 B.C.:

> Gathered in council they [the Gods] plan the attack. Mother Huber [Tiamat—Mother River—Sky Serpent]—Creator of all forms—adds irresistible weapons, has borne

monster serpents . . . so that whoever looks upon them [serpents] shall perish with fear, and they, with bodies raised, will not turn back their breast. (Jacobsen 175-176)

Thus Moses, in 1250 B.C., was not coming up with anything new when he raised up the serpent and told Israel to look upon it with faith and live and be raised up from the dead. The *Enuma elish* goes back at least 800 years before Moses. The same serpent-life-God symbolism goes back to the dawn of civilization. Jesus also made reference to the serpent as the symbol of life and resurrection:

And as Moses lifted up the serpent in the wilderness, even so must the Son of man be lifted up: That whosoever believeth in him should not perish, but have eternal life.

For God so loved the world, that he gave his only begotten Son, that whosoever believeth in him should not perish, but have everlasting life.

For God sent not his Son into the world to condemn the world; but that the world through him might be saved. (John 3:14-17)

**Fig. 36: Zapotec urn from ancient Oaxaca, Mexico, with a personage holding a flowing vase.**

**Fig. 37: A personage holding a flowing vase from a Zapotec urn from ancient Oaxaca, Mexico.**

**Fig. 38: Monument at La Venta, Tabasco, Mexico, showing the life and birth symbol at the head of a serpent (about the eighth century B.C.). Note the presence of Thomas Stuart Ferguson.**

Moses' point was simply that the serpent was a symbol of the Messiah who would come and be raised up on the cross, so that eternal life might be given, if man would only believe. John goes on to say:

> And this is the condemnation, that light is come into the world, and men loved darkness rather than light, because their deeds were evil.
> For every one that doeth evil hateth the light, neither cometh to the light, lest his deeds should be reproved. (John 3:19-20)

A brass or bronze serpent on a pole or beam was maintained as a representation of the Messiah of Israel in the chief temple of Israel from the time of Moses until the temple of Solomon was destroyed in 586 B.C. (Farbridge 75; Smith 240).

The motif of the serpent on the cross as an emblem of Christ was often used in the early Christian art of the Mediterranean

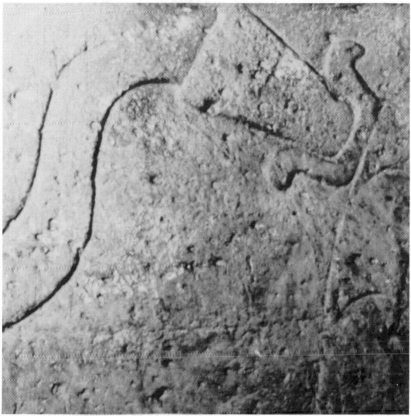

**Fig. 39: Closeup view of the life-birth symbol on monument at La Venta, Tabasco, Mexico.**

world. The serpent was a symbol of the Messiah in both the Old World and in Mesoamerica.

Since Jesus designated the serpent as a symbol of himself as God of Life in the days of Moses and again at the time of his earthly ministry, it is not surprising that we find it as one of the primary symbols in the New World. As a matter of fact, "serpent" is one of the symbolic names used in the New World in referring to the Creator-God. As has been stated earlier, *Coatl* means "serpent" or "twin" as it is found in *Quetzalcoatl*.

The serpent symbol is found in Mexico and Central America

**Fig. 40: The tomb lid of Pacal in the Temple of the Inscriptions at Palenque, Chiapas. (Courtesy of Merle Green.)**

in B.C. times. The serpent-life symbol runs rampant through the classic Maya art and architecture after A.D. 300. It is found over central and southern Mexico and in Guatemala. It was perpetuated throughout central and southern Mexico to the coming of Cortes. It appears as early as 1200 B.C.-600 B.C. at La Venta, as shown in Figures 38 and 39.

There is powerful documentary evidence of an Atlantic crossing of a group of people from the Near East so intent on being identified with the serpent symbol that they called themselves "serpent-men." They were called *Chanes,* meaning "serpent-men." Edward Herbert Thompson says of them in his book *People of the Serpent* (77-79):

> It behooves us to be very open-minded in the matter of chronology and chronological estimates, and this may be taken here to apply especially to the strange happenings chronicled by the traditions of widely separate peoples concerning the mysterious appearance on the shores of the Gulf of Mexico of the *Chanes* — the people of the Serpent. These traditions tell us, and carvings on ancient walls and stone columns sustain them, that unknown ages ago there appeared strange craft at the mouth of what is now known as the Panuco River in the State of Vera Cruz. . . . In these craft were light-skinned beings, and some of the traditions have it that they were tall of stature and blue-eyed. They were clad in strange garments and wore about their foreheads emblems like entwined serpents.
>
> . . .The leaders of the Ulmecas were ever known as Chanes, or among the Mayas, as Canob — Serpents' Wise Men — or Ah Tzai — People of the Rattlesnake. . . . They built Chichen Itza — the City of the Sacred Well. (77-79)

The Tzendal-Maya traditions come to us from the sixteenth- and seventeenth-century Tzendals, who lived in the Chiapas region in which the Chanes finally settled. These reports shed important light on the origin of the Serpent-Men of the Messiah. They were Chanes, "Serpents" of Quetzalcoatl-Itzamna. "At the head of their ancient [Mexican] calendar is placed *Nin*" (de la

Vega 9). Howard Leigh (artist living in Mitla, Oaxaca, Mexico) notes that *Nan* means "lady" in the Zapotec tongue of Mexico. *Ninhursag* meant "Lady of the rib" (Eve) in ancient Mesopotamia. Brasseur de Bourbourg, the French scholar of the last century, ties *Nin* closely to the Hebrew: "The Nin of the tzendales was the same as Cipactli of the Mexican traditions, a sea monster which figured allegorically as the father of the *Chan* [sky-serpent] race, as well as the tree [of life] with the serpent" (51-52).

*Tan-nin* (pronounced tan-neen) is Hebrew meaning "sea-serpent" or "serpent" (Strong, *Hebrew and Chaldee Dictionary*, word 8577). Thus some of the terminology from ancient Chiapas, Mexico regarding the Serpent Men is identical with ancient Hebrew terminology.

One of the New World homelands and centers of the serpent people was *Nachan,* meaning "habitation of the serpent." The serpent center, *Tamoanchan* (believed to have been in the Tabasco-Chiapas region of southern Mexico) means literally "place of the bird-serpent." After providing his reader with this information, Rafael Girard, in *El Popol-Vuh Fuente Historica,* provides an illustration of the hieroglyph for the name *Tamoanchan.* Girard's illustration is reproduced here as Figure 41. It shows a bird above a serpent, and on the body of the serpent are stars. He states that, according to the concept of the present Maya Chorti priests, the bird is a representation of the God of the Sky. It is remembered that Tiamat (*Nut* in Egypt) is a sky goddess represented by the Milky Way and the serpent symbol in ancient Mesopotamia and Egypt. Here we have in the Tamoanchan hieroglyph the identical elements in Mexico in combination exactly as found in the Near East—stars and serpents. In the National Museum in Mexico City is a large mural from Teotihuacan, great city of ancient Mexico dating to the days of Christ. Around the border of this huge mural is the body of a serpent, star-studded over its entire length—the Milky Way. Water falls from the hands of the deity portrayed in the mural.

J. Eric Thompson, Carnegie linguist, tells us that the term *Tamoanchan* "is pure Chiapan Maya: *Ta,* 'at', moan, 'the *moan*

**Fig. 41: Bird and serpent symbol of the sky god with stars on the body of the serpent. Scene from a Maya codex.**

bird,' *chan,* 'sky' or 'snake.' The complete word means 'at the moan-bird sky' or 'at the moan bird and snake,' a clear reference to this celestial realm of Maya mythology" (Tax 36). The serpent was associated with the Milky Way of the sky in Mesoamerica just as it was in Mesopotamia and the ancient Near East.

In 1912 the National Museum of Mexico published a paper by Henning, Plancarte, Robelo, and Gonzalez entitled *Tamoanchan.* In it the authors point out that *tamoanchan* was also one of several names used by the ancients in referring to their ancient, and now unidentified, lost capital.

Herman Beyer, linguist, identified the heavenly *Tamoanchan* with the Milky Way (Henning et al. 43). Rafael Girard and others have pointed out that *tamoanchan* was the sky home of deity where there were water and rain in the center of the sky, the source of rain, the Milky Way (25).

The late Sylvanus G. Morley, in his *The Ancient Maya,* describes an art object of ancient Mesoamerica which helps further in identifying the serpent with the Milky Way in that region, just as the two are associated in Bible lands:

> Across the sky stretches a serpent-like creature with symbols of constellations [including a patee cross representing the four world directions] presented on its side and signs for solar and lunar eclipses hanging from its belly. From its widely opened jaws, as well as from the two eclipse signs, pours a flood of water, falling down on the earth. Below the heavenly serpent, the Old Woman Goddess [Tiamat or Nut!] with long talon-like fingernails and toenails, patroness of death and destruction, a writhing serpent on her head, . . . holds an inverted bowl from which also gushes a destroying flood. Finally at the bottom stands *Ek Chuah,* the black God of War, the *Moan bird* of evil omen on his head; he holds in his right hand two javelins and in his left a long staff, all three pointing downward. (214)

There is some confusion of two Maya deities in Morley's description. Ek Chuah, the black God of War, is now known as the God M of the Maya pantheon with the calendar name 7 Death

Fig. 42: Miscellaneous Monument 60 from Izapa, Chiapas, with the glyph for "7 Death" (between 300 to 1 B.C.).

(Figure 42) and is associated with the planet Jupiter. The deity with the Moan bird and destroying flood is the Maya God L with the calendar name 1 Death and is associated with the planet Mars.

Rain — the dew from heaven — came from the sky river. One of the names for the Messiah in Mesoamerica was *Itzamna,* which means "the dew from heaven." The primary symbol of *Itzamna,* as for Jehovah, was the serpent, the emblem raised up by Moses in similitude of the Messiah, who was raised up in Israel 1200 years after the time of Moses.

In Sumerian myths dating to the third millennium B.C., El lived at the source of the Two Deeps, or center of the Milky Way, which flowed away from him in opposite directions and was regarded as his seed or life power. The Milky Way was also thought of by Phyllis Ackerman as the river of heaven, symbolized by the undulating serpent. Thus the serpent representing water and life force is one of the oldest symbols of deity known to humanity and is related directly to the undulating streams from the flowing vase shown in Figure 43.

### The Flowing Vase (Milky Way)

The flowing vase, which represents this creative utterance, has been identified in Sumerian art on cylinder seals, in full-round sculptured works, and in ceramics (Van Buren).

Mesoamerican figures holding flowing vases have been discovered in Oaxaca at Monte Alban, dating to the sixth century B.C. A particularly fine example is a large hollow clay figure unearthed ca. A.D. 1300 in Mayapan. It is the god Chac holding a flowing vase in each hand (photograph in Covarrubias plate 50).

### The "Little Man"

During the 1930s, Alfonso Caso, a Mexican archaeologist, discovered just above bedrock at Monte Alban in Oaxaca a remarkable stone monument about five feet tall (Figure 43). It is carved to represent a bow-legged figure with its head in profile to the right. The face is of a "little man." Between the large figure's legs are more glyphs of unknown meaning.

The larger figure represents the ancient Sumerian astral god Apsu and the Egyptian god Khephri while the small person on their abdomens is Mummu, above the flowing vase that represents the energy of the life force. Ackerman's description of the Sumerian figure could apply equally well to the Mesoamerican one:

> The phallic "Little Man" or Bes type [Bes was lion-headed dwarf  that kept evil spirits at bay], is commonly drawn with legs bowed in such  wise as to create a void pattern of a glans; and Dr. [A Leo] Oppenheim  suggests

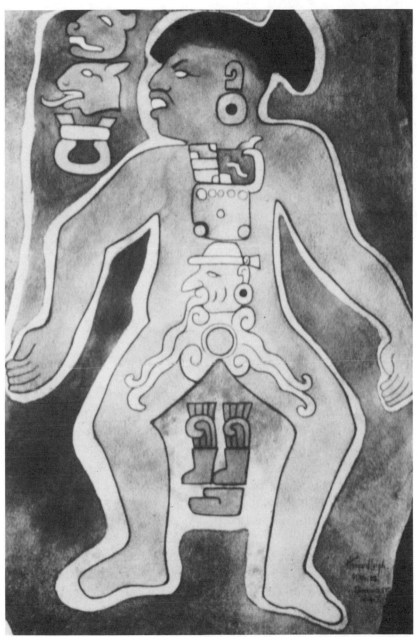

Fig. 43: The "Little Man" symbol from Danzante 55 monument from Monte Alban, Oaxaca, Mexico, about 500 B.C.

that one of the undeciphered lines [from the Sumerian epic *Enuma elish*] concerning Mummu speaks of his legs as "too short to run." . . .

Mummu was a dwarf of the Bes type. But an extensive study of the Bes type indicates that the figure originated as a phallus-personation, corresponding to the widespread notion, and designation of the phallus as the "Little Man"; and the phallus is so depicted, for example, on some of the Maori gods, the "Little Man" being an exact miniature replica of the god himself. This identification of the Mummu as a phallus personation explains the old "Enuma elish" [Babylonian epic of creation].

"Mummu" is interpreted by later Babylonians as meaning "Creative Utterance" or "Life-Force" and this . . . "Utterance" with "Life-Force" would, therefore, be the semen. . . .

All this means that in one branch of this astral cosmogony, the Milky Way was regarded as the creative semen of the Sky-god. (10-11)

## The Sacred Bucket

Another art motif of considerable interest is the sacred bucket, with parallels in both the Old and New Worlds. In *One Fold and One Shepard,* Figures 16 and 24 show Assyrian examples from about 700 B.C. being held in the hand of a religious personage.

An interesting parallel is a bas-relief from La Venta in the state of Tabasco, Mexico, which was uncovered in a 1955 expedition jointly undertaken by the National Geographic Society, the Smithsonian Institution, and the University of California. Radiocarbon dating of the site establishes occupation at 1200 B.C. to 600 B.C., and this particular artifact seems to have been made in 600 B.C. It shows a being seated upon a serpent whose head is raised above the man's. He holds the bucket toward the rattles at the end of the serpent's tail (Figure 5, page 9).

### Serpent and S Glyph

Some of the ancient connections made between the serpent and the sky have already been discussed. In Sumerian mythology, rain came from the Milky Way, nourishing young plants as milk nourishes young animals and, as the stream of seed from the god, partaking directly of his generative powers (Ackerman page 9). An echo of this same belief appears in Job 26:13, "By his spirit he hath garnished the heavens; his hand hath formed the crooked [undulating] serpent." Miguel Covarrubias cites the belief that the "White-Cloud-Serpent" or Milky Way gave birth to the original creative couple, the Lord and Lady Sustenance.

As Figures 44 and 45 show, the high civilizations in both the Old and the New World demonstrate a fascination with the serpent motif and incorporated it into their art. On a Sumerian cylinder seal are two felines with snakelike necks intertwined in a graceful symmetrical design dating from about 3300 B.C. Frankfort comments that the symbol represents the god of the bringer of the fertilizing rain and is sometimes accompanied by the Imdugud bird, "which represents the dark clouds of the storm" (33 34).

The Mesoamerican design appears in the Mixtec Codex Vienna dating from about A.D. 1350, which is located in Vienna, Austria. It is much more stylized, but even so, the feet and curved tail of the animals suggest feline shapes.

The association of serpents and the simple or double S-shape with fertilizing rains and clouds is part of the mythological structure of both the Old and the New World. The undulating shape of the S, reminiscent of the serpent, is a logical pictorial depiction of a river (or the Milky Way — sky-river and source of rain).

Bedrich Hrozny, professor of oriental languages in Prague, described S-shapes on the oldest cylinder seals discovered to date. They come from Uruk (biblical Erech) in Mesopotamia and date from about 3600-3100 B.C.:

> Some of the designs on these seals depicting animals with their long necks interwoven, appeared — under Sumero-

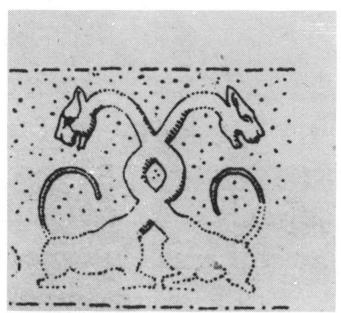

**Fig. 44: Jemdet Nasr drawing of the serpent-necked felines (ca. 3300 B.C. Sumerian culture of southern Mesopotamia).**

**Fig. 45: Stylized serpent-necked design from the Mixtec Codex Vienna.**

> Akkadian influence—early in Egypt. . . . Indeed, the
> cylinder seal itself appeared temporarily in Egypt during her
> earliest dynastic period, where it was used in the same way
> as in Sumer, Viz. in the sealing up of clay vessels. But in the
> Nile Valley the cylinder seal was soon replaced by the native
> scarab. (36)

In Old World archaeology this design is sometimes referred to as the guilloche pattern and seems to have first been created in metal, possibly gold wire, as ornamental work. "In the earlier forms the helix or S curve, seems to have prevailed probably brought from Egypt, and then in Syria contracted or consolidated, into the rope pattern" (William Hayes Ward).

An excellent example of the double-S glyph is a fresco from the Temple of the Tepantitla at Teotihuacan, not far from Mexico City, and dating from about A.D. 500 (Figure 46). It depicts a jaguar from whose mouth arises a "spiral scroll, signifying speech or song." Directly beneath his jaws is a design made of three interlocked S's "symbolizing water," from which droplets of rain emerge (Groth-Kimball and Feuchtwanger). The double S-glyph is also a symbol of the jaguar paw (Brotherston 256).

A variation the S-glyph is that of the seven-headed serpent, a symbol of the Sumerian storm god Ningishzida of the city of Lagash. In Figure 47, a Sumerian mace head dating to the third millennium before Christ and the seven heads are seen in the center with two lion-headed eagles, in Mesopotamian art a representation of rain clouds (Frankfort 32). It is noteworthy that the jaguar of southern Mexico symbolized the god of rain, Tlaloc to the Aztecs. Cocijo, the Zapotec god of rain, symbolized by a jaguar mask, controlled the earth's fertility as a result (Covarrubias 182-83).

The book of Chilam Balam of Tizimin, a product of sixteenth century Yucatan, includes the statement: "We invoke *ah vuc dhapat,* the seven-headed serpent . . ." (Makenson 48). A 1949 dictionary of Spanish-Maya refers to a traditional "fabulous serpent of seven heads" (Solis Alcala). Budge notes that the

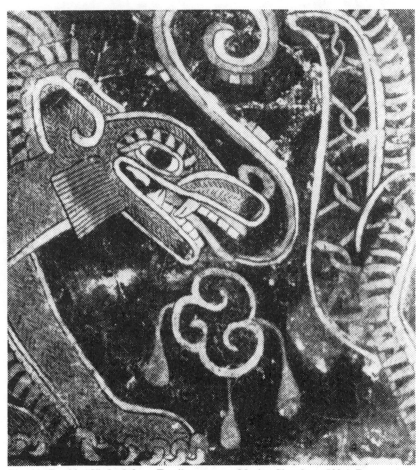

Fig. 46:  Double "S" glyph from Teotihuacan near Mexico City about 500 A.D.

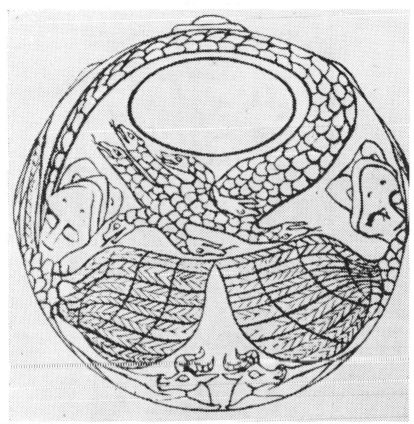

Fig. 47: Seven-headed serpent and lion-headed imdugud eagle from southern Mesopotamia about 3000 B.C.

seven-headed serpent was the emblem of Ea, god of the River of the Great Serpent (Milky Way) (132).

A marvelous example, Figure 48, found in El Tajin near Papantla in the state of Veracruz on the Gulf of Mexico, was called to our attention by retired Professor Floyd Carnaby of Utah State University. It shows a seated human figure with seven serpent heads emerging from the neck. Jose Garcia Payon, a Mexican archaeologist, calls it a representation of the deity Chicomecoatl, an important vegetation goddess. Her name, which means "Seven Serpents," is referred to as "Seven Ears of Corn." He further observes that the seven serpents "radiate in the

**Fig. 48: Late Classic Monument from El Tajin, Veracruz, Mexico, illustrating 7 serpents in place of a decapitated human head.**

form of the Jewish ritual candelabrum" (122; Covarrubius 184). This particular carving dates to the Classic era, about A.D. 250-900.

## Altars and Incense Burners

Another interesting cultural parallel with religious significance is the altars and incense burners found on both hemispheres, each marked by four horns on the corners or sometimes a profusion of horns in various patterns.

Bible-readers are familiar with references to the horned altar:

> And thou shalt take of the blood of the bullock, and put it upon the horns of the altar with thy finger. (Exod. 29:12)
>
> Take of the blood of the bullock, and the blood of the goat, and put it upon the horns of the altar round about. (Lev. 16:18)
>
> And Adonijah feared because of Solomon, and arose, and went, and caught hold on the horns of the altar. (1 Kings 1:50)

Exodus 30:1 mentions the biblical altar of incense, in a sense a miniature or symbolic altar. What would be the symbolism of the horns? The bull and cow, along with the serpent and felines, represented the life force of vitality and fruitfulness. In Egyptian art, the lower side of the horned cow is shown studded with stars, representing the Milky Way. It would be appropriate to apply such symbols of strength, power, and fertility to the altar used in approaching deity.

## Sacred Mountains

An interesting passage from Isaiah reads:

> And it shall come to pass in the last days, that the mountain of the Lord's house shall be established in the top

of the mountains, and shall be exalted above the hills; and
all nations shall flow into it.

And many people shall go and say, Come ye, and let us
go up to the mountain of the Lord, to the house of the God
of Jacob; and he will teach us of his ways, and we will walk
in his paths: for out of Zion shall go forth the law, and the
word of the Lord from Jerusalem. (Isaiah 2:2-3)

When Abraham built his altar called Bethel, it was on top of
a mountain. Throughout southern Mexico and Guatemala, the
remains of ancient altars and shrines appear on mountain tops.

We have already mentioned the importance of the stepped
temple as a representation, both in the Old and the New Worlds,
of the sacred mountain. The Sumerians of the fourth millennium
before Christ used the terraced or staged temple tower. To this
the Zapotecs and Mixe of Yalalag in Oaxaca believe that the giver
of water and life is a water shepherd who lives in mountain
springs. Floods are, it is believed, caused by the water serpent,
the great river of the sky; and during storms, they claim to see the
water serpent emerging from the storm clouds.

It is interesting that in the Sumerian system, *Shakhura*
("waiting room, antechamber") referred to the shrine or temple
on top of the temple tower, while the outer chamber before the
"Holy of Holies" on the ground-level temples at a later period in
Sumer was called by the same name.

These stepped temples have been documented as late as the
fifth century B.C. The Greek historian Herodotus tells of visiting
Babylon in the fifth century B.C., where he saw a temple tower
with seven stages, each painted a different color.

In comparisons to the temple towers of Mesopotamia with
those of Mesoamerica (Figure 49), some striking similarities
emerge. Both were usually laid out on the points of the compass.
Sun-dried adobe bricks were used in both areas. For example, the
Temple at Ur (Figure 50), dating from 2100 B.C. on the
Euphrates, and the New World temple towers at Cholula,
Teotihuacan, Kaminaljuyu and Chichen Itza (Figure 51) are each
a solid mass of sun-dried adobe brickwork, all dating back to

Fig. 49: The Quetzalcoatl pyramid of Cholula, Puebla, Mexico, in alignment with Mount Popocatepetl. (Photo by Daniel Bates. Courtesy David A. Palmer and the Society for Early Historic Archaeology.)

Fig. 50: The "Mountain of the House of God" (or Ziggurat) from Ur, southern Mesopotamia about 2100 B.C.

**Fig. 51: The Temple of Kukulcan at Chichen Itza, Yucatan, Mexico, dating from the tenth century A.D.**

near the time of Christ. The pyramid at Cholula is larger than any pyramid in Egypt, measuring 1,132 feet at the base.

The Maya word for their temple towers is *Ku,* the same word for God. *Hunab Ku* designated the Maya father-God of the universe. Thus the concept of the temple as an artificial mountain made holy by the presence of God was also well-known in the New World. Each of the four sides represents one of the cardinal directions. Sometimes each is painted a different color, representing the four directions (north, south, east and west). A similar pattern of color-coding directions has been observed in pre-Christian Mesopotamia, Egypt, and China as well as

Mesoamerica (Kelley 7). Tozzer confirms that the linking of a color to each of the cardinal directions was customary for both Maya and Aztec (Landa 135). Alfonso Caso, noted for his important archaeological work at Monte Alban, confirms that the Aztecs assigned red to the east, black to the north, blue to the south, and white for the west (133).

Although these Mesoamerican structures are sometimes called pyramids, Joseph Lindon Smith, for one, observes that the Kaminaljuyu pyramid, which he made a special trip to see, had "not even a remote similarity" to the pyramids constructed by the Egyptian Pharaoh Cheops and his family. Instead, the Maya pyramid was "flat-topped and rectangular, only about sixty feet in height and made chiefly of adobe without a facing of stone." He found in it echoes of the Sumerian ziggurat (a stepped pyramid) (305). In 1949, Alberto Ruz of Merida, Yucatan, excavated the ruins of Palenque in Chiapas, discovering a secret stone stairway beneath the floor of the Temple of Inscriptions, which stands atop a Pyramid. The stairway, blocked with stones, led into a secret burial chamber and tomb within the pyramid (Figure 52). In this burial chamber was a stone tomb vault; hieroglyphics adorned the walls of this tomb, and a beautifully carved tree of life constituted the ornamentation on the tomb lid. In the tomb was a male wearing a wide collar of tubular beads in the form of a breastplate. The style is reminiscent of the typical Egyptian wide necklace. A full-reconstruction of this pyramid-tomb may now be seen in the National Museum in Mexico City.

It seems persuasive to other observers, including us, that the ancient builders of this structure knew not only the ancient pyramid designs of Mesopotamia but also those of Egypt, for the stone stairway, the sealing of the passageway, the interior crypt, and the stone sarcophagus vault are a uniquely Egyptian combination.

We mention only seven temple towers dating back to Pre-classic times that have been discovered: one at Teotihuacan near Mexico City, one at Cholula in Puebla, four more at Cuicuilco under a fall of volcanic lava on the southern outskirts of Mexico City which date to about the time of Christ by radiocarbon

**Fig. 52: Cross-section of the Temple of Inscriptions at Palenque, Chiapas, Mexico, showing the location of Pacal's Tomb.**

methods, and one at Uaxactun in Guatemala dating between 200 B.C. and A.D. 150 and ornamented with Olmec jaguar masks over white stucco. The temples on their summits have disappeared and little is known of their design, but the Maya temples of the Classic era were designed with an interior corbeled vault consisting of stone slabs, each higher stone projecting farther into the room. This design originated in Mesopotamia and was also used in Egypt, Syria, India, and Greece during the second and first millennia B.C. (Frankfort 21).

## The Cross

Another interesting artistic motif is the cross. The patee cross in Figures 53 and 27 is an ancient solar symbol found among the Assyrians, Zapotecs, Teotihuacan, and Maya.

This same distinctive shape is the glyph for the 260-day Tonalamatl in the calendar system dating to the first millennium B.C.

Fig. 53: An Assyrian patee (Maya Kan) cross from Ninevah about 800 B.C.

An interesting variation is the cross within a cross. This device appears on a Babylonian seal of the first dynasty dated at about 2,000 B.C. (Figure 54). It also appears in Hittite art dating to about 1500 B.C. (Ceram 86). Figure 55 appears on a vase in the Howard Leigh collection in the Frissel Museum at Mitla in Oaxaca. The vase comes from Oaxaca and dates to 550-200 B.C. Another example is found on a pottery bowl from the Frissel Museum in Mitla. A fourth example appears on a lintel in Cuilapan, Oaxaca in 1904 that dates from A.D. 400-950.

Ackerman, describing the cross of the Sumerians dating from third millennium B.C., explains it as a cosmological and geographical symbol:

> Eventually in the *Enuma elish* . . . Tiamat [the Sumerian goddess associated with the Milky Way] in her turn is slain, and her hide is split in two and stretched across the heavens. The description is a bit confused, but a careful analysis indicates with reasonable probability that it was used to mark the celestial equator and meridian. The Milky Way is a rough equivalent of the equator and the meridian when it lies, respectively, East-West and North-South; hence the use of Tiamat's hide (or body) to define the imaginary lines. The equator-meridian cross (Four Quarters motif) is the most frequent seal-type in about the second quarter of the third millennium B.C. (14)

## The Pentad

Among the astral-conscious Sumerians about 2700 B.C., the North Star figures prominently. These ancient astronomers considered it to be at the center of a great theoretical cross in the sky formed by the two major directions of the Milky Way. When it lay east-west, it was regarded as the equivalent of the equator. When it lay in a north-south direction, it was considered the equivalent of the meridian (Ackerman 14).

A ring symbolized the rotating constellations among the Sumerians. A transfixing ring represented the North Star. Figure

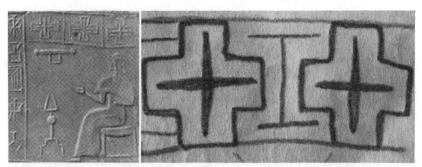

Fig. 54 (left): A cross within a cross from southern Mesopotamia about 2000 B.C. Fig. 55 (right): A cross within a cross from Monte Alban, Oaxaca, Mexico.

56, danzante carved slab elements from Monte Alban dating about 500 B.C., shows the classic pentad. According to Ackerman, "The main triad of Polaris and the twin terminal constellations is, therefore, sometimes supplemented by these secondary twins, inserted between the older and more important twins and the pole. This makes a pentad, and five is a sympathetic number to this system since it refers also to the four quarters and the center" (17-18).

The pentad glyph appears in the symbolism of Monte Alban dating to about 500 B.C. During the Classic and Postclassic periods in Mexico, the same glyph also represents five Venus years, according to Edward Seler and Raul Noriega.

## The Star of David

The Star of David, a six-pointed star formed of two, often interlaced equilateral triangles, is an ancient symbol of Judaism and is now the emblem of the state of Israel. Dating from at least the first millennium B.C., it is often referred to as Solomon's Seal.

Figure 57 is a remarkable representation of the Star of David within a circle with a feathered tail. It was found in Uxmal, a Mayan site dating from about tenth century A.D. D'Alviella comments on this identical carving and notes that the feathered

**Fig. 56: A pentad (5) transfixed by a stick from Monte Alban, Oaxaca, Mexico about 500 B.C.**

tail "suggests in a striking manner the pennated tail of certain Assyrian, Phoenician, and Persian Globes" (226). An example from seventh century Assyria shows a winged circle with a feathered tail (Figure 58).

### The Life-Birth Symbol

One of the oldest religious symbols in the world is the curving upside-down U or omega-shaped sign that represents birth. It appears on many of the boundary stones used in Babylonia to mark dividing lines between private plots dating from 1350-650 B.C. It also appears on many early cylinder seals (Ferguson 1958: 119-120).

This symbol was associated with the Sumerian "earth-mother" goddess Ki, or Ninhursag, who was regarded as "the mother of the land," the midwife of heaven and earth.

It also appears as a symbol of fertility and childbirth in

**Fig. 57: A Star of David
symbol from Uxmal, Yucatan,
Mexico about 1000 A.D.**

Sumerian, Babylonian (Figures 59 and 62), Assyrian, Egyptian, Palestinian, and Hittite art. It is found in identical form and with identical associated symbols in Mesoamerica as well. It appears at Monte Alban (Figure 61), La Venta, Cerro de las Mesas, and in the state of Chiapas. It appears many times in the Mixtec Nuttall Codex (Figure 60) and in the Mixtec Vienna Codex (Vaillant 54). In both the Near East and Mesoamerica the symbol occurs with many variations (Figure 63).

It can take a variety of forms, from a shape so flattened that it is barely curved, upside-down with the opening pointing upwards, and with a variety of ornaments, but the general shape with the terminal curls is consistent.

**Fig. 58: Winged circle with a feathered tail from Assyria about 800 B.C.**

**Fig. 59: A symbol of life or birth from ancient Babylon about 600 B.C.**

**Fig. 60: A symbol of life or birth from the Mixtec Codex Nuttall page 75, in the eleventh century A.D.**

Fig. 61: A symbol of life or birth on a Zapotec Urn from ancient Oaxaca, Mexico.

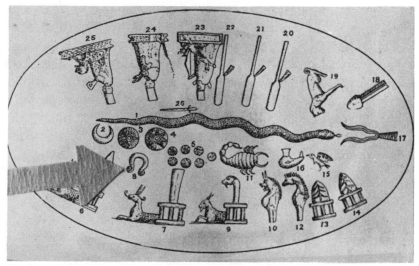

Fig. 62: A Babylonian zodiac with the life or birth symbol, about the sixth century B.C.

Fig. 63: The life, childbirth, and fertility symbol rendered in several variations from both the Near East and Mesoamerica.

On the boundary stones and cylinder seals of ancient Babylonia, this life symbol appears frequently with other astral symbols, including the serpent (Milky Way), the crescent moon, two stars, and seven dots, possibly representing a constellation. Moon, stars, and dots appear in Figure 64, a Zapotec artifact dating from the A.D. 100-400. Ward states, "The seven dots are among the most common emblems of the late period, but are not found in the first or middle Babylonian empire" (Ferguson 1958: 123). He also adds that some of the dots have stars within them.

**Fig. 64: A Zapotec symbol of life or birth with celestial symbols from ancient Oaxaca, Mexico.**

Hinke explains the reason for the presence of astral deity symbols on the boundary stones:

> It seems . . . that most public monuments were placed . . . under the protection of the Gods, to guard them against destruction by ill-disposed persons. A conspicuous example is furnished by the famous stela of Hammurabi, containing his code of laws, in which twelve of the great Gods are invoked to punish anyone who abolishes his judgments, over-rules his words, alters his statues, defaces his name, and writes his own name in its place." (Ferguson 1958: 123)

The life-birth symbol is found on the headdresses of Figure 37 from Mexico, in Figure 58 in connection with the feathered globe from Assyria, on two gold breastplates from Monte Alban, and on the ends of scepters or staffs in Middle Empire Babylonian cylinder seals (see Ward, Figures 414, 416), where it is related to the flowing vase. Ward documents that it is sometimes formed by serpents (408).

In several examples—Figures 65-67—the symbol appears as part of the headdress or coiffure of Mesoamerican figures, paralleling the same use in Babylonian, Egyptian, and Palestinian art (Figures 68, 69). Jade had particular associations with life in Mesoamerica. The fact that the Ninhursag symbols in Figures 65-67 are carved from jade strengthens the view that the symbol retained its original Old World meaning in Mesoamerica. (See Figure 37, which shows the life symbol as a woman's headdress from ancient Mesoamerica.)

The parallels are particularly compelling when we examine Ninhursag in greater detail. According to Oppenheim, she was known as "the mother of the land" and as the "great-grandmother" and "the Lady of Heaven." She was the main female figure in the Babylonian pantheon, where she was also known as Ishtar. She was the goddess and symbol of childbirth, new life, rebirth, and resurrection. "Present in human and animal reproduction, . . . she manifests herself wherever and whenever man or animal creates new life. . . . [She also] is linked to the cyclic phenomena of vegetal life, . . . the annual disappearance

Fig. 65: A symbol of life or birth on a piece of jade from ancient Guatemala.

Fig. 66: A symbol of life or birth on a piece of jade from ancient Guatemala.

Fig. 67: A symbol of life or birth on a piece of jade from ancient Guatemala.

and rebirth of vegetation" (70-71).

A female goddess of birth and rebirth with the same symbol appears in the Dresden Codex and the Madrid Codex, two of the three hieroglyphic books that have survived from the pre-Conquest Mayas of southern Mexico and Guatemala. Maya scholar J. Eric Thompson identifies her as:

> Ixchel [pronounce Ish-chel, an interesting sound-alike for the Babylonian Ishtar], the moon goddess, . . . patroness of childbirth, procreation, . . . and growing crops, . . . "our mother," "lady," . . . "mistress. . . ." We have an explanation of the fact that the curl of hair, the symbol of

**Fig. 68: The life or birth symbols associated with the goddess Ninhursag of ancient Mesopotamia and the goddess Hathor from ancient Egypt.**

> the moon goddess is also the symbol of the earth sign. . . .
> Ixchel was the patroness of childbirth, sexual relations,
> disease, the earth and its crops, water, and the art of
> weaving. (297-308)

Thompson points out that the hair-curl symbol of Ixchel is closely associated with the sign of the planet Venus in these codices. Oppenheim tells us that Ishtar, goddess of childbirth in Mesopotamia, was "worshipped as Evening and Morning Star [Venus]" (71).

An interesting interpretation comes from Samuel Noah Kramer, curator of the tablet collections from Mesopotamia at the University Museum, University of Pennsylvania. His translation of a Sumerian cuneiform tablet that dates from about 2000 B.C. identifies Ninhursag/Ninti as "the Lady of the Rib." Kramer suggests that Ninhursag can be associated with the Eve figure of the Old Testament (145, 149).

Fig. 69: The symbol of life or birth from ancient Palestine.

**Calendars**

The Mesoamerican calendars were extremely sophisticated. These people knew the exact time periods of the orbits of the five planets around the sun (visible to the eye), and how they aligned with each other at different times of the year as they interacted with the sun and the moon.

Calendars of high precision were based on many similar astronomical observations and calculations. In both the Near East and Mexico, the true solar year had been worked out to the seventh decimal point, 365.241987 days. In both lands, the exact time of the cycles around the sun of Mercury and Venus had been worked out, an achievement not accomplished in Europe until Kepler in the seventeenth century.

In May 1958, the Mexican scholar Raul Noriega, a man who was not afraid to examine carefully the relationships between the ancient Near East and Mesoamerica, was able to announce that he had deciphered numerous signs and glyphs of ancient Mexico, hitherto imponderable and undeciphered. Noriega frankly states that he found the basic method of solving the riddle of Mesoamerican calendar and astronomical glyphs by studying the astronomy and mathematics of ancient Mesopotamia. His primary Near East source was *Tabletas Astronomicas Cunciformes,* by O. Neugebauer.

Noriega shows that in both the Near East and Mesoamerica, the ancients knew the time of the lunations of the moon, 29.53058857 days; of the cycles of Mercury, 115.8774 days; of Venus, 584 days; of Mars, 780 days; of Jupiter, 398.8846 days; and of Saturn, 378.0919 days. The ancients did not express the fractions of a day as accurately as we do today, but the ancients of both regions did use multiplication and division, working in high figures (Noriega 265-57).

The ancient Egyptians had a calendar with a year of 360 days plus five supplementary days, and the five supplementary days were regarded as unlucky. The ancient Mayas had exactly the same system, also regarding the five supplementary days as unlucky.

Constellations representing the four directions and the

solstices (the times of the year when the sun is farthest north and farthest south of the equator) and equinoxes (the two times of the year when the sun crosses the equator, making night and day of equal length in all parts of the earth, March 21 and September 21, 22) are identical to those of the early Israelites (Job 9:9) and the ancients of Mexico and Guatemala (Figure 70): the Bear for the North, Orion for the South, Pleiades for the East, Scorpion for the West (two of the four names having the same meaning).

In ancient Egypt in the Middle Kingdom period, there are some references to the standard civil calendar. This calendar was twelve months of thirty days each. At the end of the twelfth month the Egyptians added five more days,which brought the year to 365 days. That makes a striking parallel to a 360-day Mesoamerican calendar and also to the 365-day Mesoamerican calendar, which lacks the leap-year accountability. The Maya

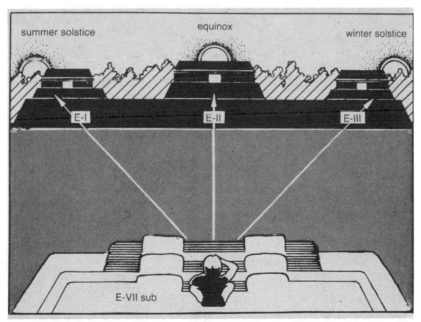

**Fig. 70: Temple E-VII at Uaxactun, El Peten, Guatemala, depicting the observation points for the spring and autumn equinoxes and the summer and winter solstices.**

called their 365-day calendar the *haab*. The Maya knew about the leap year, but ritually their system wouldn't work the way they wanted it to work, if they dealt with leap year directly. These complex Maya calendars were studied and understood by the elite and the priests.

At the same time there was a lunar calendar which dealt with the agriculture cycle that had to use the leap year. The Maya knew that 1,508 years of 365 days is equivalent to 1,507 years of 365.2422 days with the leap year in it. The codices of Oaxaca illustrate the symbols of how the Maya account for this. There is an example in one codex from Coixtlahuaca, Oaxaca, where three of the solar-leap year cycles ended at A.D. 1412. This takes one back to 3109 B.C., five years after the base date for the Maya Long Count calendar system. They started counting years forward from the base date year, 3114 B.C. So the Mayas knew how to deal with the leap year when it was necessary, and it was of course necessary for agriculture.

## Secret Combinations

Certain calendar days were fatalistic or bad for a person's birthdate. The days were classified to be good, bad, or indifferent. If persons were born on a bad day, then no matter what they did they could not overcome what they were destined to become.

The long count calendar was tied not only to astronomy, but also with astrology and numerology. Lounsbury explains, "The power and use of Maya astronomy was to learn the habits of celestial powers so as to make predictable the hazards of living under their influence. . . . But in its interpretive edifice and its applications it pertained rather to the domain of astrology, demonology, and divination" (804).

The people who organized and managed secret combinations were closely associated with the priests and others who were politically powerful. Secret combinations are made for gain and power. They were made by taking secret oaths and covenants and usually involved the murder of people who had something the secret combination wanted. Often children who were not in line to inherit properties or political rule would murder their own family members in order to obtain power, properties, and wealth.

In many of the sophistications of the ancient calendars of Mesoamerica, the priests tried to find, through the mysteries of the planets, constellations, and their movements, the knowledge that allowed them to exercise predictive power over the people. This was all connected with astrology, demonology, and divination. Secret combinations used the calendars in devious ways. As more research is done with calendar systems, more evidence will probably be found showing that secret societies attempted to use the knowledge of astrology and demonology as a tool to exercise power over the local populations.

The Mayas appear to have received some information regarding the calendars from the Zapotecs (Moran and Kelley 163-64; Kaufman 112).

The Mayas used this 360-day calendar year in the Long Count system right up to the arrival of the Spaniards in the 1500s.

The 360-day calendar year was prevalent in early Sumer/ Shinar of southern Mesopotamia. It appears that the 360-day calendar was also used by Noah. "In the second month, the seventeenth day of the month, the same day were all the fountains of the great deep broken up, and the windows of heaven were opened. And the rain was upon the earth forty days and forty nights. . . . And the waters returned from off the earth continually: and after the end of the hundred and fifty days the waters were abated. And the ark rested in the seventh month, on the seventeenth day of the month" (Gen. 7:11-12; 8:3-4). These passages show that 150 days were exactly five months, which would mean that each month had 30 days. Twelve months of 30 days each is a 360-day calendar year.

The book of Numbers Chapter 14, verse 34, mentions that a day will be as a year in prophecy, "Even forty days, each day for a year, shall ye bear your iniquities, even forty years." Phrases like seven times or three and a half times occur in the Bible. In the book of Revelation, three and a half times turns out to be 1,260 days or 1,260 years. Thus, by dividing 1,260 by 3½ (i.e., three and a half times), the result is 360. So the length of one "time" is 360 days. In prophecy these 360 days would equal 360 years.

## Hamlet's Mill

The concept of Hamlet's Mill in mythology throughout the Old World and in the New World focuses on a view of the cosmos or the universe as being a large grinding mill. The universe is pictured with the earth at the center, with an imaginary line going straight up to the North Pole at the top of the sky and another imaginary line going down to the South Pole underneath the earth. As the earth revolves on its axis, it tilts and creates an imaginary circle up around the North Pole in the upper sky and a similar imaginary circle around the South Pole. That same circle would form an imaginary band around the earth called the ecliptic path. This ecliptic path is traveled by the sun, which completes the full circle once a year, every 365-1/4 days. (A model of this is seen in Figure 71.) These three circles in the model are referred to as the Circle of the Equinoctial Precession. To briefly explain the Equinoctial Precession, we must imagine the earth again, surrounded by a 360 degree circle in a band whose width is between 23½ degrees south latitude to 23½ degrees north latitude. Within this band travel the visible planets and the visible constellations. This imaginary 360 degree circular band has been divided into twelve segments known as the solar zodiac. Each of the twelve signs of the zodiac occupies approximately 30 degrees of the 360 degree circle; thus 30 times 12 equals 360 degrees. Once a year each of these twelve signs occupies approximately one of our calendar months, so that once every year each sign of the zodiac will have had its 30 days in our life. The Equinoctial Precession phenomenon is a concept that visualizes the rising of a constellation on the east horizon on the 21st of March. This is the spring equinox. There is a gradual slippage westward of the night-time constellations. Modern-day astronomers indicate that this slippage is approximately 50 seconds per year and therefore would not be noticeable except

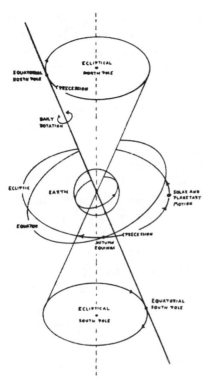

Fig. 71a: The concept of
Hamlet's Mill showing the
Precession of the Equinoxes.

Fig. 71b: Northwest African
example of Hamlet's Mill.

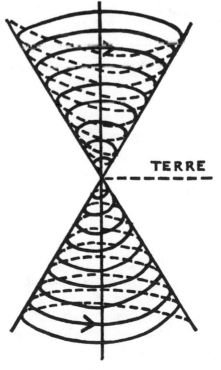

with the passage of many years. However, in Mesopotamia the priests were beginning to observe this phenomenon by the fourth millennium B.C. From ancient Mesopotamia the concept diffused throughout the Old World and into the New World as well.

Back in about 4326 B.C. the spring equinox would have fallen in the constellation of Taurus the Bull. At the rate of 50 seconds of movement of the night-time sky per year, it would take approximately 72 years before one degree of the 360 degree imaginary circle could be recorded. If one degree takes 72 years, then the 30 degrees that make up the sign of Taurus would last 2160 years (30 x 72). The spring equinox would begin in the zodiac sign of Aries the Ram in 2166 B.C. Aries the Ram then would be the spring equinox of the zodiac sign for the next 2160 years, or down to 6 B.C. The next zodiac sign would be Pisces the Fish. This is significant, because the zodiac sign Pisces is connected not only with prophecies in the Old Testament but with other major Near Eastern religions like Zoroastrianism. In the Near East it was a sign for the prophecy of a coming prince or Messiah. Pisces is also associated with the House of the Hebrews in Near Eastern mythology. It is possible that this date of 6 B.C., near the spring equinox, would be near the time of the birth of the Savior.

Another phenomenon associated with the equinoctial precession is the concept that the constellations and the planets travel in this zodiac path around the earth. These constellations and planets can be seen from the earth as it turns on its axis while circling the sun. This whole idea of rotating planets, constellations, etc., is the basis of the concept of Hamlet's Mill and its grinding motion.

In Egypt, we see the center line of the universe with the North Star at the top and two deities turning the mill (Figure 72). One deity is Seth; the other deity is Horus. In the Hindu material from India, we see the mill set upon a tortoise, a long snake representing the Milky Way; several heads on the snake are pulled back and forth in churning fashion. The deity Vishnu sits at the top at the North Star (Figure 73). In Mesoamerica we see

Fig. 72: **Egyptian gods Horus and Seth rotating the churn.**

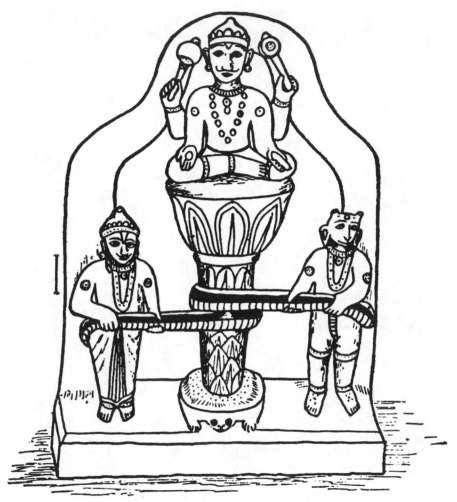

**Fig. 73: A Hindu example of churning the Milky Ocean.**

the same concept in the Maya Codex Madrid, in the form of the churn and a long path. A sun symbol on the path represents the sun traveling through the heavens and several individuals and pulling or churning along the sun's path (Figure 74).

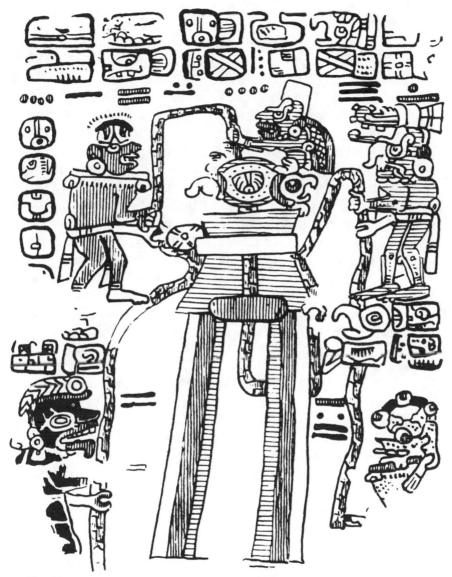

**Fig. 74: A scene from the Maya Codex Madrid illustrating the churning of the Milky Way.**

**The Volador Ceremony**

A spectacular ritual from ancient Mesoamerica needs to be researched more intensively and compared with the Old World scenes of the "churning Milky Ocean" (Figures 72-74) (Mesoamerica, India and Egypt). This ritual parallels the pentad design in the "Volador" ritual from Mesoamerica. One man, the center, shouts, dances, and plays music on top of a rotating platform located atop a very high pole. Four "flyers" leap off the rotating platform with the ropes tied around their waists and descend to the ground like "falling rain." The ritual is connected to petitions for rain and fertility. In India the "churning Milky Ocean foam" is related to sperm. Further symbolism involves the center figure on top of the churn or pole as representing the polar star and the pole or column the spindle of the universe (see *Hamlet's Mill*, p. 162). The Mesoamerican "Volador" ritual is widespread in Mesoamerica (Dahlgren de Jordan 280-286) but needs in-depth ethnographic documentation before the ritual disappears from the Mesoamerican scene. It is probable that the rain god Tlaloc and the four Tlaloques are the actors in the "Volador" ritual.

In summary, the theme of the "little man" or *Mummu* and the flowing vase symbols of the water coming out of the flowing vase would both fit into the ninth row or the bottom row of Table I. The flowing vase would represent the Milky Way and the water-carrier constellation, with water or milk spilling out and flowing through the night-time sky. The "little man" represents the direction south and the area of Eridu. The heavenly Eridamu, which is on the edge of the Milky Way, parallels the earthly Eridu and is also near the star of Sirius, which is the bright star out in the southern part of the night-time sky.

The theme of the felines fits in very nicely with the ninth row, the row connected with the planet Saturn; in the New World the feline is the jaguar and particularly Tepeyollotl, the Heart of the Mountain (Figure 75), which is considered to be the God of Merchants and of Secret Societies in ancient Mesoamerica and connected with the planet Saturn, as is the lion in Mesopotamia.

Fig. 75: A Late Preclassic Monument from Tuxtla Chico near Izapa, Chiapas, Mexico, showing the god Tepeyollotl. This deity represents the "heart of the mountain," the merchants, and secret societies. (Photo by Daniel Bates. Courtesy David A. Palmer and the Society for Early Historic Archaeology.)

The section on the life-birth symbols connected with the Sumerian Goddess Ninhursag is associated with the eighth row in the chart, and the Goddess is represented by the planet Venus. These life symbols are associated with the planet Venus in the Near East and in Mesoamerica.

The sixth row, connected with the planet Mercury, involves some of the themes in this chapter. (The theme of the serpent and the S-glyphs and particularly the seven-headed serpent, which would be associated with the Mesopotamian god Ningishzida. This same theme occurs in Mesoamerica on monuments from the Mexican states of Veracruz and Yucatan with an individual who has been decapitated. Seven serpents are shown in place of his head.)

Also, the serpent and the S-glyph are connected with the planet Mercury in ancient Mesoamerica, just as the serpent deity Ningishzida was connected with the planet Mercury in Mesopotamia and other parts of the Near East.

Also connected with the planet Mercury is the concept of purification, particularly in the form of a God of Healing. In Egypt this was the God Thoth, who also, besides being the God of Healing, was the God of Writing. In Mesoamerica it was Ixtlilton, the little black God of Healing. The "Volador" ceremony described above adds another theme to the sixth row.

For the third row, which represents the planet sun, we have the theme of the wing globe or the winged sun disc, but this symbol isn't common in the Near East or Mesoamerica. The wing bird is the eagle in both areas.

For the second row, connected with the front head of the eclipse demon, we have the concept of the Tree of Life, as mentioned earlier in this chapter.

The pentad correlates with the first row. The pentad of four dots with a center dot represents the North Star. The center dot and the twin constellations forming five dots are a symbol that would correlate with the concept of the god Tlaloc. Tlaloc represents the center big tree or the Tree of Knowledge of Good and Evil, and the four surrounding trees of the four directions represent the Tlaloques in Mesoamerica. On an astronomical level, Tlaloc represents the direction of the Milky Way at two different times of the year, one at summer solstice and one at the winter solstice. In the winter the Milky Way runs across the sky in an east-west direction; in the summer it runs in the north-south direction. If one places the east-west and north-south Milky Way patterns in the same location, they form a cross in the night-time sky. In the Mayan area of Mesoamerica, the name of the underworld is the name of the Milky Way at the winter solstice, or Xibalbey. We have a name for the Milky Way at the summer solstice called Sacbey, which is also the name of a causeway between Chichen Itza and the archaeological site of Coba in the Yucatan Peninsula. Finally, each row of Table I is represented in Mesoamerica by one of the nine lords of the night (Figures 76-78).

Fig. 76: The nine lords of the night: Xiuhtecutli, Itztli, Piltzintechtli, Cinteotl, Mictlantecuhtli, Chalchihuitlicue, Tlazolteotl, Tepeyollotl, Tlaloc (Aztec version).

Fig. 77:  The Aztec symbols for the nine lords of the night.

Fig. 78: The Maya symbols for the nine lords of the night.

And behold, there shall a new star arise, such an one as ye never have beheld; and this also shall be a sign unto you. And behold this is not all, there shall be many signs and wonders in heaven. (Helaman 14:5-6)

Chapter Seven
# RELIGIOUS AND CULTURAL PARALLELS

---

*The Book of Mormon is the keystone of our religion — the keystone of our testimony, the keystone of our doctrine, and the keystone in the witness of our Lord and Savior.*

President Ezra Taft Benson
General Conference, April 1986

(*Ensign*, November 1986, p. 6)
Used by permission

The Mexican historians of the sixteenth and seventeenth centuries provided voluminous information of a Messiah who died for all mankind. These histories parallel the Bible and Book of Mormon accounts of Christ.

Harold Gladwin, an archaeologist from Santa Barbara, California, in his book *Men Out of Asia,* said of Old and New World parallels:

> If new facts turn up which refute your ideas, then you must obviously revise your hypothesis since you cannot change the facts, and, in this instance, we were soon confronted with the indisputable fact that many of the fundamental traits of high native American civilizations are not to be found in northeastern Asia, but are characteristic of southern Asia and the Near East. . . . The prototypes of culture traits in North America, north of Mexico, were almost exclusively confined [in the Old World] to China and northeastern Asia. The prototypes of those culture traits which are distinctive of Mexico, Central America, and the Andean region, can be traced exclusively to Polynesia,

Melanesia, India, and the Near and Middle East. (178, 257-58)

Joseph Lindon Smith, who worked with art and archaeology for some of the world's great museums, spent time both in Egypt and in Mesoamerica. He observed:

> In Japan, China, and other Asiatic countries, there was nothing I saw that reminded me of the great Maya achievement in building in Yucatan, Honduras, and Guatemala. . . . Even in the temples of Angkor Wat and Angkor Thom, situated in the same kind of jungle surroundings, there were no similarities. It was in Egypt, of all countries, that I found striking features in common between the material cultures of the Maya and the Egyptians. In Egypt, the approach to a temple was through a series of great courts leading to enormous pylon gates. The idea of space in an approach to temples was carried out by the Maya with the same sense of majesty and space, and through similar great courts, but they used, instead of pylons, carved monoliths of incredible size. (300)

Nearly fifty years ago, Dr. Alfred Vincent Kidder, the foremost authority on the archeaology of Mesoamerica, and Colonel Charles A. Lindberg made the first reconnaissance flights over Yucatan and Guatemala in search of ancient cities. Thereafter, as chief of Carnegie Institution's field program in Mesoamerica, he spent the greater part of twenty years in directing excavations in the Maya area of southern Mexico, Guatemala, and Honduras.

Concerning the remains he helped uncover near the outskirts of Guatemala City, Kidder wrote in his 1946 Carnegie report that the culture is "on the level with, and extraordinarily like, those of our own cultural ancestors of the ancient Near East or Palestine." And the remains date as far back as several centuries before Christ.

The script of an ancient people is usually considered to be the most complex part of their civilization. It is also one of the best ways to identify a specific culture. In October 1957, Eduardo Martinez, a staff member of the New World Archaeological Foundation, excavated a cylinder seal at Chiapa de Corzo, Chiapas, Mexico (Figures 79-83). Eventually four other seals were found in strata dating 300-600 B.C. On May 22, 1958 photographs of impressions of Seal 1 were sent to Dr. William F. Albright, then an international authority on bibilical languages and archaeology. Albright observed that the seal contained "several clearly recognizable Egyptian hieroglyphs." When he examined photographs of the impression on the seal, he observed that they resembled the seals of 3000 B.C. Mesopotamia in certain respects. This clay seal immediately sparked controversy. Rudolph Anthes, Egyptologist at the University Museum in Philadelphia, pointed out the resemblance of the triangular glyph to the Egyptian hieroglyph meaning "given." However, additional examples would need to be found and studied before firm conclusions could be reached.

In the early 1960s, Pierre Agrinier gathered a 600 word vocabulary from a Zapotec village in Oaxaca, Mexico. Linguists found that 18% of these 600 words appeared to be cognate with Hebrew. Because of this high relationship, linguists suggested that more research be done. This research was done under the direction of Morris Swadesh, a professor of linguistics at the National University of Mexico, who before his death was considered one of the top linguists in the world. Dr. Swadesh pioneered research on language families to reconstruct proto-language vocabulary in the distant past. He also developed a special technique of language analysis that dates the separation of two languages in the same family (e.g., Canaanite and Hebrew in the Semite language family). Swadesh possessed large data bases for the world languages and used computers in his analysis.

**Plant Life Elements**

George Carter, professor of geography at Johns Hopkins University, reported in February 1957:

When we Europeans discovered them, . . . the Indian peoples of Mesoamerica were practicing agriculture, making pottery, raising some domesticated animals, practicing metallurgy, using practically all the known techniques of weaving, living in organized city states, even empires, and having great capitals that would rival Rome or Athens or Thebes or Babylon. . . .

The work that was to reopen the Diffusionist controversy began with an attempt by a group of botanists to untangle the relationships of the cottons of the world. This group of botanists included Hutchinson, Silow, and Stevens who teamed up on this job, using the modern techniques of genetics. They soon found that they could divide the cottons of the world into three groups: (l) the wild and domestic cottons of the Old World, (2) the wild cottons of the New World, and (3) the domestic cottons of the New World. The New World domestic cottons   particularly interested them. When they studied cells under high-powered microscopes, they found that they contained twice as many hereditary units (chromosomes) as did the other cottons. Further, they could tell that there were two sets of chromosomes there, one the Old World type and the other the New World type. The most probable explanation they could find was that man had brought a domestic cotton from the Old World into the New, and that the two cottons had crossed, combined the full sets of chromosomes from both plants, and created this new plant.

They then did a very interesting thing. They examined the New World domestic cotton and carefully catalogued all its characteristics. Next they searched the cottons of the world to see just what two cottons, if combined, would give them these characteristics. They found the answer in an Asiatic domestic cotton and in a Peruvian wild cotton.

They succeeded in crossing these two plants and producing a near-duplicate of the American domesticated cotton.

Cotton seeds are not particularly tough. Plant men do not believe that they can float around the ocean and remain alive. To have arrived in America, they must have been carried by someone. (10)

Fig. 79: Seal 1 from Pit 78 at Chiapa de Corzo, Chiapas, Mexico about 600 B.C.

Fig. 80: Seal 2 from Chiapa de Corzo, Chiapas, Mexico.

Fig. 81: Seal 3 from Chiapa de Corzo, Chiapas, Mexico.

**Fig. 82: Seal 4 from Chiapa de Corzo, Chiapas, Mexico about 400 B.C.**

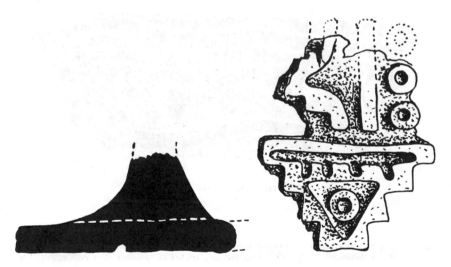

**Fig. 83: Seal 5 from Chiapa de Corzo, Chiapas, Mexico with a bar-and-dot number 8 (about 500 B.C.).**

Some scholars have told the world that there was an absolute separation of Old World and New World plants (Heiser 10-11). Others have long believed that some New World plants were imported in ancient times. But recent discoveries throw new light on the question. In 1953, Carter wrote,

> Some plants positively were pre-Columbian in the Old World and the New World. . . . There is a formidable list of plants, most of them related to the Middle-American—Southeast-Asian areas, that range all the way from probable to possible cultural transfers. The long-held doctrine of the absolute separation of Old World and New World agricultures is no longer tenable. The plant evidence should be re-examined without bias. (71)

Carl O. Sauer, distinguished chairman, Department of Geography, University of California (at Berkeley), wrote in 1952 in his book *Agricultural Origins and Dispersals,* "The trans-Pacific carriage of cotton, the true gourd, sweet potato, and coconut appears proven, I should say, even for the coconut, as due to the deliberate action of man" (Ferguson 1958: 52).

Recently a discovery of domesticated barley was reported from a Hohokam archaeological site near Phoenix, Arizona. The author mentions that "nearly half of the samples yielded barley" (Adams 32). The author goes on to suggest that the domesticated barley may have come from Mexico. This represents the first discovery of barley in the New World. The Hohokam culture dates between 300 B.C. to A.D. 1400.


## Men Across the Ocean

The absence in ancient Alaska, Canada, and the United States of these many cultural and religious elements common to the Near East and Mesoamerica indicate that they were not all brought over the land bridge connecting Siberia and Alaska. Atomic energy dating by carbon-14 places the beginnings of complex society in Mesoamerica at 2500 B.C., with no primitive underpinnings to indicate that all the elements did not developed independently, step by step.

The only plausible explanation is the one given by the early histories of Mesoamerica—that some of it came by boats to the central part of the New World. But how could people have made it across the ocean hundreds, even thousands, of years before Columbus?

In 1950, Thor Heyerdahl, a Norwegian explorer, focused the world's attention on his balsa raft with its square sail as he crossed the South Pacific from Peru to the Tuamotu Islands. His historic voyage is recounted in his *American Indians in the Pacific: The Theory Behind the Kon-Tiki Expedition.*

A young German graduate of the medical school at the University of Hamburg, Dr. Hannes Lindemann, has twice crossed the Atlantic in simple crafts. In 1955, he used a twenty-four foot dugout canoe. In the fall of 1956, he used a seventeen-foot rubberized canvas craft on a collapsible wooden frame with an outrigger made from an inner tube (Lindemann 1957).

On 21 September 1958, DeVere Baker, an American ship builder, drifted into the Hawaiian Islands on his raft *Lehi* after bobbing 2,100 miles for sixty-nine days across the Pacific from Redondo Beach, California. Also in 1958, a sixty-six-year-old Frenchman, Eric de Bisschop, made it from South America to the South Sea island of Manikiki, only to be killed when his raft broke up on a reef.

Two additional scholars summarize other contemporary transoceanic voyages:

> Merrien lists 120 modern intentional *solo and two-man* long voyages. Among these are a 17-day voyage from the Cape Verde Islands to Martinique by a pair of Estonians in a 29-foot sloop; a 30-day Atlantic crossing in a 24-foot 8-inch sailing craft by a toeless, fingerless sailor; William Verity's 68-day passage from Florida to Ireland in a home-built, 12-foot sloop; a sail-less, oar-propelled crossing by two men from New York to the Scilly Islands in 55 days in a dory 17 feet, 8 inches long; a solo, 93-day crossing from Japan to

San Francisco in a 19-foot sloop; a 68-day raft drift from California to Hawaii; a solo voyage in a converted Indian dugout canoe (bottom length, 3 feet) from Vancouver directly to the Cook Islands, a journey of some 5,500 miles in 56 days, followed by an ultimate landing in England; a solo, 162-day journey in a 19.5-foot schooner 6,500 miles from San Francisco to Australian waters without a single port of call; the solo, three-year, 46,000-mile, round-the-world voyage of Joshua Slocum in the *Spray* (36 feet, 9 inches); the round-the-world journey of Vito Dumas in a 32-foot ketch, a journey that included a direct 7,200-mile run in the Roaring Forties from the Cape of Good Hope to New Zealand, on to Valparaiso, Chile (5,400 miles in 72 days), and then around the Horn; sixty-six-year-old Francis Chichester's 28,500-mile, one-stop circumnavigation via Cape Horn in a 54-foot ketch; the voyages of Eric de Bisschop—including one with a single companion from Hawaii to Cannes in 264 sailing days in a double canoe, one by bamboo sailing raft some 5,000 miles into the southeastern Pacific from Tahiti, and one by raft from Peru 5,500 miles to Rakahanga; the 7,450-mile pontoon raft journey from Peru to Samoa by seventy-year-old William Willis (1965), who eventually sailed 3,000 additional miles to Australia, though suffering an abdominal hernia, a fractured sacrum, and partial paralysis; four other raft journeys from Peru, with safe landings ranging from the Galapagos to Australia; a journey by three Americans in an old Polynesian outrigger from Oahu to San Francisco; a trip down the Amazon and on to Miami by an eighteen-year-old in a leaky, 19-foot dugout fitted with sails, including a run of over 850 miles on the Atlantic; a solo, 72-day crossing of the Atlantic in a 17-foot canvas foldboat; an island-hopping expedition by a sixteen-year-old in a 24-foot sloop from California to South Africa, including a 2,300-mile run under jury rig due to a dismasting; and a solo voyage in a 6-foot sailboat from Casablanca to Florida in 84 days. Even transatlantic races for loners have now been established. (Jett 17-19)

Edwin Doran, Jr., investigating trans-Pacific voyages, mentions
that:

> Of sixty cases of inadvertent drifts of Japanese junks into
> the Pacific, at least a half dozen reached the coast of
> America between Sitka and the Columbia River and another
> half dozen were wrecked on the Mexican coast or
> encountered just offshore. Survivors of such drift voyages
> were not uncommon, and Japanese slaves were held by
> Salmon Indians of the northwest coast of America when
> they first were visited by Whites. Drift voyages between Asia
> and America not only are clearly possible but actually have
> occurred repeatedly in historic time. In view of the ability of
> rafts to sail close-hauled against the wind in remarkable
> effective fashion, a phenomenon noted repeatedly and with
> great surprise by early Western mariners who encountered
> rafts off the coast of Ecuador and Peru, an even greater
> feasibility for early transpacific raft voyages can be inferred.
> There appears to be no question that rafts could have
> crossed the Pacific, repeatedly and in appreciable number.
> (133-35)

These intrepid modern sailors were duplicating ancient
voyages, incomplete records of which have survived in
fragmentary reports. The sailors of Crete during the first and
second millennia B.C. traveled from the Mediterranean Sea to
Britain and back. About 950 B.C., "King Solomon made a navy
of ships in Ezion-geber [an Israelite port off the northeast corner
of the Red Sea], which is beside Eloth, on the shore of the Red
Sea, in the land of Edom. And Hiram [king of Tyre in Phoenicia]
sent in the navy his servants, shipmen that had knowledge of the
sea, with the servants of Solomon. And they came to Ophir, and
fetched from thence gold, four hundred and twenty talents, and
brought it to king Solomon" (1 Kgs. 9.26-28). Also, between
608-594 B.C., Necho II of Egypt sent out an expedition that went
around Africa (Herodotus 306).

Thus, both in modern and ancient times, transoceanic
voyages are clearly possible. In fact, the feat was not unique.

America has long been a melting pot for many people and many cultures. Ancient times were no exception. There are many indications that other groups came to Mesoamerica anciently. The cultural pattern is a giant jig-saw of complexity. Each group of colonizers brought its own piece of the puzzle, to be blended with the indigenous population.

## Other Immigrants

The essays of Stephen C. Jett and Edwin Doran, Jr., dealing with documented transoceanic voyages in historic times, have already been mentioned. However, Meggers, Evans, and Estrada (1965) take voyages a step further in establishing probable Japanese colonization of a South American site. The Valdivia culture of Ecuador, which dates back to nearly 3,000 B.C., produced ceramics that have close parallels with Jomon pottery from ancient Japan, which dates before 3000 B.C. Reporting records from historic times of Japanese fishermen caught in storms and landing on the coast of Ecuador, the authors hypothesize a probable Japanese origin for the Valdivia culture.

Recent important works investigating possible Southeast Asian sources of influence upon Mesoamerica include "The Trans-pacific Origin of Mesoamerican Civilization: The Preliminary Review of the Evidence and Its Theoretical Implications" by Betty Meggers of the Smithsonian Institution. This paper focuses on the Shang Dynasty of China and the Olmec civilization of Mesoamerica, maps their territories, and analyzes parallel symbols, artifacts, and monuments. Her conclusion is that a fairly strong case can be made for some type of trans-Pacific contact between the two.

Chinese archaeologist Paul Shao, who did his graduate work in America and is now a resident of the United States, has published *Chinese Influence in Pre-Classic Mesoamerican Art* and *The Origin of Ancient American Culture,* a full-length treatment of Chinese influences in Mesoamerican civilizations. His interest, initially triggered by a visit to Mesoamerican sites where he was greatly excited by the similarities he saw between Chinese and Mesoamerican monuments and artifacts, has not lessened after several years of concentrated work upon the topic.

David H. Kelley, an anthropologist from the University of Calgary, found several distinctive features of the Maya Long Count calendar that paralleled features of the Hindu calendar of northern India. For example, certain plant, animal, and deity names have artistic similarities. Both use a Four-World Age system with associated colors. The base date in both systems is a cataclysmic flood in the distant past. According to Kelley, the Hindu calendar dates from 3102 B.C., associated with the mass planetary conjunction at the time of the flood. A mass planetary conjunction occurs when the five visible planets — Venus, Mercury, Mars, Jupiter, and Saturn — appear on the east horizon on the same evening. This event occurs approximately every 179-180 years. The Maya Long Count system dates from 3114 B.C. and is associated with the destruction of the earth by flooding. Both systems at one point switched from a seven-day to a nine-day week, and both added two eclipse deities to bring the seven deities of the seven days up to nine deities for the nine-day week.

The seven-day week was associated with the same planetary bodies in both systems. Perhaps not coincidentally, our own seven-day week uses the same planets in the same order: sun (Sunday), moon (Monday), Mars (Tuesday), Mercury (Wednesday), Jupiter (Thursday), Venus (Friday), and Saturn (Saturday). This particular order of days was first set among the Greeks during the Hellenistic period, who imported them into the Indus Valley and West Pakistan as part of Alexander the Great's wars of conquest between 331-323 B.C. Thus, Kelley also argues that it is possible to date the departure of the Hindu migrants from this area to the Mayas of Mesoamerica as no earlier than the first century B.C. The research of Shao and Kelley suggests that other Old World colonists may have come to Mesoamerica during the Book of Mormon time period. If so, they could have had an impact on the Book of Mormon peoples. Two recent publications are significant in the evaluation of possible voyages and migrations to the New World: Nigel Davies' *Voyages to the New World*; and Irving Rouse's *Migrations in Prehistory: Inferring Population Movement from Cultural Remains.*

John L. Sorenson's essay "The Significance of an Apparent Relationship between the Ancient Near East and Mesoamerica" is important. He presents a table of over a hundred cultural features shared by both Mesoamerica and the Near East (water confined beneath the temple, zero concept, and navel of the world concept).

Long distance trading is another interesting area of research. Robert Chadwick compared the strong parallels between cultures dating from about 500 B.C. at Tlatilco, in the Valley of Mexico, Monte Negro, in Oaxaca, and Paracas on the south coast of Peru.

In a separate presentation, Chadwick cited Ezekiel's lamentation for the seaport of Tyre, "a merchant of the people for many isles," which includes an enumeration of more than thirty cities or countries included in its merchandising network. He then concluded: "Although we can't say definitely that Ezekiel's chapter 27 description of long-distance trading the 'prospector' colonies' intrusions in the New World at Tlatilco, Monte Negro, and Paracas refer to the same event, it seems likely this may be the case" (10).

In summary, transoceanic voyages in very simple crafts were possible in ancient times and have been replicated in our own century. The numerous cultural and religious parallels between the Biblical and Book of Mormon cultures indicate that immigrants from several Old World cultures, including the Near East, have come to Mesoamerica. It seems probable that some of the colonizers were descendants of one of the tribes or branches of the family of Jacob.

Nephi wrote:

> For I came out from Jerusalem, and mine eyes hath beheld the things of the Jews, and I know that the Jews do understand the things of the prophets, and there is none other people that understand the things which were spoken unto the Jews like unto them, save it be that they are taught after the manner of the things of the Jews. (2 Ne. 25:5)

## NOTES TO CHAPTER SEVEN

1.           Atomic energy dating by carbon-14 determinations, a post-war achievement of infinite importance to archaeology, places the very high ancient culture of Mexico in the second millennium before Christ. It appeared full blown, with agriculture, cities, ceramics and textiles. There is nothing primitive underlying this culture from which it developed step by step.

If there were Israelites in Mesoamerica centuries before Christ was born, they should have left things behind. A list of religious and cultural traits common to both Mesoamerica and the Near East has been prepared. Many of the elements are uniquely shared by only those two cultures, while other elements are common to other societies also. This list includes Palestine and surrounding lands. Dr. W. F. Albright has said:

Situated between the two principal foci of ancient Eastern civilization, Egypt and Mesopotamia, Palestine drew continuously from both. Nearly all important elements of ancient Oriental material culture originated in one or the other of these lands, and inevitably spread from them through Syria and Palestine. The culture of Palestine was more or less mixed in all periods, containing Egyptian and Mesopotamian components as well as elements from other minor sources. Substantially, the same is true of the literature, learning, and religion of Syria and Palestine. Thus the people of Palestine became acquainted with all significant developments of ancient Eastern civilization. (253)

Study the list carefully. The more complex the element, the less likely the chance of its being invented independently in Mesoamerica. The fewer elements found in Siberia, Alaska, Canada, and the United States, the less likely the probability of transfer by land.

Authorities cited can be identified by means of the bibliography at the end of this book.

2. **Belief and Ritual Elements**
    1. Books, with long strips of paper folded like a screen, each fold forming a page five to six inches wide (Thompson 169; Funk and Wagnalls 112).
    2. Colors representing four quarters of world.
    3. Creation story very similar between Genesis, Babylonians, and Mayas (Kramer 12).
    4. Cross as symbol of god of life (175ff.)
    5. The game of Parchesi (Sorenson 228, n.3)
    6. Pyramid burial of dignitaries (as at Palenque, Mexico).
    7. Truncated pyramids ("mountains of God") (Sorenson 229).
    8. Mythological monsters of sky and earth, including celestial dragon (Sorenson 235).
    9. Religious traditions of creation by God, first parents, great flood, great tower and confusion of tongues, darkness before creation (see Ch. 3).
    10. Underworlds, one below the other (Thompson 226-227; Funk and Wagnalls 222).
    11. Duality concept: good versus evil, an eternal struggle (Morley 215; Thompson 227, 223, 250).
    12. Astral worship (Funk and Wagnalls 83; this book, Chapter 5).
    13. Astrology (Thompson 18, 140, 249).
    14. Astrology almanacs (Thompson 138).
    15. Astronomy (Thompson 55, 70, 79; Funk and Wagnalls 83).
    16. Calendars of high precision based on similar astronomical observations and calculations.
    17. Constellations representing the four directions, solstices and equinoxes.
    18. Zodiacal sequence (twelve symbols in the Old World, thirteen in Mesoamerica—the scorpion and serpent being common in both) (Morley 311; Aveni 199-204).
    19. Venus cycles (Thompson 144).
    20. Lime sizing of paper writing surfaces (Thompson 169; Funk and Wagnalls 716).
    21. Lunar time count (Morley 306).
    22. New Year Renewal ceremonies (Vaillant 200; Frankfort).
    23. Sacred "books of God" (see Ch. 8).
    24. Seven-day time cycle or week (Jakeman; Thompson 144).
    25. Signs for numerals and of relative value according to position

(Thompson 155).

26. Poetic religious literature with typical Old Testament type antiphons (Thompson 170).

27. Incense burners and altars with horns projecting at the top or from four corners (Sorenson 231).

28. Incense burners, cone-shaped, with triangular windows (as seen in the Louvre and Guatemala Museums).

29. Circumcision, with stone knife used in the operation (Landa 114).

30. Flint blades with entwined serpent handle used in human sacrifice (Breasted Figure 9; Morley Figure 14).

31. Baptism, the ancient Maya term for it being *caput sihil,* meaning "to be born again," a biblical term for the same rite (Ferguson 1958:156).

32. Serpent of seven heads—a symbol (Ahuucchhapat in Maya) (Ferguson 1958:95).

33. Feline (leopard,jaguar, cat, etc.) thrones (as in Egypt and at Chichen Itza in Mexico).

34. Feline-skin garb for important priests in ceremonials (Ferguson 1958:111).

35. Feline symbols (Ferguson 1958:110).

36. Bearded men and gods (as found at La Venta, Mexico; von Wuthenau (1975) and Magleby (1979:1-51).

37. Pot held by a deity with flowing streams coming out from it in opposite directions (Ferguson 1958:180-81).

38. "S" glyph representing clouds and water in early Babylonia and in early art in Mexico (Ferguson 1958:92).

39. Sacred bird, symbol of highest God, directly above sacred tree, in elaborate and identical ancient tree-of-life symbol (Ferguson 1958:85).

40. Tree-of-life symbol, with sacred bird representing God, a priest on each of two sides of tree and facing tree, one with scepter, and the earth monster beneath the tree (Ferguson 1958:175-82).

41. Belief that God would ultimately destroy the world by fire in the final age (Ferguson 1958:41).

42. Double-headed eagle (or condor) (Ferguson 1958:128).

43. Art style showing head in profile view, but the eye and upper torso of human body in full frontal position, in conventionalized, unrealistic Egyptian and Maya form (Ferguson

1958:112).

44. "Bes" as a phallic symbol (Ferguson 1958:77).
45. Earth monster, symbol of opposition and death (Thompson 220).
46. Eternity-of-time idea (Thompson 140; Isa. 60.15; Deut. 33.27).
47. Eye symbol — all-seeing eye of God, or eye of the sky (Morley 223).
48. Red, symbolic color: the color of Bee Crown in Egypt, the "Red Crown" (Deseret Crown); red the color of the Maya bee god of Mexico (Thompson 225).
49. Suffering for sin — concept that individual suffers for his sins and society suffers for the general transgressions of its members (Landa 106; Bible).
50. Supreme being — creator God — and His Son (Thompson 232).
51. Totemism (symbols representing clans or lineages).
52. Blocking (with stones) of staircases leading to tombs within pyramids (as in Egypt and Palenque, Mexico).
53. Four corners of the earth, or four quarters of the world recognized (Ferguson 1958:102).
54. Priesthood with temple rituals.
55. Temples and religious structures dominant in architecture.
56. Sky divided into a plurality of heavens in horizontal layers, one above the other (Thompson 225; Funk and Wagnalls 152).
57. Decimal system (indicated but not established beyond question in Mexico; Jakeman).
58. Hieroglyphs (Ferguson 1958:22-24, 224).
59. Historical annals (Ferguson 1958:136).
60. Mathematics (addition, subtraction, multiplication into high figures).
61. Paper or writing surface made from fiber of a tree, and also from plants, fiber pounded to cloth-like consistency and covered with thin lime sizing (Thompson 169; Funk and Wagnalls 716).
62. Parchment (Landa 78).
63. Sundials (Morley 144, 145, 146).
64. Sun worship and symbolism (Thompson 227; and as in Egypt).
65. Venus as Morning Star and Evening Star (Thompson 145).

66. Zero date of one aspect of Maya calendar as 3114 B.C. (GMT correlation); and dynastic dating in Egypt begins about 3100 B.C. (Regarding the zero concept, see Thompson, 155, 158.)
67. Burials beneath floors of houses, and urn or jar burials of infants (as found by New World Archaeological Foundation near Tehuantepec and as in Israel; Landa 131).
68. Burial of sacrificial victims beneath foundation of building upon its erection.
69. Embalming, including removal of viscera (Mason 76, 221; Hayes 303, 320).
70. Shaft burial chambers (106; Peterson 292).
71. Burial of attendants with deceased dignitary, to accompany master to next world. (Thompson 218; Funk and Wagnalls 118).
72. Red ocher, a mixture of hydrated oxide of iron with clay, used to cover body of deceased (Peterson 223; Frankfort 116; Mason 48, 58).
73. Ceramic incense burners covered with a white wash (exhibits from Iran in Louvre; Museum, Mexico City).
74. Feline decoration on incense-burning stands.
75. Offerings of incense, food, blood, and flesh.
76. Carved stelae (as found at Tikal, Guatemala, by Edwin Shook).
77. Fertility figurines (Ferguson 1958:114).
78. Figurines of ceramic, of pregnant women and figurines with the eye pupils punctuated, also with small punched holes at corners of the mouth (Ferguson 1958:56, 321).
79. Blood-letting (Thompson 60, 187, 189, 195, 248; Funk and Wagnalls 110).
80. Blood sacrifice (blood from sacrificial victim was sprinkled over ritual area) (Lev. 1.5; Thompson 249).
81. Flaying of sacrificial victim (Morley 237).
82. Sacrifice of doves and quail (Ferguson 1958:164).
83. Self-mutilation (Thompson 60; Funk and Wagnalls 118).
84. Slaying of sacrificial victims by pushing them from a height.
85. Holy water used in purification rite (Ferguson 1958:108).
86. Libations (pouring wine or liquid on the ground or on a sacrifice), including use of wine in ceremony (Ferguson 1958:108).
87. Aspergillum (a brush for sprinkling water) in sprinkling

(Landa 323; Funk and Wagnalls 755).

88. Rain-inducing ritual.

89. Crescent moon glyph (Figures 62 and 64).

90. Eagle symbolism (Peterson 290).

91. Foreshortening in art (reducing or distorting a represented object in order to create a three-dimensional effect) (Thompson 173).

92. Fresco mural painting of life scenes (as at Chichen Itza, Bonampak, Teotihuacan).

93. Painting on stucco (as at Bonampak, Chichen Itza, Teotihuacan).

94. Morning star symbol of deity.

95. Bird masks worn by priests (Ferguson 1958:228).

96. Confession (Thompson 256).

97. Cylindrical altars (Ferguson 1958:164).

98. Fasting, individual and community, including fasting for the dead (Thompson 60, 135-36, 189, 253).

99. Fleur de lis (Ferguson 1958:83).

100.High headdresses designed to convey identification of the deity portrayed (as in Egypt and among Mayas).

101.Large fans in ceremonies (as at Bonampak, Mexico).

102.Phallic symbols (as at Chichen Itza, Mexico).

103.Rubber in Central America and frankincense in Arabia called "the blood" of the trees producing them.

104.Sacred seer stones (Ferguson 1958:235-236).

105.Sacred things uncontaminated by human touch.

106.Salt not eaten during periods of fasting (Thompson 60).

107.Scapegoat idea (Ferguson 1958:162).

108.Small sweat rooms with steam apparatus.

109.Transubstantiation (a change into another substance) concept.

110.Linguistic borrowing by Zapotec-speakers located in Oaxaca, Mexico, from Semitic-speakers (Agrinier 4-5; Smith ms.).

111.Compass-point orientation of buildings (as at Teotihuacan; Thompson 76).

112.Festivals at the end of certain periods of time (Ferguson 1958:154).

113.Sarcophagus of stone used for royal burials (as at Palenque, Mexico).

114.Figurine cults (Peterson 262).

115.Human sacrifice (Ferguson 1958:108).

116. Black magic (Landa 314; Ferguson 1958:309).
117. Burnt offerings of all or parts of animals (Landa 114; Ferguson 1958:164).
118. Divinations and black magic (Landa 314).
119. Omen days of good and bad luck (Thompson 139).
120. Gods in image of man (Chapter 8; Thompson 264).
121. Perspective in art.
122. Swastika or gama cross (Keleman plate 193).
123. Childless women considered shameful.
124. Continence or self-restraint in connection with certain occasions, particularly by priests (Thompson 60, 135, 238, 253).
125. Dancing, essentially in religious ritual (Thompson 257; Funk and Wagnalls 165).
126. Idolatry (Ferguson 1958:45).
127. Marks worn to impersonate gods.
128. Pottery vessels with life scenes painted on them (Thompson 177).
129. Religious pilgrimages (Thompson 114).

3. **Social Elements**

1. Armies of 10,000 men per unit (Bible mentions such armies, as does the *Book of Mormon* and Bernal Diaz for Mexico).
2. Names of persons chosen according to day of birth or some special circumstance at birth (Funk and Wagnalls 605; Morley 464).
3. Parasol (umbrella) as token of rank.
4. Civic centers (Ferguson 1958:76; Teotihuacan, La Venta, Chiapa de Corzo are examples).
5. Crested war helmets (Landa 122, 172).
6. Cupbearers.
7. Dowry payments by groom (28; Morley 188).
8. High priest elected from a certain lineage (Thompson 249; Funk and Wagnalls re "Priesthood").
9. Litters for carrying prestigious persons (Morley plate 88; Thompson 218; Mason 74; Hayes 92, 122).
10. Moats, artificial — surrounding cities for defensive purposes, supplemented by walls (Ferguson 1958:285).
11. Nose rings (Isa. 3.21; Keleman plate 215).
12. Palisades (to enclose with poles).
13. Quilted armor (Landa 121; Hunter and Ferguson 273-76).

14. Slings (Peterson 163).
15. Intentional deformation of the skull (Ferguson 1958:273).
16. Modification of head shape of infants (Thompson 40).
17. Trepanation (highly technical surgical procedure on skull; Mason 223; Louvre Museum).
18. Tattooing and scarification (Mason 81; Landa 293).
19. Hornets used in warfare (Ex. 23.28; Deut. 7.20; Peterson 163).
20. Genealogy records (Thompson 249).
21. Helmets for warriors (326, exhibit 137; Vaillant 51).
22. Shields, including woven material (Peterson 163).
23. Short skirts for warriors.
24. Slavery (Thompson 126, 193, 221).
25. Spears (Ferguson 1958:265).
26. Spouses selected by parents with consideration for preference of candidate for marriage (Thompson 211; Funk and Wagnalls 553).
27. Stabbing instruments (Ferguson 1958:108, 265).
28. Walled or fenced fortified cities, with city gates (Ferguson 1958:85; Peterson 293).

4. **Political Elements**
   1. Finger rings of gold (Isa. 3.21; Keleman plate 228).
   2. Crown of gold (Keleman plates 220, 229).
   3. Theocracy (Morley 163, 210; Mason 74).
   4. Thrones (Thompson 58, 60, 70, 77, 89, 111).

5. **Economic and Subsistence Elements**
   1. Beekeeping and stingless bees. The word in early Egypt for bee DSRT (Deseret) was apparently known in Mesoamerica, and with the same meaning (Ferguson 1958:250).
   2. Beeswax (Thompson 262).
   3. Bottle gourds, dried fruit shells used as bottles (any of a family of climbing plants bearing fleshy, many-seeded fruit) (Thompson 239; Ferguson 1958:52).
   4. Chickens
   5. Coconuts (Ferguson 1958:52).
   6. Common beans (in Maya *bul,* Hebrew *pul).*
   7. Cotton, of 13-chromosome variety (Ferguson 1958:20-21).
   8. Grain amaranths (any of several plants such as cockscomb and prince's feather).

9.  Irrigation (273; F. Peterson, *Ancient Mexico* 45).
10. Lima beans (excavated by Edwin Shook, see Ferguson 1958:263).
11. Pottery spindle whorls (Thompson 77, 88; Peterson 268; Prov. 31:19).
12. Red dye (cochineal) obtained from the dried bodies of small plant lice (Thompson 159; Funk and Wagnalls 142).
13. Sweet potatoes (Ferguson 1958:52).
14. Wild bees (Thompson 262; Funk and Wagnalls 273; Deut. 32:13).
15. Agriculture, with cultivation (Thompson 160).
16. Fish catching by poisoning water with plant juices that stupefy fish—including the use, apparently, of poisons derived from plants from a common ancestor (in America the plant was *Tephrosia toxicaria;* in southern Asia it was *Tephrosia candida*).
17. Fishhooks (Thompson 185).
18. Maize (existence in the Old World is controversial).
19. Markets, including specialized markets.
20. Metates (hollowed out stone used to grind seeds and grain) (saddle querns).
21. Net fishing (Thompson 181).
22. Pearls (Thompson 69).
23. Eagles (Peterson 290).

6.  **Technological Elements**

1.  Bottle-shaped, underground cisterns. A unique and striking cultural parallel between ancient Israel and Yucatan-Guatemala-Mexico is the peculiar bottle-shaped underground cistern for the storage of water during dry seasons. In 1934 Bible archaeologist Nelson Glueck discovered seven such cisterns at the ruins of Sela, ancient Bible community in Eastern Palestine. His diary reports the discovery as follows: "Difficult of approach, and commanding a wonderful view over Petra, the position . . . corroborates the biblical passages which refer to Sela as an inaccessible nest. On the flat top of the acropolis are seven pear-shaped cisterns filled with debris. The rainwater was led to them by channels cut in the rock surface" (32).

In June 1955, Sela was again visited by an expedition of

the American School of Oriental Research. William H. Morton reports on the cisterns as follows: "These cisterns are plastered throughout and bottle-shaped in outline, each having a small mouth about two feet in diameter, but rapidly expanding to a diameter of 8 to 10 feet. . . . Rockcut channels angling across the natural slope of the incline serve to divert surface rainwater into the cistern mouths" (32). Reporting on the discovery of many of the underground bottle-shaped pits in Guatemala and Yucatan, Carnegie archaeologist A. Ledyard Smith says: "There is no doubt that in northern Yucatan, where paving and gutters have been found around the entrances and the walls were covered with plaster, in some cases bearing designs of water symbols, chultuns (bottle-shaped pits) served as cisterns." He describes one of the Central American pits as follows: "Cut out of living rock, it had a circular shaftlike entrance just large enough to admit a man. The neck of the entrance extended about 40 cm. above the natural rock and was built of small stones and marl with a collar at the top to receive a capstone. The entrance, cut through the hard limestone crust, led down to a small bottle-shaped chamber with a foothold cut in the east and west sides" (17, 48, 84-85). O. G. Ricketson Jr. gives the diameter of the circular rooms as measuring up to 2.28 meters—that is, up to about 8 and 1/2 feet (123).

Edwin Shook and Michael D. Coe have each observed that these bottle-shaped cisterns were in use over a wide area of Mesoamerica during Preclassic times—i.e., before to 250 A.D. Thus we have a parallel with the Near East involving a highly technical thing—a bottle-shaped cistern for the storage of water, about eight feet in diameter, plastered, cut into living rock, with small aperture, and with channels on the surface above to direct rainwater into the cistern. The experts say the chultuns may have also had other uses in the New World.

2. Breastplates worn by high priests, divided into twelve segments (Thompson plate 19; Funk and Wagnalls 867).
3. Casting by lost wax process (Vaillant 147).
4. Cement, the principle ingredient being limestone raised to a temperature sufficiently hot to burn out the carbon, used for plaster, stucco and mortar in Egypt, Near East and Mesoamerica (as at Chiapa de Corzo and Teotihuacan,

Mexico; Peterson 282-83).

5. Cubit as unit of measurement from the elbow to the tip of the finger (demonstrated at Yagul by David Vincent 1958).

6. Dyeing designs on cloth and pottery by coating with removable wax on the parts not to be dyed, the batik method (Peterson 50, 255).

7. Purple dye obtained from shellfish by technical process (Morley 209; Thompson 159; Funk and Wagnalls 142).

8. Wheeled toys of pottery (Ferguson 1958:103).

9. Turquoise mosaics (Hayes 307; Ferguson 1958:159).

10. Panpipes (syrinx) (288, exhibit 133; Gladwin 273).

11. Battle trumpets, including conch-shells (Thompson 185).

12. Trumpets and carved trumpets or twisted trumpets and conch-shell trumpet (Thompson 185, 195, 200, 257, and plate 17; Funk and Wagnalls 599).

13. Cylinder seals with identical designs (Ferguson 1958:51).

14. Stamp seals (Ferguson 1958:25).

15. Altars of unworked stones (as in Israel and at Cuicuilco, Mexico).

16. Alabaster or onyx vases (as in the National Museums of Mexico and Egypt).

17. Aqueducts (as at Palenque, Mexico; Thompson 64).

18. Arch, both corbelled (a stepped arch), and true (one true arch has been found in Maya architecture).

19. Asphalt surfaced walls.

20. Avoiding the use of glaze, though known, in ceramic art.

21. Bas relief in stucco (as at Palenque, Mexico).

22. Beaten sheets of gold and silver and copper (as in Museum at Oaxaco, Mexico).

23. Bells of copper and bronze worn on ankles and wrists (Thompson 184).

24. Blast furnaces (Vaillant 148).

25. Blowgun (Thompson 124).

26. Boats with sails (Heyerdahl 514-620).

27. Bone carving and bone awls (Ferguson 1958:205).

28. Boots or shoes with upturned toes (as at La Venta, Mexico; Albright 211).

29. Brocade textiles (Thompson 180 and Figure 84).

30. Bronze (Thompson 184).

31. Caps peaked or pointed like nightcaps (Hunter and Ferguson 318).

Fig. 84: A Maya weaver from Highland Guatamala.

32. Celts of copper (Thompson 184).
33. Ceramics decorated with groups of 4 or 5 wavy lines in red paint produced with multiple-brush applicator (as found at Chiapa de Corzo and other Preclassic sites).
34. Copper tubing (Thompson 21, 69; Peterson 27).
35. Damask (silk or linen material woven into elaborate patterns) (Morley 405-409).
36. Drain pipes of ceramic (Thompson 179).
37. Ear plugs (Ferguson 1958:51, upper right).
38. Fez (Gladwin 270).
39. Filigree (ornamental work in gold or silver wire) work in metals.
40. Games of chance with counting board (Vaillant 204).
41. Gauze weaving (Gladwin 12).
42. Iron age processes (blast furnaces, smelting and casting).
43. Iron pyrite mirrors and hematite (Thompson 21).
44. Jade carving (*Lapidary Journal* 14.4:296ff.).
45. Jewel boxes of shell (Thompson 185).
46. Kiln-fired bricks and kiln-made lime (*Southwestern Journal of Anthropology* 16:428-41).
47. Kilts (short plaited petticoats worn by men) (Lloyd 237).

48. Lapis lazuli and jade, as symbolic sacred stones.
49. Large double canoe with planks and superstructure and sails and rudder-oar (Heyderdahl 513ff.).
50. Lime plaster (as at Chiapa de Corzo, Mexico).
51. Maces (Morley 164; Mason 74; Hayes 12, 19, 24).
52. Masonry construction (all over Mesoamerica).
53. Mechanical stone thrower for use in war (Thompson 160).
54. Mirrors (Thompson 21, 183, 218).
55. Carved mother of pearl (Keleman 282).
56. Obsidian blades (see Mesopotamian exhibit, University of Pennsylvania Museum).
57. Oil lamps.
58. Pattern-burnishing decoration in ceramic art.
59. Reservoirs lined with stone or cement (Thompson 25, 76).
60. Resist painting (a protective coating that resists the paint) of ceramics (Frederick Peterson 45).
61. Rubbing paint of a contrasting color into the incised or engraved patterns in ceramic art.
62. Rudder-oar on boats (Heyerdahl 513ff.)
63. Sculptured sphinx images.
64. Stone-lined water drains (as at Teotihuacan, Mexico).
65. Umbrella (Ferguson 1958:228, lower right of exhibit 109).
66. Unleavened bread (tortilla) (Funk and Wagnalls 272).
67. Wire or threads of gold in textiles (Exodus 39:3; Peterson 219).
68. Headrests (typical Egyptian-type headrest have been found in Mesoamerica).
69. Honey-wine (Funk and Wagnalls 274; Thompson 254; Landa 92).
70. Flint-edged swords (Gladwin 272).
71. Adobe bricks (as in truncated pyramids at Cholula, Mexico and at Ur, Iraq).
72. Application of a coating or slip, usually of a contrasting color, to pottery surfaces (such pottery is found all over Mesoamerica).
73. Applique technique in ceramics (as seen in Museums).
74. Arrowheads of metal.
75. Awls (a pointed tool for making small holes in leather or wood) of bone (as in Museums of Mexico).
76. Baked clay tiles.
77. Bark cloth (Thompson 181, 191, 259).

78. Bichrome (two colors) painting of ceramics (Ferguson 1958:50).
79. Bow, arrow and quiver (Thompson 88, 124, 185).
80. Carved or sculptured clay vessels with human and animal heads and bodies (Ferguson 1958:52).
81. Ceramic dishes, bowls, ollas, etc., of plain black, white, red, brown wares (as excavated from any Preclassic site in Mesoamerica).
82. Ceramic pots with unsupported spouts (Ferguson 1958:50).
83. Ceramic storage jars (as seen in museums of many areas and Thompson 215).
84. Collars, broad and beaded, worn by dignitaries (Ferguson 1958:112).
85. Elaborate city gates (Thompson 105).
86. Embossed or raised designs on pottery surfaces (Gladwin 134).
87. Fine wood carving (as at Tikal, Guatemala).
88. Flint blades, thin and leaf-shaped, made by pressure flaking (Thompson 182).
89. Flutes (Ferguson 1958:288).
90. Herring-bone, incised designs on dishes.
91. Human features on pottery surfaces (Ferguson 1958:51).
92. Incised patterns on sun-dried ceramic surfaces before baking (Peterson 255; Gladwin 134).
93. Iron oxide pigment (Morley 350).
94. Jewelry of metal, including rings, bracelets, necklaces (Morley 350).
95. Knitting (Mason 254 and plate 50B).
96. Lapidary art (Thompson 182).
97. Large jars with four vertical handles.
98. Maps (Frederick Peterson 27).
99. Metallurgy (Ferguson 1958:20, 273).
100. Needles of bone (Thompson 187).
101. Pigments of iron oxide (red) and carbon (Morley 413).
102. Plaster floors (as at Teotihuacan, Chiapa de Corzo, etc.)
103. Plating with precious metals (Thompson 184).
104. Potter's wheel (Kluckholm's statement 53).
105. Pottery vessels covered with a thin, plaster-like stucco (Ferguson 1958:50, vessel in lower left corner of page).
106. Razors of obsidian and flint (Landa 94; Mesopotamian Exhibit, University of Pennsylvania Museum, Museums of

Mexico).

107. Red and black pottery with painted designs (Gladwin 134).

108. Red pottery ware with polished surfaces and black interiors — at 300 B.C. not known in Northeastern Asia, but known in Palestine and Mesoamerica (Ferguson 1958:50).

109. Reed mats (Thompson 215, 221; Funk and Wagnalls 100).

110. Roads, well engineered, of a baserock, surfaced with cement or with stones (Thompson 160; Keleman plate 300).

111. Robes, long and with short sleeves (Ferguson 1958:37).

112. Rope (Thompson 181).

113. Sandals (Thompson 221).

114. Stone foundations for dwellings (as at Teotihuacan).

115. Stucco masks on walls (Ferguson 1958:101).

116. Stucco walls and floors (as at Teotihuacan, Chiapa de Corzo).

117. Tapestry (Thompson 181; Gladwin 181).

118. Tetrapod (four legged) trays (Gladwin 135).

119. Textiles (turbans, Ferguson 1958:326, exhibit 136).

120. Tripod vessels (as seen in museums of Bible lands and Mesoamerica).

121. Tripod ceramic trays (Gladwin 135).

122. Tunics (Thompson 78; Vaillant 51).

123. Turbans (Ferguson 1958:326).

124. Tweezers of metal (Thompson 185).

125. Twisted-strand ceramic handles for vessels.

126. Vertical loom with ten or more working parts (Gladwin 217).

127. Wheel and axle principle known (not in use at time of Columbus — having disappeared) (Ferguson 1958:104).

128. White pottery with painted designs (Gladwin 134).

129. Repousse (raised relief by pounding from the inside) technique (Morley 432).

130. Plumb bobs (a pointed weight attached to a line dropping straight down, used by surveyors, carpenters, etc.) (Peterson 281).

As discussed in the previous chapter, in 1554 the native leaders of the ancient Guatemalan town of Totonicapan, under direct Spanish influence, recorded that their ancestors were descendants of Israel and that they were the sons of Abraham and Jacob. To understand the significance of this statement and why Jesus came to ancient Mesoamerica, it may be helpful to understand more about Abraham and the House of Israel.

7.    **House of Israel**

Abraham was a central character in the Old Testament. He was born about 1980 B.C. in Ur of the Chaldees in northern Mesopotamia. His name means "father of many nations," and he is the founder of the covenant lineage through which the twelve tribes of Israel sprang. Abraham begat Isaac, and Isaac begat Jacob, whose name God changed to Israel, which means "One who prevails with God" or "Let God prevail." It was Jacob, or Israel, who had the twelve sons whose descendants became the twelve tribes. The Jews are descendants of the tribe of Judah.

What made this family special was the covenant God made with Abraham. God commanded Abraham to sacrifice his only son, Isaac, whom he dearly loved. Abraham obeyed and had lifted the knife to slay his son when an angel of the Lord called to him:

> Lay not thine hand upon the lad, neither do thou any thing unto him: for now I know that thou fearest God, seeing thou hast not withheld thy son, thine only son from me. . . . I will bless thee, and in multiplying I will multiply thy seed as the stars of the heaven, and as the sand which is upon the sea shore. . . . And in thy seed shall all the nations if the earth be blessed; because thou hast obeyed my voice. (Gen. 22:12, 17-18)

Among the promises was that Abraham's descendants would be entitled to all the blessings of the gospel, that Christ would come though his lineage, and that Abraham's posterity would receive certain lands as an enternal inheritance (Gen. 17; 22:15-18). These promises taken together are called the Abrahamic covenant. It was renewed with Isaac (Gen. 26:1-4) and again with Jacob (Gen. 28; 35:9-13; 48:3-4).

Being an heir to the Abrahamic covenant does not make someone a "chosen person," but it does give a responsibility to carry the gospel to all the peoples of the earth (Matt. 3:9). The Jews, for example, have faithfully reserved the instructions from God as found in the Torah, which includes the five books of Moses in the Old Testament.

In approximately 925 B.C. the twelve tribes were divided into two groups. The tribes of Judah and Benjamin, called Judah, had their capital at Jerusalem. The larger group, composed of ten tribes, was called Israel. They had their capital at Samaria. When both these groups failed to keep their part of the covenant, the Lord chose to punish them:

> And the Lord said, I will remove Judah also out of my sight, as I have removed Israel, and will cast off this city Jerusalem which I have chosen, and the house of which I said, My name shall be there. (II Kings 23:27)
> . . . I will not utterly destroy the house of Jacob, saith the Lord.
> For, lo, I will command, and I will sift the house of Israel among all nations, like a corn is sifted in a sieve, yet shall not the least grain fall upon the earth. (Amos 9:8-9)

The larger group soon went into apostasy and were eventually captured by the Assyrians and carried away captive into Assyria. They are referred to as the "ten lost tribes." When they are ready to obey the gospel, they will be gathered again:

> And it shall come to pass in that day, that the Lord shall set his hand again the second time to recover the remnant of his people, which shall be left, from Assyria, and from Egypt, and from Pathros, and from Cush, and from Elam, and from Shinar, and from Hamath, and from the islands of the sea.
> And he shall set up an ensign for the nations, and shall assemble the outcasts of Israel, and gather together the dispersed of Judah from the four corners of the earth. (Isa. 11:11-12)

Chapter Eight
# THE BOOK OF MORMON: ANOTHER TESTAMENT OF JESUS CHRIST

*Now, in the authority of the sacred priesthood in me vested, I invoke my blessing upon the Latter-day Saints and upon good people everywhere.*

*I bless you with increased discernment to judge between Christ and anti-Christ. I bless you with increased power to do good and to resist evil. I bless you with increased understanding of the Book of Mormon. I promise you that from this moment forward, if we will daily sup from its pages and abide by its precepts, God will pour out upon each child of Zion and the Church a blessing hitherto unknown.*

President Ezra Taft Benson
General Conference April 1986

(*Ensign*, May 1986, p. 78)
Used by permission

About 597 B.C., in the reign of Zedekiah, representatives of three families departed from Jerusalem. Fleeing into the Arabian peninsula, the faithful band of approximately twenty people worked its way southward along the borders of the Red Sea. After eight difficult years in the Arabian wilderness (covering over 3,000 miles), they arrived in what we now call Oman.

They brought with them some precious "records . . . engraven upon plates of brass" (2 Nephi 5:12). A number of years ago this curious statement about a book of brass might have disturbed the reader. However, with the discovery of the now-famous Dead Sea Scrolls came the discovery of a book of bronze (shown in Figure 85). The "plates of brass" brought by the prophet Lehi into the new world contained the first five books of the Old Testament and the history of the Jews to the time of Zedekiah.

**Fig. 85: An engraved copper scroll from a cave by the Dead Sea (about the time of Christ).**

Interestingly, the Lords of Totonicapan, in the highlands of Guatemala in 1554, still possessed a similar manuscript. It had been passed down from generation to generation. It told of "the creation of the world, of Adam . . . and the posterity of Adam, following in every respect the same order as in Genesis and the sacred books [of the Old Testament] as far as the captivity of Babylonia [i.e., the days of Zedekiah]."

The Book of Mormon is the book of Joseph. It deals with descendants of Joseph who settled Mesoamerica about 585 B.C. They had divine help in designing their ship and in preparing for the great trans-Pacific voyage. They were led by the Lord over the wall and beyond the vineyard to isolated Mesoamerica for great and marvelous purposes of the Lord.

While it may seem obvious, the Book of Mormon is a divine effort—a work written by men who were inspired by God.

In the fourth century, Mormon, a prophet, wrote, "Therefore I, Mormon, do write the things which have been commanded me of the Lord" (3 Ne. 26:12):

> Written by way of commandment, and also by the spirit of prophecy and of revelation—Written and sealed up and hidden up unto the Lord that they might not be destroyed—To come forth by the gift and power of God unto the interpretation thereof . . . The interpretation thereof by the gift of God . . . to show unto the remnant of the House of Israel what great things the Lord has done for their fathers; and that they may know the covenants of the Lord, that they are not cast off forever—And also to the convincing of the Jew and Gentile that Jesus is the Christ, the eternal God, manifesting himself unto all nations. (Preface)

Elsewhere in the Book of Mormon the last contributor wrote:

> For none can have power to bring it to light save it be given him of God; for God wills that it shall be done with an eye single to his glory, or the welfare of the ancient and long dispersed covenant people of the Lord. And blessed be he that shall bring this thing to light; for it shall be brought out of darkness unto light, according to the word of God; yea, it shall be brought out of the earth, and it shall shine forth out of darkness, and come unto the knowledge of the people; and it shall be done by the power of God. (Morm. 8:15-16)

A relevant quotation from the Book of Mormon, credited to the scribe who recorded the departure from Jerusalem and the first events in the New World in the sixth century B.C., is as follows:

> Wherefore, the Lord hath commanded me to make these plates for a wise purpose in him, which purpose I know not. But the Lord knoweth all things from the beginning; wherefore, he prepareth a way to accomplish all his works among the children of men; for behold, he hath all power unto the fulfilling of all his words. And thus it is. (1 Ne. 9:5-6).

Incidentally, the closing of that quotation, "and thus it is," is a typical ancient Egyptian ending, as Dr. Hugh Nibley (18) has pointed out. It is also an ancient Zapotec phrase, according to Marcus in *The Cloud People* (Flannery and Marcus p. 95). (See Figure 43.)

The ancient prophet-historian Nephi also said:

> And after I had made these plates by way of commandment, I, Nephi, received a commandment that the ministry and the prophecies, the more plain and precious parts of them, should be written upon these plates; and that the things which were written should be kept for the instruction of my people, who should possess the land, and also for other wise purposes, which purposes are known unto the Lord. (1 Ne. 19:3)

> Wherefore, the Lord God will proceed to bring forth the words of the book; and in the mouth of as many witnesses as seemeth him good will he establish his word; and woe be unto him that rejecteth the word of God! (2 Ne. 27:14)

> And if they are not the words of Christ, judge ye — for Christ will show unto you, with power and great glory, that they are his words, at the last day; and you and I shall stand face to face before his bar; and ye shall know that I have been commanded of him to write these things, notwithstanding my weakness. (2 Ne. 33:11)

The Book of Mormon refers to its relationship to the New Testament as follows:

These last records, [the Book of Mormon] which thou hast seen among the Gentiles, shall establish the truth of the first [the New Testament], which are of the twelve apostles of the Lamb, and shall make known the plain and precious things which have been taken away from them; and shall make know to all kindreds, tongues, and people, that the Lamb of God is the Son of the Eternal Father, and the Savior of the world; and that all men must come unto him, or they cannot be saved. (1 Ne. 13:40)

Wherefore, the fruit of thy loins shall write [the descendants of the ancient Mesoamerican colonizers shall write the Book of Mormon]; and the fruit of the loins of Judah shall write [the Bible]; and that which shall be written by the fruit of thy loins [the Book of Mormon], and also that which shall be written by the fruit of the loins of Judah [the Bible], shall grow together, unto the confounding of false doctrines and laying down of contentions, and establishing peace among the fruit of thy loins, and bringing them to the knowledge of . . . my covenants, saith the Lord. And out of weakness he [a latter-day seer] shall be made strong, in that day when my work shall commence among all my people, unto the restoring thee, O house of Israel, saith the Lord. (2 Ne. 3:12-13)

The Book of Mormon contains a prophecy that the people of the world will resist, at first, the sacred book of the New World on the ground that the Bible is all the word of God that man needs:

And because my words [the Book of Mormon] shall hiss forth — many of the Gentiles shall say: A Bible! A Bible! We have got a Bible, and there cannot be any more Bible. But thus saith the Lord God: O fools, they shall have a Bible; and it shall proceed forth from the Jews, mine ancient covenant people. And what thank they the Jews for the Bible which they receive from them? Yea, what do the

Gentiles mean? Do they remember the travails, and the labors, and the pains of the Jews, and their diligence unto me, in bringing forth salvation unto the Gentiles?

O ye Gentiles, have ye remembered the Jews, mine ancient covenant people? Nay; but ye have cursed them, and have hated them, and have not sought to recover them. But behold, I will return all these things upon your own heads; for I the Lord have not forgotten my people. Thou fool, that shall say: A Bible, we have got a Bible, and we need no more Bible. Have ye obtained a Bible save it were by the Jews? Know ye not that there are more nations than one? Know ye not that I, the Lord your God, have created all men, and that I remember those who are upon the isles of the sea; and that I rule in the heavens above and in the earth beneath; and I bring forth my word unto the children of men, yea, even upon all the nations of the earth?

Wherefore murmur ye, because that ye shall receive more of my word? Know ye not that the testimony of two nations is a witness unto you that I am God, that I remember one nation like unto another? Wherefore, I speak the same words unto one nation like unto another. And when the two nations shall run together the testimony of the two nations shall run together also. And I do this that I may prove unto many that I am the same yesterday, today, and forever; and that I speak forth my words according to mine own pleasure. And because that I have spoken one word ye need not suppose that I cannot speak another; for my work is not yet finished; neither shall it be until the end of man, neither from that time henceforth and forever.

Wherefore, because that ye have a Bible ye need not suppose that it contains all my words; neither need ye suppose that I have not caused more to be written. For I command all men, both in the east and in the west, and in the north, and in the south, and in the islands of the sea, that they shall write the words which I speak unto them; for out of the books which shall be written I will judge the world, every man according to their works, according to that which is written.

For behold, I shall speak unto the Jews and they shall write it; and I shall also speak unto the Nephites and they shall write it; and I shall also speak unto the other tribes of the house of Israel, which I have led away, and they shall write it; and I shall also speak unto all nations of the earth and they shall write it. And it shall come to pass that the Jews shall have the words of the Nephites, and the Nephites shall have the words of the Jews; and the Nephites and the Jews shall have the words of the lost tribes of Israel; and the lost tribes of Israel shall have the words of the Nephites and the Jews.

And it shall come to pass that my people, which are of the house of Israel, shall be gathered home unto the lands of their possessions; and my word also shall be gathered in one. And I will show unto them that fight against my word and against my people, who are of the house of Israel, that I am God, and that I covenanted with Abraham that I would remember his seed forever. (2 Ne. 29:3-14)

## The Resurrected Lord

While yet in Palestine, Jesus said:

I am the good shepherd, and know my sheep, and am known of mine. As the Father knoweth me, even so know I the Father: and I lay down my life for the sheep. And other sheep I have, which are not of this fold: them also I must bring, and they shall hear my voice; and there shall be one fold, and one shepherd.

Therefore doth my Father love me, because I lay down my life, that I might take it again. No man taketh it from me, but I lay it down of myself. I have power to lay it down, and I have power to take it again. This commandment have I received of my Father. (John 10:14-18)

Jesus of Nazareth did have the power to lay his life down for his sheep and then to take it up again. He was the first to break the bands of death. As the Son of God, he had been given the power by his Father to do so. His spirit had left his body on the cross, his friends placed his body in a borrowed tomb, and three days later his spirit returned to his body, and he lived again:

Behold my hands and my feet, that it is I myself: handle me, and see; for a spirit hath not flesh and bones, as ye see me have. (Luke 24:39)

Then opened he their understanding, that they might understand the scriptures, And said unto them, Thus it is written, and thus it behoved Christ to suffer, and to rise from the dead the third day: And that repentance and remission of sins should be preached in his name among all nations, beginning at Jerusalem. And ye are witnesses of these things. (Luke 24:45-48)

## Another Witness

The other witnesses to the resurrection of Jesus the Christ were his sheep in Mesoamerica. As the descendants of Joseph, they were promised the same blessings as Abraham, Isaac, and Jacob. They were his covenanted people, and he was their shepherd. When the resurrected Messiah visited his flock in ancient Mesoamerica he said unto them:

Ye are my disciples; and ye are a light unto this people, who are a remnant of the house of Joseph. (3 Ne. 15:12)

And verily, I say unto you that ye are they of whom I said: Other sheep I have which are not of this fold; them also I must bring, and they shall hear my voice; and there shall be one fold, and one shepherd. (3 Ne. 15:21)

And they understood me not, for they supposed it had been the Gentiles. . . . But behold, ye have both heard my voice, and seen me; and ye are my sheep, and ye are numbered among those whom the Father hath given me. (3 Ne. 15:22, 24)

And I command you that ye shall write these sayings after I am gone, that if it so be that my people at Jerusalem, they who have seen me and been with me in my ministry, do not ask the Father in my name, that they may receive a knowledge of you by the Holy Ghost, and also . . . may be brought to a knowledge of me, their Redeemer. (3 Ne. 16:4)

## A Witness for the Jews

The ancient Mesoamerican prophets foresaw that their recorded witness of the Savior's visit to Mesoamerica would someday have an impact on the Jews:

> Now these things are written unto the remnant of the house of Jacob; . . . and they are to be hid up unto the Lord that they may come forth in his own due time. . . . And behold, they shall go unto the unbelieving of the Jews; and for this intent shall they go--that they may be persuaded that Jesus is the Christ, the Son of the living God; that the Father may bring about, through his most Beloved, his great and eternal purpose, in restoring the Jews, or all the house of Israel, to the land of their inheritance, which the Lord their God hath given them, unto the fulfilling of his covenant. (Mormon 5:12, 14)

> And after they have been scattered, and the Lord God hath scourged them by other nations for the space of many generations, yea, even down from generation to generation until they shall be persuaded to believe in Christ, the Son of God, and the atonement, which is infinite for all mankind—and when that day shall come that they shall believe in Christ, and worship the Father in his name, with pure hearts and clean hands, and look not forward any more for another Messiah, then, at that time, the day will come that it must needs be expedient that they should believe these things. And the Lord will set his hand again the second time to restore his people from their lost and fallen state. Wherefore, he will proceed to do a marvelous work and a wonder among the children of men. Wherefore, he shall bring forth his words [of his visit to Mesoamerica] unto them, which words shall judge them at the last day, for they shall be given them for the purpose of convincing them of the true Messiah, who was rejected by them; and unto the convincing of them that they need not look forward any more for a Messiah to come, for there should not any come, save it should be a false Messiah which should deceive the people; for there is save one Messiah spoken of by the prophets, and that Messiah is he who should be rejected of the Jews. (2 Ne. 25:16-18)

When Jesus was on the cross some of the Jewish priests, elders and scribes made a unilateral contract with the Savior. They said:

> If thou be the Son of God, come down from the cross. . . . If he be the King of Israel, let him now come down from the cross, and we will believe him. He trusted in God; let him deliver him now, if he will have him: for he said, I am the Son of God. (Matt. 27:40, 42-43)

This offer, reduced to its essence, was that if Jesus would prove that he was divine, "we will believe him." Jesus went far beyond that required by the offer. Not only did he come down from the cross, but he came back from the grave. By his performance of the resurrection, the Lord bound Israel.

### The Messiah

The people of the world need not look forward any more for a Messiah to come other than Jesus of Nazareth. There is but one Messiah — the one spoken of by the prophets of Israel, by the apostles of the early Church, and by the historians of ancient Mesoamerica. His resurrection in the Old World redeemed man from the chains of death. His New World appearance prepared a second witness of the resurrection, and that Jesus is the Christ, the son of the living God:

> And if Christ had not risen from the dead, or have broken the bands of death that the grave should have no victory, and that death should have no sting, there could have been no resurrection. But there is a resurrection, therefore the grave hath no victory, and the sting of death is swallowed up in Christ. He is the light and the life of the world; yea, a light that is endless, that can never be darkened; yea, and also a life which is endless, that there can be no more death. Even this mortal shall put on immortality; and this corruption shall put on incorruption, and shall be brought to stand before the bar of God, to be

judged of him according to their works whether they be good or whether they be evil. (Mos. 16:7-10)

It is Jesus of Nazareth that man must thank for immortality and the hope of an eternal life of peace, personal progress, happiness and joy. Through the resurrection of Jesus Christ all mankind may live again after death. But it is only through personally accepting Christ's atonement in the garden of Gethsemane that man may return to live eternally with his Father in Heaven:

And he cometh into the world that he may save all men if they will hearken unto his voice; for behold, he suffereth the pains of all men, yea, the pains of every living creature, both men, women and children, who belong to the family of Adam. And he suffereth this that the resurrection might pass upon all men, that all might stand before him at the great and judgment day. And he commandeth all men that they must repent, and be baptized in his name, having perfect faith in the Holy One of Israel, or they cannot be saved in the kingdom of God. (2 Ne. 9.21-23)

## Mormon's Farewell

The Messiah did visit ancient Mesoamerica. He knew his sheep and they knew him. They followed his teachings and lived in peace for two hundred years. But in their prosperity they soon forgot their God. Their desire for wickedness became so strong that they lost all feeling for righteousness. Their once-glorious nation was destroyed in a final battle in A.D. 375, where 230,000 troops, plus their families, were killed. Mormon, the historian, prophet and commander-in-chief of the army, gave his eyewitness report:

And it came to pass that my people, with their wives and their children, did now behold the armies of the Lamanites marching towards them; and with that awful fear of death which fills the breasts of all the wicked, did they await to receive them. And . . . they came to battle against us, and every soul was filled with terror because of the greatness of their numbers.

And it came to pass that they did fall upon my people with the sword, and with the bow, and with the arrow, and with the ax, and with all manner of weapons of war. And . . . my men were hewn down, yea, even my ten thousand who were with me, and I fell wounded in the midst; and they passed by me and they did not put an end to my life. And when they had gone through and hewn down all my people save it were twenty and four of us (among whom was my son Moroni) and we having survived the dead of our people, did behold on the morrow, when the Lamanites had returned unto their camps, from the top of the hill Cumorah, the ten thousand of my people who were hewn down, being led in the front by me.

And we also beheld the ten thousand of my people who were led by my son Moroni. And behold, the ten thousand of Gidgiddonah had fallen, and he also in the midst. And Lamah had fallen with his ten thousand; and Gilgal had fallen with his ten thousand, and Limhah had fallen with his ten thousand; and Jeneum had fallen with his ten thousand; and Camenihah, and Moronihah, and Antionum, and Shiblom, and Shem, and Josh, had fallen with their ten thousand each.

And . . . there were ten more who did fall by the sword, with their ten thousand each; yea, even all my people, save it were those twenty and four who were with me, and also a few who had escaped into the south countries, and a few who had deserted over unto the Lamanites, had fallen; and their flesh, and bones, and blood lay upon the face of the earth, being left by the hands of those who slew them to molder upon the land, and to crumble and to return to their mother earth.

And my soul was rent with anguish, because of the slain of my people, and I cried: O ye fair ones, how could ye have departed from the ways of the Lord! O ye fair ones, how could ye have rejected that Jesus, who stood with open arms to receive you! Behold, if he had not done this, ye would not have fallen. But behold, ye are fallen, and I mourn your loss. (Morm. 6:7-18)

A great civilization had passed away. The stillness of its ruins is today a solemm reminder of what happens when a nation forgets God. As if a warning, the voices of the ancient prophets of Mesoamerica cry out of the dust to us:

> Know ye that ye must come to the knowledge of your fathers, and repent of all your sins and iniquities, and believe in Jesus Christ, that he is the Son of God, and that he was slain by the Jews, and by the power of the Father he hath risen again, whereby he hath gained the victory over the grave; and also in him is the sting of death swallowed up. (Morm. 7:5)
>
> And now, I would commend you to seek this Jesus of whom the prophets and apostles have written, that the grace of God the Father, and also the Lord Jesus Christ, and the Holy Ghost, which beareth record of them, may be and abide in you forever. Amen. (Ether 12:41)

Discover for yourself the reality of the resurrection of Jesus Christ. Read the eyewitness account of his visit to a remnant of the tribe of Joseph in ancient Mesoamerica. Find out how that second witness of his resurrection can bring you closer to God and to the personal knowledge that Jesus is the Christ, the redeemer of the world.

The Book of Mormon from beginning to end is the work of Jesus of Nazareth. As you read it, notice the promise that the last writer made to you:

> And when ye shall receive these things, I would exhort you that ye would ask God, the Eternal Father, in the name of Christ, if these things are not true; and if ye shall ask with a sincere heart, with real intent, having faith in Christ, he will manifest the truth of it unto you, by the power of the Holy Ghost. And by the power of the Holy Ghost ye may know the truth of all things. (Mormon 10:4-5)

## A Modern Prophet's Testimony

Living prophets today have also given their witness of the Book of Mormon. President Ezra Taft Benson, President of the of the Church of Jesus Christ of Latter-day Saints, declared during April 1986, October 1986, and April 1987 General Conferences:

> Often we spend great effort in trying to increase the activity levels in our stakes. We work diligently to raise the percentages of those attending sacrament meetings. We labor to get a higher percentage of our young men on missions. We strive to improve the numbers of those marrying in the temple. All of these are commendable efforts and important to the growth of the kingdom. But when individual members and families immerse themselves in the scriptures regularly and consistently, these areas of activity will automatically come. Testimonies will increase. Commitment will be strengthened. Families will be fortified. Personal revelation will flow. (April 1986 General Conference, Priesthood Leadership Meeting, May 1986 *Ensign,* p. 81)

> It [the Book of Mormon] was written for our day. The Nephites never had the book; neither did the Lamanites of ancient times. It was meant for us. Mormon wrote near the end of the Nephite civilization. Under the inspiration of God, who sees all things from the beginning, he abridged centuries of records, choosing the stories, speeches, and events that would be most helpful to us. (October 1986 General Conference, November 1986 *Ensign*, p. 6)

> The Book of Mormon must be reenthroned in the minds and hearts of our people. We must honor it by reading it, by studying it, by taking its precepts into our lives and transforming them into lives required of the true followers of Christ. Speaking of the central role of the Book of Mormon in our worship, President Joseph Fielding Smith said: "It seems to me that any member of this Church would never be satisfied until he or she had read the Book of

Mormon time and time again, and thoroughly considered it so that he or she could bear witness that it is in very deed a record with the inspiration of the Almighty upon it, and that its history is true. . . .

"No member of this Church can stand approved in the presence of God who has not seriously and carefully read the Book of Mormon." (October 1986 General Conference, November 1986 *Ensign,* p. 80)

And if we ignore what the Lord has given us, we may lose the very power and blessings which we seek. In a solemn warning to the early Saints, the Lord said this of the Book of Mormon: "Your minds in times past have been darkened because of unbelief, and because you have treated lightly the things you have received. . . .

"Which vanity and unbelief have brought the whole church under condemnation.

"And this condemnation resteth upon the children of Zion, even all.

"And they shall remain under this condemnation until they repent and remember the new covenant, even the Book of Mormon" (D&C 84:54-57). (April 1986 General Conference Priesthood Leadership Meeting, May 1986 *Ensign*, p. 82)

Adults, youth, and children have borne powerful testimonies as to how the Book of Mormon has changed their lives. My life, too, continues to be changed by this sacred volume of scripture. (April 1987 General Conference, May 1987 *Ensign*, p. 4)

Nephi testifies that the Book of Mormon contains the "words of Christ" and that if people "believe in Christ," they will believe in the Book of Mormon (2 Ne. 33:10). . . .

God uses the power of the word of the Book of Mormon as an instrument to change people's lives: "As the preaching of the word had a great tendency to lead the people to do that which was just—yea, it had had more powerful effect upon the minds of the people than the sword, or anything else, which had happened unto them—therefore Alma thought it was expedient that they should try the virtue of the word of God" (Alma 31:5). . . .

God bless us all to use all the scriptures, but in particular the instrument He designed to bring us to Christ — the Book of Mormon, the keystone of our religion — along with its companion volume, the capstone, the Doctrine and Covenants, the instrument to bring us to Christ's kingdom, The Church of Jesus Christ of Latter-day Saints.

Now, by virtue of the sacred priesthood in me vested, I invoke the blessings of the Lord upon the Latter-day Saints and upon good people everywhere.

I bless you with added power to endure in righteousness amidst the growing onslaught of wickedness, about which we have heard a great deal during this conference.

I promise you that as you more diligently study modern revelation on gospel subjects, your power to teach and preach will be magnified and you will so move the cause of Zion that added numbers will enter into the house of the Lord as well as the mission field.

I bless you with increased desire to flood the earth with the Book of Mormon, to gather out from the world the elect of God who are yearning for the truth but know not where to find it.

I promise you that, with increased attendance in the temples of our God, you shall receive increased personal revelation to bless your life as you bless those who have died.

I testify that the Book of Mormon is the word of God. Jesus is the Christ. Joseph Smith is His prophet. The Church of Jesus Christ of Latter-day Saints is true, in the name of Jesus Christ, amen. (April 1987 General Conference, May 1987 *Ensign*, p. 84-85) Used by permission from The Church of Jesus Christ of Latter-day Saints.

# APPENDIX A

## History of the New World Archaeological Foundation

In 1958, Thomas Stuart Ferguson's introduction to *One Fold and One Shepherd,* boldly began:

> The number one problem of New World archaeology is—who were the people responsible for the great and advanced civilizations of Central America and Mexico dating back to the centuries from 2650 B.C. to A.D. 400? I propose a hypothetical answer to that problem--that Central America and Mexico received their very early high civilization from Mesopotamia in the third millennium B.C. and from two small groups of Israelites who made it across the ocean in the sixth century B.C. In other words, I suggest that high civilization was transferred or "diffused" to ancient Middle America by early transoceanic voyagers from Bible lands who "discovered" the New World hundreds of years before Columbus. (13)

At the time, Tom Ferguson was forty-three, an attorney, a student of Mesoamerican history since he was twenty, and president of the New World Archaeological Foundation (N.W.A.F.). Since that time, both Book of Mormon studies and Mesoamerican studies have continued to advance. Ferguson's hypothesis has been the subject of painstaking research, but though much more is known today about Mesoamerica in the periods he discusses, research must continue. However, it is also accurate to say that continued research has not disproved his hypothesis. On the contrary, the more that is known, the greater the fascination of a Mesoamerican setting for the Book of Mormon.

Thomas Stuart Ferguson was born in Pocatello, Idaho, on 21 May 1915. He married Ester Israelsen in 1940, and they had five children. He died 16 March 1983. He received his degrees in political science and law from the University of California and practiced law in Orinda, California, where in the early 1950s, their home was used as the local meeting place for members of The Church of Jesus Christ of Latter-day Saints until numbers increased to the point that other facilities were necessary.

Tom Ferguson maintained a profound interest in Mesoamerican archaeology during his adult life, an interest apparently sparked as a freshman at the University of California at Berkeley. As a freshman at U.C. Berkeley in 1934, Ferguson had an experience which gave birth to the idea which was later responsible for the creation of the N.W.A.F. In the mid-1930s the chairman of the history department at U.C. Berkeley was Dr. Herbert Bolton, a widely recognized expert in the history of the Americas. In 1919 Dr. Bolton inaugurated an undergraduate class, History 8, History of the Americas, a course still taught today at U.C. Berkeley. Dr. Bolton was also the director of the well known Bancroft Library at U.C. Berkeley.

As a freshman in Dr. Bolton's undergraduate history class, young Ferguson spoke privately with him about the Book of Mormon. Ferguson explained that he was a member of the LDS Church. Dr. Bolton was not LDS, but was familiar with the Book of Mormon and its historical claims. Dr. Bolton told Ferguson that he did not know if the Book of Mormon was a true and accurate history, but thought this an interesting question. He and Ferguson reasoned together that it may be possible to determine the historical accuracy of the Book of Mormon claims through scholarly research. They decided together that there were three possible origins of the Book of Mormon:

1.  Joseph Smith wrote a novel based on historical fact,

which historical information he borrowed from the scholars of his day, since he himself had no formal education concerning ancient America.
2. Joseph Smith wrote a fiction book not based on historical fact.
3. The book was of divine origin as claimed by Joseph Smith.

Dr. Bolton challenged young Ferguson to do research concerning the earliest high civilizations of Mesoamerica, to learn what was known and being taught by the scholarly world in or about 1830, when the Book of Mormon was published. If the results of that research revealed a general 1830 knowledge of dates, origins, places, and civilizations similar to those in the Book of Mormon, then the "borrowing" theory, was possible. On the other hand, if the research eliminated the "borrowing" theory only the "fiction" or "divine origin" possibilities were valid. Dr. Bolton suggested that because of the historical nature of so much of the Book of Mormon, archaeological and historical research could be undertaken to determine which of the "fiction" or "divine origin" possibilities was correct.

During his four undergraduate years at U.C. Berkeley, Ferguson spent considerable time doing research at the U.C. Berkeley library on the "borrowing" possibility. He concluded that the scholarly world in 1830 knew very little about the early high civilizations of Mesoamerica. The theories of the origin and dates of these civilizations could only be guessed at in 1830, and the guesses were totally incompatible with the text of the Book of Mormon. The 1830 period conventional wisdom was that early Mesoamerican civilization was a result of land bridge migrations across the Bering Straits connecting Asia and Alaska, and that the civilization first blossomed about A.D. 600—a minimum of 1200 years later than the Book of Mormon text and a completely different origin than that described in the Book of Mormon. The "borrowing" possibility was eliminated.

As Dr. Bolton had suggested, sufficient dirt archaeology and historical research should reveal the true origin of the book. If the very specific and detailed historical Book of Mormon claims could be supported and verified by research, it would verify that Joseph Smith did not write a fiction book, leaving only one plausible origin—that the Book of Mormon is a true religious history of ancient America. This would lead to the conclusion that the Joseph Smith story is true, and that in fact Joseph Smith was chosen by the Savior of the world as a modern-day prophet to restore His Church to the earth. This line of reasoning motivated Ferguson to eventually found the N.W.A.F.

Ester recalls during their courtship that she was sometimes piqued by his passion for the Book of Mormon and once complained to her mother, "I think I'm going out with the Book of Mormon." Her mother wisely asked her to think about the many less desirable preoccupations a man could have. Throughout their married life she staunchly supported her husband's efforts.

M. Wells Jakeman, another student of Mesoamerican archaeology, recalls long, frequent, and enthusiastic studies, many of them focused on a translation of the writings of Don Fernando de Alva Ixtlilxochitl, a native Texcocan (a city in the Valley of Mexico) in the sixteenth century, who wrote a history of central Mexico. Tom Ferguson and Wells Jakeman founded the Itzan Society, an organization interested in archaeology and the Book of Mormon that functioned in California between 1938 and about 1944.

In February 1946, Tom Ferguson made his first trip to Mexico in the company of J. Willard Marriott. In his lifetime Tom made approximately 25 trips to Mexico. J. Willard Marriott wrote in a letter to Tom's wife, Ester, dated 17 March 1983, referring to Tom, "We spent several months together in Mexico looking at the ruins and studying the Book of Mormon archaeology. I have never known anyone who was more devoted to that kind of research than was Tom. I remember when he was with the F.B.I., he would arise at 4:30 or 5:00 AM and read the Book of Mormon and information he could find pertaining to it." His last trip was about a month before his death in February 1983. He was accompanied on this trip by Elder Howard W.

Hunter of the Quorum of the Twelve of the Mormon Church and other members of the BYU New World Archaeological Foundation Advisory Board (Figure 86).

**Fig. 86: NWAF Board members visiting in Mesoamerica in 1983. This was Thomas Stuart Ferguson's last visit to Mesoamerica before his death the following month. Elder Howard W. Hunter is seated in front right and Thomas Stuart Ferguson is standing on the far left.**

Tom Ferguson first approached the President of Brigham Young University, Howard S. McDonald, about establishing a Department of Archaeology. He also discussed the proposal with Elder John A. Widtsoe of the Quorum of the Twelve, who was something of a mentor to young Ferguson, encouraging him in his interest and efforts. Tom Ferguson was able to convince officials of BYU of the benefit to the University of having such a department.

In conversations with these men and others, Tom Ferguson suggested to President McDonald that Wells Jakeman, who had received his Ph.D. in ancient history from Berkeley, would be an excellent candidate for a professorship in archaeology at Brigham Young University, with a view toward organizing a department. In the spring of 1946, Wells Jakeman joined the BYU faculty, and the new department was formed the following December.

The new Department of Archaeology (now Anthropology) sponsored its first field trip in 1948 to western Campeche, a state in southeastern Mexico. Wells Jakeman, Tom Ferguson, and W. Glenn Harmon, a lawyer, participated in that first of many expeditions in the department's distinguished history of training dozens of students who have gone on to receive higher degrees and to work as professional archaeologists. The department has had a very positive influence on hundreds of students since its founding.

The year 1946 was important for a third reason as well. William E. Gates, a noted Maya scholar, was a great collector and photographer of Mesoamerican manuscripts until his death in 1940. Tom Ferguson, then working as an FBI agent on an assignment, had been asked to interview Mrs. Gates on another matter, but their mutual interest in archaeology led them into further conversation. When Ferguson learned that the Gates collection was for sale, he recommended to BYU and officials of the Mormon Church that BYU purchase it. Jakeman, on request, evaluated the collection and made the same recommendation. The university then obtained a substantial portion of this collection. Now housed in the archives of the Harold B. Lee Library, it contains many documents, manuscripts, and photographs that would not otherwise be available to scholars. This great collection will benefit scholars and students for many years to come.

All who knew him remember Tom Ferguson as confident and optimistic, quick to see the possibilities of an idea, possessed of the driving energy to do the necessary work to bring a project to fruition, and enthusiastic enough to persuade others of the merits of a position. Neil K. Holbrook, speaking at Ferguson's funeral, said that he could never hear the Rodgers and Hammerstein song "Cockeyed Optimist" without thinking of Tom. His success in these ventures only deepened his love for Mesoamerican archaeology. He had written *Cumorah Where?* in 1947 and followed it in 1950 with *Ancient America and The Book of Mormon,* which he co-authored with Milton R. Hunter, a General Authority of the Mormon Church. Shortly after the publication of *Cumorah Where?* Ferguson was invited to give a slide lecture on archaeology and the Book of Mormon to the President of the Mormon Church, George Albert Smith, and to all of the General Authorities of the Mormon Church at the Lion House in Salt Lake City. Ferguson discussed Book of Mormon geography, placing it in Mesoamerica. Ferguson was well received by the General Authorities of the Church. This was a beginning for Ferguson to make several friendships with General Authorities of the Church, many of which lasted throughout his life. In 1951, he was ready for an enormous undertaking: the establishment of an organization to expand field research on Mesoamerican civilizations.

He began in a thoroughly sound way by enlisting the aid of two of the nation's most prominent Mesoamerican archaeologists: Dr. Alfred V. Kidder of the Carnegie Institution, and Dr. Gordon R. Willey, professor of archaeology at Harvard University. Although Ferguson's chief interest was in developing an archaeological base for the Book of Mormon, he had the wisdom and intellectual temper to understand that such a venture must be thoroughly professional and scholarly. Otherwise it would be dismissed as the zealous views of a small and unprofessional group.

The following is a description of the founding of the New World Archaeological Foundation given by Thomas Ferguson in 1956:

> In the summer of 1951, Dr. Alfred V. Kidder, for twenty years director of archaeological work in Central

America for the Carnegie Institution, Dr. Gordon Willey, Professor of Central American archaeology at Harvard University, and the writer had a series of discussions concerning the status of archaeology in Mexico and Central America. It was agreed that it was unfortunate that so little work was being carried on in so important an area and that something should be done to increase explorations and excavations. Work done in the twenty years from 1930 through 1950, largely by the Carnegie Institution staff under the direction of Dr. Kidder, in Guatemala, Honduras, and Yucatan, had provided the world with an excellent outline of the history and culture of the ancient Maya from the Classic period (beginning about 400 A.D.) down to A.D. 1500. Further, fragmentary information concerning the highly important Preclassic (2500 B.C.-300 A.D.) culture had come to light during the 1930's and 1940's. By 1950, it was known that the little-known Preclassic people occupied parts of central and southern Mexico from A.D. 400 backwards in time for some centuries before Christ.

In the 1951 discussions it was agreed that there were exciting archaeological and early documentary clues telling us that knowledge of great worth could be expected from extensive explorations and excavations of Preclassic sites. But there were no funds available for the work. None of the great financial foundations of the United States were informed or interested. Few people knew of the Preclassic civilizations and fewer still realized the potential values that could come from the excavations. The necessary preliminary work had all been done—the stage was set for unfolding the story of the amazing Preclassic peoples. The pioneering had been accomplished by the work of the Carnegie men on the Classic Maya (A.D. 300-A.D. 900, which now could be distinguished from the Preclassic materials) and more particularly by the discovery and identification of various Preclassic sites and materials by Eduardo Noguera, Pina Chan, George Vaillant, Pedro Armillas, Alfonso Caso, and others near Mexico City, Puebla and Oaxaca, Mexico; by Alfred V. Kidder, Edwin Shook, and Jesse Jennings near Guatemala City; by Matthew Stirling, Philip Drucker, and M. Wells Jakeman in Veracruz and Tabasco, Mexico; by

Gordon F. Ekholm and Richard S. MacNeish near Tampico, Mexico; in northern Guatemala by Alfred V. Kidder, Sylvanus G. Morley, Robert Smith, A. Ledyard Smith, Oliver Ricketson, and J. Eric Thompson. By 1950 the limited excavations made by these men had prepared the way for a major effort with respect to the things and peoples of Mexico and Central America prior to A.D. 400.

Despite the amazing discoveries made between 1930 and 1950, work on the Preclassic was virtually at a standstill in 1951. The result of the discussion was that we agreed to set up a new organization to be devoted to the Preclassic civilizations of Mexico and Central America—the earliest known high cultures of the New World. Dr. Kidder and Dr. Willey agreed to select a committee of skilled archaeological advisors and suitable field directors. The writer agreed to solicit needed funds and to assist in field explorations and in the selection of promising sites for serious excavations.

It was decided that the area drained by the Grijalva River should be explored for Preclassic sites. The Grijalva River, being the first major water course southerly from Mexico's narrow neck of land, the Isthmus of Tehuantepec, could and should be rich in Preclassic sites. Although the Grijalva drainage area was virtually unknown archaeologically, Preclassic sites had been found to the south in highland Guatemala, to the east in lowlands Guatemala, to the west in Oaxaca, and to the northwest along the Gulf Coast of Mexico in Veracruz.

With a promise of needed funds in our possession, Dr. Kidder addressed a letter to the distinguished and gracious head of Mexico's archaeological program, Dr. Ignacio Marquina, director of the National Institute of Anthropology and History, Mexico City as follows:

> A group of persons interested in New World prehistory, of which Mr. T.S. Ferguson of Orinda, California, is President, I [Alfred Kidder], First Vice-President, and of whose Advisory Committee Drs. Gordon Willey and Gordon F. Ekholm are members, is in process of organizing

a new institution to be incorporated under the laws of California as the New World Archaeological Foundation.

The purpose of the Foundation is to carry on explorations and excavations to add to knowledge of Mesoamerican archaeology and to test several theories as to the origin of the high civilizations of the Americas: 1) That they were autochthonous; 2) That, as set forth in the Book of Mormon, they were derived from ancient Israel; 3) That their rise was due to stimuli from some Asiatic source.

Mr. Ferguson is an advocate of the second of these theories; Dr. Ekholm, as you know, views with some favor the third; I feel that, although the problem is *still unsolved,* these civilizations were essentially the product of native American Indian creativeness. So all shades of opinion are represented!

In discussing the Foundation with Mr. Ferguson, to whose interest and energy its organization has been due, he made it clear to me that he, and those of his friends who have contributed financial support, are primarily concerned with discovery of the truth and that the results of such fieldwork as may be done are published as purely factual reports. . . .

Mexico kindly granted the Foundation the permit to explore and excavate along the Grijalva. On October 20th, 1952 the State of California officially acknowledged the incorporated status of the New World Archaeological Foundation as a non-profit, scientific, fact-finding body. On March 3, 1954 the U. S. Treasury Department recognized that the Foundation was exempt from tax under the Internal Revenue Code and that bequests, legacies and gifts to the Foundation are deductible under Federal revenue laws. The officers were: Thomas Stuart Ferguson, president; Alfred V. Kidder, first vice-president; Milton R. Hunter, vice-president; and Scott H. Dunham, secretary-treasurer. The directors were Scott H. Dunham, Thomas Stuart Ferguson, J. Poulson Hunter, Alfred V. Kidder, Nicholas G. Morgan, Sr., LeGrand Richards, and Ernest A. Strong. The late Dr. John A. Widtsoe was a director until his death. The advisory committee of archaeologists is made up of the following scholars, Alfred V. Kidder, Pedro

Armillas, Gordon F. Ekholm, M. Wells Jakeman, and
Gordon Willey.

Tom Ferguson enlisted the help of his friend J. Willard
Marriott to arrange for an interview with the First Presidency in
April 1951. After an unsuccessful attempt to meet with the First
Presidency of the Church, he and Alfred Kidder presented a plan
for archaeological work in Mesoamerica, including funding in
the amount of $150,000. This plan had already been discussed with
Elder Widtsoe, who had also discussed it with other Church
General Authorities. An answer was delayed until, on 14
December 1951, Tom Ferguson wrote to David O. McKay,
President of the Church, reminding him of the visit and reporting
in tantalizing detail upon the status of the project:

> Seven months have passed since the plan was
> submitted. Dr. Kidder writes me inquiring concerning your
> action upon the plan. Since the plan was submitted some of
> the great men in archaeology have agreed to serve on the
> project without pay. Among these is Dr. Gordon Willey,
> Professor of Mexican and Central American archaeology at
> Harvard University. Pedro Armillas, leading Mexican
> archaeologist, has also stated his willingness to serve.
>
> You will be interested to know that these noted men
> and others, including Thor Heyerdahl (author of *Kon Tiki*)
> and Marcus Bach (author of *Faith and My Friends*) have
> read *Ancient America and The Book of Mormon* by Milton
> R. Hunter and me—and are expressing interest in the Book
> of Mormon.
>
> If the work is undertaken as suggested, important
> scholars throughout the world will become better informed
> concerning the Book of Mormon. If the anticipated
> evidences confirming the Book of Mormon are found,
> world-wide notice will be given the restored gospel through
> the Book of Mormon. The artifacts will speak eloquently
> from the dust. According to Brother Pierce, former Mission
> President, we will make many good and important friends
> for the Church in Mexico if the work is undertaken.
>
> Brother Widtsoe and other Authorities who have

shown special interest in this matter may talk with you in the
near future, I am advised. Dr. Kidder and I will be happy to
furnish any additional information you may desire.

Joseph Anderson, secretary to the First Presidency, responded
on 20 December:

> President McKay has received and has carefully read
> your letter of December 14, in which you called attention to
> an earlier correspondence. You inquire as to whether or not
> President McKay feels that the Church should undertake the
> financing of some archaeological research in chosen Latin
> American areas at an estimated minimum cost for five years
> of work of $150,000.
>
> President McKay, along with other members of the
> First Presidency, has given careful consideration to this
> matter, and they have reached the conclusion that while they
> are not without a keen appreciation of both the importance
> and the value of archaeological studies that shall revolve
> about Book of Mormon history, and hope that sometime it
> may be undertaken, nevertheless they do not feel that the
> Church is in a position at this particular time to take on this
> work. They regret this very much, but such is the conclusion
> that seems to be necessary at this time.
>
> President McKay would be happy to have you express
> to Dr. Alfred V. Kidder, Dr. Gordon Willey, and Pedro
> Armillas his grateful appreciation for their kind offers of
> cooperation. He also wishes to thank you for your sustained
> interest in this great subject.

Three weeks later, Ferguson wrote again to the First
Presidency on 12 January 1952:

> Dr. Alfred V. Kidder and I wish to thank you for
> having considered our plan for archaeological work in
> southern Mexico.
>
> Inasmuch as you have not seen fit for the Church to
> finance the work at this time, we now propose to organize a
> non-profit California corporation through which to finance

and carry out the work. . . . It will be financed by contributions from private individuals and corporations and will be independent of the Church. No references will be made to the Church in any of the publications or writings of the Foundation.

The directors of the proposed corporation will be, for the most part, very prominent business executives. Some will be members of the Church and some will not be. The officers will be scholars expert in the ancient high civilizations of the New World.

Dr. Kidder suggests that I be President of the corporation because upon me and a few of my good friends will fall the major task of raising the funds. I will take an active part in the Foundation to the end that the Church receives the full benefit of any discovered evidences relating to the Book of Mormon. I anticipate that many important artifacts will be discovered confirming the Book of Mormon. I will endeavor to channel such artifacts into the possession of the Church wherever it is possible to take them out of Mexico.

Through my present connections with leading archaeologists at Harvard, Carnegie, and in Mexico, I can obtain casts of the more important artifacts now in museums. These, together with anticipated discoveries could provide Salt Lake City with an outstanding museum.

My purpose in writing you is not to ask for an endorsement of the foregoing. Rather, we simply want to inform you so that you will know of our plans. I would like to know if you object to our going forward with them. If you do not object, we will establish the corporation at an early date. Thereafter if asked by members of the Church if we know of the attitude of the Church toward the work of the Foundation, we will state that the organization has no connection with the Church other than that some members of the Church have participated in its activities—that there is no official connection with the Church.

An early reply will be appreciated. Thank you.

Again, a reply came back from Joseph Anderson, dated 18 January 1952:

>        Your letter of January 12 addressed to the First Presidency has been received in which, acknowledging my letter to you of December 20, 1951, you set out plans for the organization of a non-profit California corporation which will undertake exploratory work in Latin America along the lines which you have heretofore set out in your communications to the First Presidency.
>
>        The First Presidency directs me to say that they see no objection to the organization of a non-profit corporation of the kind you suggest, nor do they see any objections to the projected activities in which this corporation would engage.
>
>        Indeed, the Brethren feel that careful exploratory work may very well develop faith-promoting corroborative evidence of the historical value of the Book of Mormon. The Brethren feel that it may be that no discovery will be made which shall establish the historical value of the Book of Mormon. They incline to feel that the faith now required to accept the book is a very considerable factor in the faith of the Restored Gospel, belief in which is the result of faith therein.
>
>        The Brethren direct me to say that they wish you well in your undertaking and will await with deep interest a report on the progress of your work and particularly on the result of your exploratory operations.
>
>        The Brethren have noted your statements as to your position in letting it be known that this is not a Church undertaking and they are in entire accord with your declared intention.

With characteristic zeal and enthusiasm, Tom Ferguson had traveled throughout California speaking at church firesides, Rotary Clubs, Kiwanis luncheons, and any other group who would hear him. He wrote hundreds of letters and, with the utmost effort, scraped together $3,000, a painfully small sum but sufficient to fund the year's short field expedition.

In the winter of 1952-53, the Foundation's first expedition

began work on the lower Grijalva, near the mouth of the river, close by Villahermosa in the state of Tabasco. Professor Pedro Armillas was Field Director, assisted by William Sanders (graduate student in archaeology from Harvard University); Roman Pina Chan, a Mexican archaeologist; John Sorenson and Gareth Lowe (both graduate students in archaeology from Brigham Young University). The expedition worked until June of 1953 exploring and test pitting from Villahermosa up-stream to the south toward Tuxtla Gutierrez. It was determined that there were no major Preclassic sites along the Grijalva between the Gulf of Mexico and Tuxtla Gutierrez, Chiapas. The search was narrowed greatly by this exploratory work of the first season. Numerous Preclassic sites were discovered.

Some of N.W.A.F.'s major goals were producing a topographic map, digging excavation trenches and pits at key sites, doing some selected major excavations at one or two important sites, and cataloging and preserving any artifacts found.

As the season progressed through the winter of 1953, it became clear that there were few Preclassic sites on the lower Grijalva and that most settlements there dated from the Classic and Postclassic (A.D. 900-A.D. 1519). In April and May, as the archaeological season drew to a close, Tom Ferguson, who joined the expedition late, and John Sorenson left the rest of the crew to conduct a brief reconnaissance of the area on the upper Grijalva near Tuxtla Gutierrez, capital of Chiapas, and as far southward toward Guatemala as La Concordia. They picked up artifacts from the surfaces of twenty-two sites, made notes, and obtained information on a number of Preclassic sites in the area.

Upon returning to Provo, Utah, John Sorenson was assigned to analyze the surface finds, review the notes, and write the report on the first reconnaissance. There was general agreement that at least a dozen Preclassic sites merited further excavation; and the report, published in 1956, strongly recommended concentrating on the upper Grijalva Basin. The enthusiasm generated by this first expedition, however, was tempered by the problem of funds.

Thus, it was without official backing that Ferguson put together funding for the first field expedition; but he did not give up. Before flying down to join the field expedition in the spring of 1953, Ferguson made another presentation to the First Presidency. On 9 April 1953, he asked for $30,000 for the 1954 field season and $30,000 more for each of four additional years for a total of $150,000. He followed it up with a letter to the First Presidency the next day:

> This is to supplement the oral presentation of Thursday morning *April 9, 1953*. Additional points need to be made to assist you in deciding whether to sustain work in Book-of-Mormon lands.
>
> The golden age of the Nephites was that which followed the crucifixion and New-World appearance of Christ. Following the crucifixion many cities were built and were occupied for several hundred years: "And the Lord did prosper them exceedingly in the land; yea, insomuch that they did build cities again where there had been cities burned. Yea, even that great city of Zarahemla did they cause to be built again" (4 Ne. 7-8). Thus, the destructions and changes at the time of the crucifixion did not render archaeological pursuits hopeless. On the same point, it should also be noted that most of the geographical helps found in the Book of Mormon are in the portion abridged by Mormon and many of the geographical statements reflect Mormon's fourth-century views.
>
> Approximately half of all the verses of the Book of Mormon relate to history, geography, culture, and related matters. Ferguson classified every verse, one by one. Surely the Lord required all of this material to be included for a purpose—else would he not have preserved for the latter days only a theological work like the New Testament, devoid of matters lending themselves to proof?
>
> Under any view of Book of Mormon geography, southern Mexico and Guatemala are included. Great interest was shown in discoveries made by John Lloyd Stephens in the region in question during the lifetime of the Prophet. In

fact, while the Prophet was editor of *The Times and Seasons* this statement appeared: "It will not be a bad plan to compare Mr. Stephens' ruined cities with those in the Book of Mormon: light cleaves to light, and facts are supported by facts. The truth injures no one. . . ." There follows an extensive quotation concerning the archaeological discoveries of Stephens, the pioneer in Central American archaeology. (*Times and Seasons,* 1 October 1842, 3.927-28. See also the following references in *Times and Seasons*: 2.440-42; 3.818, 858-60, 911-15.)

Our Secretary-Treasurer is one of the finest C.P.A.'s in San Francisco, a Latter-day Saint. He was the tax adviser for several years to Mr. William Randolph Hearst, and he is now adviser to the Hearst estate. He will make regular reports to you concerning all expenditures, etc., should you make it possible for the work in Middle America to go forward.

The source of our income and support for the work can be kept strictly confidential if it is desired. The Church cannot afford to pass up title to Nephite works of art and handcraft; the Church cannot afford to let all of the priceless artifacts of Book of Mormon people fall into other hands. We can make wonderful use of them in missionary work and in letting all the world know of the Book of Mormon. We cannot afford to let this work go undone now that we are so well prepared to undertake it.

As mentioned Thursday morning, we need $15,000.00 now for 1953, and $30,000.00 per year for four additional years.

This time, Ferguson's persistence and persuasiveness paid off, for a letter dated 17 April 1953 arrived, signed by J. Reuben Clark, Jr., second counselor, for the First Presidency:

Reference is made to your letter of April 10, and to the oral explanations which you made on Thursday, April 9, before a group of the Brethren. The matter of your request was taken up by the First Presidency and given careful consideration. The following conclusions were reached.

It is to be distinctly understood that this contribution is to cover your request for funds to complete your operations for the current year. This is not a commitment either expressed or implied for any future contributions by the Church.

We of course, wish you the fullest success in your efforts to discover something that will help to coordinate American archaeology with the Book of Mormon.

With only the summer and fall to raise funds to finance another expedition from January through June 1954 and with most of the readily available sources exhausted, Ferguson was unable to procure the additional sums desired and no field work was done during 1954.

However, Tom Ferguson did not give up. Edwin Shook, then finishing Carnegie Institution's final season of excavation, was persuaded to take a brief "vacation" in late April and early May to join Ferguson and friends from California in making a quick reconnaissance on the upper Grijalva to select excavation sites.

The survey included the following sites in the southern state of Chiapas, Mexico: Comitan, Esperanza, and Chiapa de Corzo (possibly Sidom in the Book of Mormon). Shook's only test pit (Figure 87), sunk on the bank of the Grijalva, produced a very nice late Preclassic pot with a radiocarbon date of A.D. 258. (Refinements in radiocarbon dating techniques later located it more accurately at about the time of Christ.) On the basis of his visit, Shook recommended Chiapa de Corzo as one of the most important sites in the upper Grijalva time period and recommended more work in the Acala-area of Chiapas.

Shook then returned to finish his Maya project; and armed with this persuasive analysis, Ferguson persisted in his proposals to the First Presidency. Ferguson appealed to his good friend J. Willard Marriott for assistance. The following day Ferguson had an appointment with President McKay which Marriott had arranged. This time, he succeeded. As the family tells it, during this private meeting, President David O. McKay listened to Tom

**Fig. 87: The 1955 test-pit Edwin Shook at Puerto Mexico near Acala, Chiapas, Mexico. At this time Shook was the field director of the Carnegie Institution's last archaeological season at Mayapan, Yucatan, Mexico.**

Ferguson's proposal and asked the specific amount he was requesting. Ferguson replied, "Only about the amount that it would take to build a chapel."

President McKay gave him a penetrating glance. "We build $50,000 chapels and $250,000 chapels. Which did you have in mind?" Tom Ferguson promptly replied, "A $250,000 chapel." That was the amount granted, sufficient to underwrite five years' work in a generous way (1955-1959).

Tom Ferguson moved from a partnership to a sole law practice, and his hard-driving pace continued. His wife recalls that he would spend long periods of almost day-and-night work at the office, since income was directly related to volume, using the funds of this busy period to stabilize the family finances and provide more support for NWAF. It was during this period that Ferguson spent approximately half of his working time away from law, devoting this time to administering the affairs of the NWAF, giving speeches, studying and writing about the archaeology and history of ancient America and their relationship to the Book of Mormon. These intense periods of concentration on his legal duties would alternate with "working vacations" he would give himself to inspect field operations, lecture (sometimes attracting more than 2,000), or carry out research projects of his own. He made twenty-five trips to Mexico and Central America. Neil Holbrook, himself a lawyer, speaking at Tom Ferguson's funeral, termed him "a lawyer's lawyer." Had he given more time to the practice of law rather than to the uncompensated time in archaeology, he would have been one of America's most famous jurists today (2-3).

With the assurance of funds, the NWAF moved quickly. The second season of field work began in November 1955 at Chiapa de Corzo in the state of Chiapas. Dr. Heinrich Berlin, of Mexico City, who had done the earliest work in the area, was named field director, assisted by Gareth Lowe. The staff also included Richard Madison, Lorenzo Allen, Eduardo E. Martinez, a Mexico City topographer, and Bruce W. Warren. Except for Martinez, all were students of archaeology at BYU.

At that time, two general hypotheses were in print on the origins of the Chiapanec Indians of Chiapas. One hypothesis saw them as arriving in the area from Oaxaca in the north in the Classic period, while the other saw them as coming from Nicaragua in the south during the Postclassic period. (Eventually, NWAF established the people as coming out of central Mexico around A.D. 600, later than the Book of Mormon period.)

Berlin made a brief reconnaissance in January and February of 1941 around Chiapa de Corzo and Tuxtla Gutierrez. He made test excavations at the mouth of El Sumidero Canyon, and made finds of a plumbate-pottery dated at about A.D. 1000. His report was not published until 1946 in *American Antiquity*. Otherwise, Matthew W. Stirling, Director of the Bureau of American Ethnology, had excavated a site near Ocozocuautla, Chiapas, and found Preclassic materials. Robert Russell, an amateur archaeologist, had made a quick trip in 1953 as far as Acala on the Grijalva and reported finding Preclassic pottery in a cave on the middle Grijalva. Arden King of Tulane University had reported finding baskets and other materials usually not recovered in this part of the world in a cave in western Chiapas, including black and white pottery in the late Preclassic and Early Classic. This was the sum total of information about the area when the NWAF began its work there.

In the first six weeks at Chiapa de Corzo, the NWAF workers dug about twenty-five test pits and trenches (Figure 88). It was an exciting season. The site turned out to be much bigger than anticipated, extending further back into Preclassic times than either the Sorenson or Shook explorations had hypothesized. After the Christmas break, the group moved up river to Acala, where Berlin directed excavations (Figure 89) and Lowe, assisted part-time by both Madison and Warren, conducted reconnaissance along the upper Grijalva in preparation for future efforts.

**Fig. 88: One of the first test-pits at Chiapa de Corzo, Chiapas, Mexico in November of 1955.**

**Fig. 89:  Excavations in Mound K of the Ruiz site, Chiapas, Mexico in 1956.**

**Fig. 90:  Field workers at the site of Santa Rosa, Chiapas, Mexico in 1956.**

Acala turned out to have important Preclassic occupation that had extended into early Postclassic times; but the reconnaissance efforts during the same time period turned up the most exciting materials. Close to the Guatemalan border, they searched a valley about thirty miles long and about ten or fifteen miles wide, where they located numerous sites. Most had Preclassic occupation and some were entirely Preclassic. The largest in the area, Santa Rosa (possibly Zarahemla in the Book of Mormon), was clearly of such importance that a change of strategy was called for.

However, Lowe's efforts to refocus the expedition's energies on the new site alienated Berlin, who resigned because Santa Rosa had not been part of the original plan. His criticism in high places resulted in a ban on excavation for NWAF for several weeks, but other NWAF representatives were able to change Ignacio Marquina's mind before the onset of the rains made it impossible to do any work. Marquina was then the director of the National Institute of Anthropology and History of Mexico. In only a fortnight they found caches of artifacts that established the importance of the site of Santa Rosa (Figure 90).

Lowe was named field director to replace Berlin. He wrote the annual report and rented a large building in Tuxtla Gutierrez, the capital of the state of Chiapas, to serve as NWAF headquarters, to serve as barracks for field personnel, and to store field materials.

Until 1959, most of the NWAF's resources would be concentrated on sites in the upper Grijalva (Figures 91-93). Beginning in the fall of 1956, extensive excavation occurred at Chiapa de Corzo, with some side reconnaissance trips. One of the most important discoveries was Tomb 1 at Chiapa de Corzo where four human femurs were uncovered, two of them carved (Figures 94-95). They produced a sensation, not only because of the elaborateness of the carving, but because they dated to the first century A.D.

In October 1957, while the workers excavated in the main plaza,they found a cylinder seal with an unusual set of designs

Fig. 91:  A mound excavation at Santa Rosa, Chiapas, Mexico in 1956.

Fig. 92:  A Late Preclassic jar (ca. the time of Christ) from
Santa Rosa, Chiapas, Mexico.

Fig. 93: Part of the archaeological site of Laguna Francesa, Chiapas, Mexico, 1957.

Fig. 94: Excavating Tomb 1 at Chiapa de Corzo, Chiapas, Mexico, in 1957.

Fig. 95:  Museum display of Tomb 1, Chiapa de Corzo, Chiapas, Mexico, in 1958.

Fig. 96:  Intriguing cylinder seal from Pit 78 at Chiapa de Corzo, Chiapas, Mexico, in 1958.

(Figure 96). They were copied and sent to William F. Albright, dean of Near Eastern archaeologists, who said they were imitation Egyptian hieroglyphics of the sixth century B.C. Tom Ferguson carried on an intensive correspondence regarding the cylinder seal with various scholars, including Professor Rudolph Anthes, an Egyptologist at the University of Pennsylvania.

The NWAF board of directors decided to authorize an extensive excavation in the main plaza at Chiapa de Corzo in hopes of finding more hieroglyphic evidence. The rainy season

Fig. 97: Stela 2, Chiapa de Corzo, with the earliest known Long Count calendar date.

was approaching rapidly when Warren was assigned in June 1958 to put in a grid of test pits through the plaza area to reaffirm the basic stratigraphy for Chiapa de Corzo and also to look for more seals. Thirty test pits later, all of them dug with spades, the stratigraphy was thoroughly verified; but disappointingly, only a few more cylinder seals had come to light, none of them in the style that had caused such excitement.

In the year 1957, the University of Chicago initiated a "Man and Nature" project in the highlands of Chiapas about fifty miles away. Part of the work included an archaeological survey of part of the highland Mayan area. The Chicago project quite naturally overlapped with NWAF's work. T. Patrick Culbert's archaeological summary of Chicago's project became his Ph.D. dissertation, which the NWAF published in 1965.

NWAF experienced dynamic growth during 1957-58. Ambitiously, it undertook numerous projects to solidify its reputation with the profession in general and attracted students from other universities who participated in field projects. Tom Ferguson wrote his very popular *One Fold and One Shepherd* with up-to-date results from the field and published it in 1958. William T. Sanders came from Mississippi State University and conducted an archaeological project at Santa Cruz, the results of which NWAF published in 1961. Donald Brockington came with Augustin Delgado and did more extensive excavations at Santa Rosa, while Carlos Navarrete excavated at San Agustin, an interesting Preclassic site near Tuxtla Gutierrez. Fred Peterson, a Mesoamerican scholar and author, joined the foundation and conducted an archeological survey in the area of Santa Marta, finding an important rock shelter in the process.

NWAF hired Dr. John Alden Mason, recently retired from the University Museum at Philadelphia, to edit the New World Archaeological Foundation reports. Augustin Delgado, after finishing his work at Santa Rosa, was assigned to the Juchitan area on the western side of the Isthmus of Tehuantepec. All this activity resulted in excellent relations for the NWAF with a number of important institutions, including the Mexican government.

As that season closed, however, another crisis was emerging over the future of NWAF. The Church formed a committee to make proposals about the Church's funding of archaeology. NWAF and BYU's Department of Archaeology were involved. Several meetings were held in 1958 on campus chaired by BYU president, Ernest L. Wilkinson. M. Wells Jakeman, the chairman of the Archaeology Department, Gareth W. Lowe, NWAF field director, and Ross T. Christensen BYU professor of archaeology, were asked to define what they felt the future of archaeology should be and how it should be handled by the Church. The NWAF was completely independent at that time, although BYU allowed it to recruit students for field projects and gave them a certain amount of academic credit for such projects. There was, however, no financial or political connection between the two organizations.

The funding ran out in May 1959, midway through the season, and all field personnel left except for Frederick Peterson, acting field director, and Bruce W. Warren. They both worked on the artifact collection in the Tuxtla Regional Museum.

By the most fortunate of coincidences, the Mexican government, as part of its ongoing series of Round Tables focusing on some area of Mexico, had chosen Chiapas as the topic for the international conference, scheduled for September 1959 in San Cristobal. Peterson and Warren, asked to prepare displays for the visiting scholars, promptly began preparing all of the excavated material for display in the Regional Museum in Tuxtla Gutierrez. It was organized by time periods within each locale – not only Chiapa de Corzo but also the survey materials brought together by the different reconnaissance expeditions and test excavations at other sites.

The exhibit was featured as one of the highlights of the conference and was extensively viewed. As acting field director, Peterson made a point of asking delegates to send letters to Church officials appraising the importance of the materials and chronological sequence and expressing dismay at the lack of funding for continued work. Some directors of large museums and personnel from several universities as well as renowned scholars in Mexico wrote such letters.

In May 1960, Ferguson invited LDS Church and BYU officials to come to Mexico for an on-site visit. Elder Mark E. Petersen and Marion G. Romney of the Quorum of the Twelve apostles, represented the General Authorities, while Ernest L. Wilkinson and Joseph T. Bentley, president and comptroller respectively of BYU, represented the university. They were met by Daniel Taylor, who represented the Church schools in Mexico. Initially they were reserved and reluctant, but they were impressed by the museum exhibit and by El Mirador, a major Preclassic site in Chiapas that had been first excavated by NWAF personnel in 1957. Elder Romney reported his strong sensation that "something important happened here." They were thoroughly enjoying their visit by the time they reached Izapa (possibly either "the city beyond . . . in the borders by the seashore") [Alma 65:31] or the city of Judea [Alma 56:9, 15, 18, 57; 57:11]. Izapa is an important Pacific Coast site that was briefly studied by Matthew W. Stirling in April 1941. Here they viewed Stela 5, one of about eighty Preclassic monuments discovered at the site. (M. Wells Jakeman believes Stela 5 contains some important Mesoamerican and Near Eastern parallels on the Tree of Life theme.) Upon his return, Tom Ferguson jubilantly reported to his family that both General Authorities during the plane ride back had expressed enthusiasm for the project.

Those who had accompanied Ferguson returned to recommend continued Church support but also suggested that the NWAF be attached to and administered through BYU. The purpose would still be the same: to investigate the origins of the high civilizations of Mesoamerica but not to discuss direct connections with the Book of Mormon, but rather to allow the work to stand exclusively on its scholarly merits. This decision would protect the archaeologists from pressure to find a "Book of Mormon connection" that might endanger the scholarly objectivity of their work, but it also made the project less accessible to the average Latter-day Saint, whose only interest in Mesoamerican archaeology was the Book of Mormon. Still, it is accurate to say, as John L. Sorenson observed in 1955: "From the beginning, the New World Archaeological Foundation has held to a policy of objectivity. While an underlying Mormon hope for illuminating results in relation to the Book of Mormon was clear enough, the operational rule was always impeccably down-the-line archaeology" (Nelson 16).

This change took place effective 1 January 1961, with Elder Howard W. Hunter of the quorum of the Twelve Apostles as chairman of the board, a position he still holds as of this writing. Tom Ferguson became secretary of the board of directors and held that position until his death in 1983. Under this new system, BYU-NWAF was the sole source of funding for all Church-sponsored archaeological fieldwork in Mesoamerica. The emphasis on gaining scholarly credibility lasted from 1961 to 1975. A major find came in December 1961 with the discovery of fragments of a broken stela (Figure 97) at the so-called Peanut Field site in Chiapa de Corzo. One fragment, termed Stela 2 for identification purposes, contained the oldest Long Count calendar date system (that was used by the Maya) found in Mesoamerica to date. It was dated 9 December 36 B.C.

Also toward the end of November 1961, the organization for the project at Izapa was completed. Gareth Lowe, the field director, took most of the NWAF personnel and moved to Tapachula, a large city near the ruins of Izapa (Figure 98) and close to the Guatemalan border, where he began a four-year excavation project. Ferguson had been interested in an excavation at this site as early as 1957, when he decided that its many monuments would supply art materials paralleling Near Eastern mythic themes.

The site was a rich one — eighty monuments and several mounds (Ekholm; Lowe; Norman). A serious problem was looting. One stela with a crocodile design (Figure 99) was actually loaded on a truck and taken as far as Tapachula before the police were able to recover it. The site rewarded excavation efforts through the 1964 season, and more work was done at El Mirador, particularly in 1965. One of the most important finds was a portion of codex screenfold book measuring about three by four inches and in lumps about three-fourths of an inch thick, in

**Fig. 98: View of part of the ruins of Izapa, Chiapas, Mexico.**

extremely fragile condition. It was sent to Aero-Jet Laboratories in San Ramon, California, where different methods of analyzing the material were tried. A section of several pages was recovered and dated to the Early Classic (fourth century A.D.), but the original material was in a severe state of deterioration. It was stored carefully to await the development of more sophisticated techniques.

In June l962, Thomas A. Lee became NWAF's assistant field director, a position he held until 1975, when he became the field director. Also in 1962 more explorations were carried out in Chiapas (Figure 100). In the fall of 1965, the Mexican government asked the NWAF to cooperate in a salvage operation. The Mal Paso dam on the Grijalva was nearing completion, and the artificial lake it would create would flood practically all of the middle Grijalva.

From the fall of l965 through the spring of l966, the NWAF concentrated its energies on the area in a heroic effort that

**Fig. 99: Stela 25 at Izapa, Chiapas, Mexico.**

**Fig. 100: Airplane used in archaeological explorations in eastern Chiapas, Mexico, in 1962.**

located and mapped 100 sites and tested the most promising ones. San Isidro (possibly the city of Aaron in the Book of Mormon), the largest in the area and rich in Preclassic materials, showed fascinating connections to other areas, but the work was terminated by the rising waters in June 1966.

Three years later, the Mexican government again requested NWAF collaboration on an archaeological survey of Angostura Canyon, where another dam was planned. A 1970 field crew found many sites not located in earlier reconnaissance. The rising waters covered about 100 sites, including Santa Rosa. Some NWAF personnel shifted their attention to Campeche and other sites on the Pacific Coast.

In 1973-74, because of the flooding on the upper Grijalva, NWAF personnel decided to spend more time on the upper tributaries above the flooded areas. Tom Lee and James Murray White, a graduate student, did reconnaissance in the area and found Ocos horizons pottery, the earliest pottery found on the Pacific Coast of Chiapas.

As a result of this promising find and other factors, Lee

proposed a Maya project for the upper tributaries of the Grijalva which would work straight up to the Spanish period and through to 1821, the date used to begin the modern historical period. This decision represented a shift in the purpose and philosophical direction of NWAF away from a specialization in the Preclassic time period most closely linked to Book of Mormon times. It also precipitated a reorganization. Although Tom Ferguson protested this movement away from the foundation's original purpose, he continued to support Mesoamerican archaeology in general and to serve as secretary to the Board of Directors. Since 1961, the budget had come from Church general funds through BYU, not directly from the university, although Bentley had represented its interests well as a member of the board of directors until he was called to be a mission president in South America in 1975. In the following internal reorganization at Brigham Young University, Leo P. Vernon was named vice president of research and given general oversight, among other responsibilities, for the NWAF. Lowe was named director of NWAF, a newly created position, and Lee became field director.

This particular project of the upper tributaries of the Grijalva extends up to the present and has produced several important discoveries of figurines, pottery, and architecture. Deanne Matheny, now a law student at BYU, has completed a dissertation in Anthropology for the University of Utah on the site of Lagartero. Many BYU students have been involved in excavations. Pierre Agrinier has been working near Comitan at Tenam Rosario, and one masters thesis has emerged from that project. Much of the material is Classic, Late Classic, Post-classic, and colonial.

By October 1985, the NWAF publication series had produced forty-nine major publications, with several more at press or in preparation. These reports are "extremely valuable to archaeologists and are a must for any serious student of Mesoamerican archaeology" (Nelson 15). NWAF publications are mailed to almost all major university and archaeology departments in the country. Numerous NWAF articles have been published in leading archaeology journals and similar publications. Many leading Mesoamerican archaeologists have consulted with NWAF and benefited from their publications and work. NWAF is also the unquestioned leader in Mesoamerican archaeology, simply because of the extent and volume of its work. The Carnegie Institution, despite its fine work from the 1930s to 1955, worked only three months of the year instead of year round, as did NWAF personnel.

When John Sorenson was a student at Brigham Young University, Ferguson had a great influence in directing him to pursue the study of archaeology and the Book of Mormon. While Sorenson was a graduate student at BYU, Tom Ferguson took him on his first archaeology trip to Mexico in 1953. This was a very successful trip and increased Sorenson's interests in further study of the Book of Mormon. Sorenson went on to become a great scholar of Mesoamerican archaeology and the Book of Mormon. He became the department chairman of Archaeology and Anthropology at BYU. His recent outstanding book, *An Ancient American Setting for The Book of Mormon* (Deseret Book, 1985), contains one of the best discussions of the geography of the Book of Mormon ever published.

As Nelson pointed out in his 1983 appraisal before a professional group,

> Thomas Ferguson has either directly or indirectly influenced thousands of people's thinking on archaeology. He has directly influenced many people through his books and lectures. The Ferguson family is still receiving letters from people who have read his books and been impressed by them. He has had a great influence on professional archaeology through the Department of Archaeology at Brigham Young University, the Gates Collection, and the New World Archaeological Foundation.
>
> Many of us are the benefactors of his foresight and vision, his incredible drive and energy, and his ability to see a need and to organize a solution and see it through to fruition. We need more who are willing to sacrifice their time, talents, and money for the benefit of projects such as these. Thomas Stuart Ferguson's legacy in the founding of

the Archaeology Department at Brigham Young University, the obtaining of the Gates Collection, and as founder of the New World Archaeological Foundation stands as a shining example to us all." (Nelson 16-17)

## Final Tribute

It is appropriate to conclude this tribute to Thomas S. Ferguson with his testimony of the Book of Mormon. In 1982, the year before he died, he included a photo of himself and his wife and their testimony in several copies of the Books of Mormon that he distributed to non-Mormons.

We have studied the Book of Mormon for 50 years. We can tell you that it follows only the New Testament as a written witness to the mission, divinity, and resurrection of Jesus Christ. And it seems to us that there is no message that is needed by man and mankind more than the message of Christ. Millions of people have come to accept Jesus as the Messiah because of reading the Book of Mormon in a quest for truth. The book is the cornerstone of the Mormon Church.

The greatest witness to the truthfulness of the Book of Mormon is the book itself. But many are the external evidences that support it.

# APPENDIX B

## An Allegory of the House of Israel

### (V. Garth Norman)

> And there shall come forth a rod out of the stem of Jesse, and a branch shall grow out of his roots. (Isaiah 11:1)

Lehi taught that the Gentiles and the house of Israel:

> should be compared like unto an olive-tree, whose branches should be broken off and should be scattered upon all the face of the earth . . . And after the house of Israel should be scattered they should be gathered together again; or, in fine, after the Gentiles had received the fullness of the gospel, the natural branches of the olive-tree, or the remnants of the House of Israel, should be grafted in, or come to the knowledge of the true Messiah, their Lord and their Redeemer. (1 Ne. 10:12, 14)

One of the most intriguing Mesoamerican correspondences to Biblical and Book of Mormon metaphors is a connection between human history and trees. Different stages of human existence are associated with a sacred tree. The Yacatec Maya believe that roots of a giant ceiba tree reach into the underworld paradise beneath the earth, from which the spirits of the dead can ascend on a path up the tree through its branches into the highest heaven. The highland Maya Indians of Chiapas believe their ancestors came through the roots of the sacred *yaxche* tree of life or abundance (Thompson 1950: 71-72).

The Mixtecas Indians of Northern Oaxaca Mexico express their origin in the codices in pictographs showing a man emerging from a split tree trunk in symbolic birth (Figure 16). According to Fray Antonio de los Reyes, who recorded a Mixtec tradition at Apoala in 1593, the birth of their original ancestral king occurred through being lopped off a tree as a branch (Furst 1977: 184-185, 211).

The most graphic depiction of human descent symbolized in a tree is a Postclassic generation tree of the Xiu family of Mani, Yacatan, in which a tree sprouts from the loins of the Maya king (Morley 1946: Plate 22). Names of his descendants are recorded on branches and fruits of the tree.

In different contexts the broken Tamoanchan tree-trunk represents three major stages of history: the ancestral tree (land of birth or origin), the earthly paradise tree (goal of migratory traditions), and the heavenly paradise tree (destination of resurrected spirits). The Cakchiquel (Maya tribe in highland Guatemala) manuscript of Totonicapan (Recinos 1953: 45) tells of sacred places called Tulan that correspond to the three Tamoanchans of other traditions as the chosen homeland in Mesoamerica, the western place of birth and origin, and heaven. "From the west we came to Tulan, from across the sea; and it was at Tulan where we arrived." References to all three mythical and ancient legendary Tamoanchan/Tulans may be found on the Izapa Stela 5 tree-trunk dating to at least 300 B.C. (discussed below).

In the Totonicapan manuscript thirteen chiefs of twelve tribes (one didn't marry) of the Quiche nations are repeatedly referred to as the "trunk and root" of the tribal families (Recinos 1953: 169, 170, 172). This correlates perfectly with the human aspects in the Stela 5 tree with its twelve roots (Figure 18). In the *Popol Vuh*, sacred book of the Quiche maya, Balam-Quitze is referred to as "the root" *(xe)*, meaning first or original priest leader of the Cavec tribe. Also in the *Popol Vuh,* roots connected to a common "trunk" constitute a "single family," and different tribes of the Quiche family "trunk" are referred to as "branches" (Recinos 1950: 171, 227, 228; 229, n. 5). Names of trees are commonly used as proper names of Maya chiefs, tribes, and cities (Norman 1976: 207).

These are just a few of the many references to human symbolism in trees that could be cited from Mesoamerica. They have been selected to illustrate possible connections to the unique and very important Book of Mormon account of the Allegory of the Olive-Tree in Jacob 5. A detailed discussion of the Mesoamerican historical meaning of the tree-trunk on Izapa Stela 5, found in Norman 1976 (pp. 109-214), compares in many details to Jacob's allegory.

Following is a brief overview of the Allegory of the Olive-Tree, with some historical parallels as a foundation for beginning comparative studies.

### Establishment and Nourishment Period

A tame olive tree was nourished in a vineyard. It grew, waxed old and began to decay. It was then nourished and preserved for a time. Young and tender branches grew, but the main top of the tree began to perish (Jacob 5:3-6).

### Grafting Preservation Period

The Lord plucked off the withered branches and burned them. He also took the young and tender branches and grafted them in other parts of the vineyard. The servant grafted in wild branches in their places, and digged about, pruned, and nourished the tree (7-14).

### Production and Righteousness Period

After a long time, the master and his servant went into the vineyard and beheld that the wild branches "had sprung forth and began to bear (good) fruit." They went where the natural branches were hid. The first and second branches had brought forth much (good) fruit. Another branch had brought forth fruit also. Of the last tree, planted in a good spot of ground, only part brought forth good fruit, while the other part produced wild fruit. The Lord and his servant nourished all the fruit of the vineyard (15-28).

### Corruption and Scattering Period

As the time of the end drew near, the Lord and his servant went in the vineyard again. All the fruit had become corrupt. "And the wild fruit of the last had overcome that part of the tree which brought forth good fruit, even that the branch had withered away and died" (29-40).

### Regrafting, Restoration and Pruning Period

The Lord and his servant went to work in the corrupted vineyard. "They took from the natural tree [(Gentiles)] which had become wild and grafted in unto the natural trees which also had become wild. And they also took of the natural trees which had become wild and grafted into the mother tree (Israel)." Other servants (though few in number) are called and instructed: "let us go to and labor with our might this last time to prune my vineyard." (End to follow the last pruning.) They are instructed to pluck off the most bitter wild branches and graft in the branches, beginning at the last, "that they may be first, and that the first may be last." "They labored with all diligence. . . even until the bad had been cast away out of the vineyard (Kingdom of God) . . . and the trees had become again the natural fruit; and they became like unto one body; and the fruits were equal." (41-74)

### Harvesting and Destruction Period

The servants are called up. The vineyard has been nourished and pruned for the last time and the bad has been cast away. The Lord says, "For behold, for a long time will I lay up of the fruit of my vineyard unto mine own self against the season, which speedily cometh. . . . And when the time cometh that evil fruit shall again come into my vineyard, then will I cause the good and the bad to be gathered; and the good will I preserve unto myself, and the bad will I cast away into its own place. And then cometh the season and the end; and my vineyard will I cause to be burned with fire. (75-77)

## Historical Parallels to the Allegory of the Olive Tree

### Establishment and Nourishment Period

Abraham (born about 1980 B.C.), Isaac, and Jacob were the covenant fathers of the house of Israel (Abr. 2:10-11; Gen. 12:1-5; 13:14-17; 17:5-7, 15-19; 28:12-15; 1 Ne. 17:40). The Lord named Jacob, Israel. The house of Israel took root and grew through Jacob's twelve sons. During their 450 years in Egypt they became greater in number and strength than the Egyptians (Ex. 1:9; Acts 13:20). They began to decay under Egyptian bondage because they could not worship the Lord properly. So the Lord appointed Moses (born just about 1300 B.C.) to deliver them (Ex. 3:7-10). Israel was pruned, digged about, and nourished through the ministry of Moses and succeeding prophets, but it never emerged as a righteous nation. Young and tender branches (righteous individuals) emerged, but the nation as a whole never did.

### Grafting Preservation Period

During the later half of the Mosaic dispensation, the "young and tender branches" of righteousness which had grown in Israel were separated in order to preserve them and develop righteous fruit (people). The ten tribes were taken captive into Assyria in 721 B.C. and shortly afterward escaped into the north. They became a righteous branch (3 Ne. 15:20) and are to return in these latter days (Gen. 18:11-12; D&C 110:11). Prior to the destruction of Jerusalem in 586 B.C., Lehi and his colony were separated to preserve a righteous branch and produce good fruit (Jacob 2:25; 1 Ne. 2:1-2). Mulek also led a group from Jerusalem at the time of this destruction; they were led to America, as was Lehi, and eventually joined with the Nephites (Omni 15,16). At the time of Lehi's departure, most of the children of Israel had already been "led away." Nephi said, "they are scattered to and fro upon the isles of the sea. . . . We know that they have been led away" (1 Ne. 22:4).

Finally the wild branches (Gentiles) are grafted in after the natural branches still on the mother tree have become corrupted. After the Jews rejected the Gospel of Jesus Christ, the Apostles left them and went among the Gentlies (Acts 18:4-6). (See Amos 9:8-9.)


**Production and Righteousness Period**

During a short period of about a decade after Christ (the apostolic ministry), the Gospel "sprang forth" among the Gentiles and "began to bear fruit." The Epistles of the Apostles give an account of this period. The branches of Israel which had been led away before Lehi's time (first two branches cited) had brought forth much fruit. The third and fourth branches might refer to the Mulekites and Nephites. The fourth branch compares with the Nephites and Lamanites in that "only a part of the branch brought forth tame fruit" (Jacob 5:20-25).

During this visit of the Lord and his servant, it is seen that the four trees mentioned, which contain the natural branches, are good and have produced "much fruit," with the exception of the last tree, which was part good and part bad. At this time, the natural tree upon which the wild branches had been grafted had not produced a lot of good fruit like the other trees but had only "sprung forth and begun to bear fruit" (Jacob 5:17). Therefore, we may logically place this inspection time during the early part of the development of the Church of Jesus Christ among the Gentiles.

The wording of the allegory in other parts suggests literal interpretation rather than figurative. This visit is the first time that the Lord personally assists the servant in nourishing it (Jacob 5:28). Before this time the Lord instructs his servant (prophet) to do the work of pruning, digging, and nourishing in striving to establish the Kingdom (Jacob 5:10-12), while the Lord only works directly in destroying the wicked branches and placing the young and tender branches in other parts of his vineyard (Jacob 5:9, 13). Before this time, the *trees* and *branches* are nourished (people collectively — branch, ward, church), but at this point the Lord personally nourishes the *fruit* (contact with the individual people). The fruits are the people (Jacob 5:74). In view of these points it is significant to note that as the God of Israel, Christ never came personally among the house of Israel until after his resurrection (Matt. 28). He dwelt among the people of Enoch (Moses 7:16, 69), but the dispensations of Abraham and Moses never progressed to the point where they were able to be gifted with Christ's personal presence. It wasn't until after Christ's earthly mission was completed that he again came among men as the glorified God to bless and instruct them. While preaching to the Jews, Jesus said: "And other sheep I have, which are not of this fold: them also I must bring, and they shall hear my voice; and there shall be one fold, and one shepherd" (John 10:16). The Book of Mormon gives an account of Christ establishing His church among these other people. He repeats the above passage and tells them that they were the other sheep (3 Ne. 15:13-24). From the time of Lehi's exodus, the Nephites knew these circumstances. While in the Near Eastern wilderness Nephi taught his brothers "that the house of Israel was compared unto an olive tree, by the spirit of the Lord which was in our fathers; and behold are we not broken off from the house of Israel, and are we not a branch of the house of Israel?" (1 Ne. 15:12). Christ at this same visit said that the Father has separated the other tribes from them (the Jews); and it is because of the Jews' iniquity that they know not of them (3 Ne. 16:1-3).

At the time when the Lord visited the righteous Nephites in America, there were also many unrighteous Lamanites in the land. In the allegory the Lord saw the partly bad tree, and spoke of destroying the branches that produced bad fruit, but the servant prevailed upon the Lord to "prune it and dig about it, and nourish it a little longer, that perhaps it may bring forth good fruit" (Jacob 5:27). It is significant that after Christ established his Church among the Nephites in A.D. 30, it was only a period of approximately two years until all the Nephites and Lamanites were converted to the Church of Christ (4 Ne. 1-2).

### Corruption and Scattering Period

Following a period of righteousness throughout the tribes of Israel, a time came when all of the branches became corrupt. The Lord made another visit, observing the wild branches first (Gentiles), and saw that they had become corrupt (Jacob 5:30). After the Apostles of Christ established His church among the Gentiles, a "great and abominable church" took away from the gospel "many parts which are plain and most precious; and also many covenants, . . . that they [its priests] might pervert the right ways of the Lord" (1 Ne. 13:26-27). Historically this took place between A.D. 90 and 100. The book of Revelation evidently refers to this period. (See Rev. 6:9-12.) The Lord then went into other parts of his vineyard and observed total corruption throughout. By A.D. 300 the descendants of Lehi on the American continent had all become extremely wicked (4 Ne. 1:45), and by A.D. 375 the Lamanites had completely destroyed the Nephites (Morm. 6:5, 15; see Rev. 12:17; 1 Ne. 11:35; 15:16-18). The prophecies of Isaiah refer to this period of total corruption before the restoration (2 Ne. 20:16-21).

### Regrafting, Restoration and Pruning Period

The Book of Mormon is most clear on this particular period. There are well over a hundred references to the latter-day restoration of the gospel. Because this is in our time and we are familiar with it, we will not take the space to outline these events. The allusions of the allegory are quite clear.

### Harvesting and Destruction Period

The Book of Mormon is not very explicit on this millennial period, except for the Savior's teachings (3 Ne. 24-25). This is likely because these events are being withheld from our knowledge until a yet future day, and because John the revelator was appointed to record this period (1 Ne. 14:20-27). First Nephi 22:16-26 describes this period briefly.

# BIBLIOGRAPHY

NOTE: All references to the New World Archaeological Foundation are abbreviated NWAF; references to The Society for Early Historic Archaeology are abbreviated SEHA.


Ackerman, Phyllis. "The Dawn of Religions." *Ancient Religions: A Symposium.* Ed. Vergilius Ferm. New York: Philosophical Library, 1950. 3-24.

---. "Stars and Stories." *Myth and Mythmaking.* Ed. Henry A. Murray. New York: George Braziller, 1960. 90-102.

Adam, Leonhard. *Primitive Art.* Baltimore: Penguin Books, 1954.

Adams, Daniel B. "Last Ditch Archaeology." *Science* 4 (1983): 28-37.

Agrinier, Pierre. "Linguistic Evidence for the Presence of Israelites in Mexico." Newsletter and Proceedings of the S.E.H.A. 112.1 (28 Feb. 1969) Provo: SEHA. 4-5.

Albright, William Foxwell. *Archaeology and the Religion of Israel.* Baltimore: John Hopkins UP, 1946.

---. *The Archaeology of Palestine.* Baltimore: Penguin, 1949.

---. "The Biblical Period." Reprinted from *The Jews: Their History, Culture and Religion.* Ed. Louis Finkelstein. New York: Harper Brothers, 1950.

---. *From the Stone Age to Christianity Monotheism and the Historical Process.* New York: Doubleday, 1957.

Alvarado, Tezozomoc, H. *Cronica Mexicana Escrita Hacia El Ano de 1598.* Notes de Manuel Orozco y Berra. Mexico City: Editorial Leyenda, 1944.

Andrae, Walter, ed. *Coloured Ceramics from Assur, and Earlier Ancient Assyrian Wall-Paintings, from Photographs and*

Water-Colours by Members of the Asher Expedition Organized by the Deutsche Orient Gesellschaft. K. Paul, French, Trench, Trubner, & Co. Ltd, 1925.

Andrews, E. Wylls. Archaeology of Southwestern Campeche. Carnegie Institute of Washington. Contribution 40, 1943.

Arte Prehispanico de Mexico. Mexico City: Instituto Nacional de Anthropologia e Historia, 1946.

Ashton, Dore. Abstract Art Before Columbus. New York: 1957.

Audrain, Michel. The Glory of Egypt. London: Thames and Hudson, 1955.

Augur, Helen. Zapotec. Garden City, New York: Doubleday, 1954.

Aveni, Anthony F. Skywatchers of Ancient Mexico. Austin: U of Texas Press, 1980.

Bancroft, Hubert H. The Native Races of the Pacific States. 5 vols. San Fransisco: The History Company, 1883-86.

Barker, James L. The Divine Church. Vol. 2. Salt Lake City: Deseret Book, 1951.

Bass, Robert Wauchope. "Documentary Evidence of Identity of the Maya Great-Great Cycle Doctrine and the Ancient Near Eastern Equinoctial Precession Doctrine." Ms. Provo, 1975.

Ben-Gurion, David. Rebirth and Destiny of Israel. New York: Philosophical Library, 1954.

Bennett, Wendel C. Ancient Arts of the Andes. New York: Museum of Modern Art, 1954.

Birrell, Verla L. The Book of Mormon Guide Book. Salt Lake City: Verla Birrell, 1948.

Blanton, Richard E. Monte Alban: Settlement Patterns at the Ancient Zapotec Capitol. New York: Academic Press, 1978.

Blom, Frans. Conquest of Yucatan. Boston: Houghton Mifflin, 1936.

Brainerd, George W. "Early Ceramic Horizons in Yucatan." The Civilizations of Ancient America. Ed. Sol Tax. Vol. 1 Selected Papers in the 29th International Congress of Americanists. New York: Cooper Square, 1951. 72-78.

Breasted, James Henry. A History of Egypt. New York: Scribner's, 1948.

Briggs, Lyman J., and Kenneth F. Weaver. "How Old Is It?" National Geographic Magazine Volume 114 (August 1958): 234ff.

Brinton, Daniel G. The Abbe Brasseur de Bourbourg and his Labors. Vol. 1. Philadelphia: Lippincott's Magazine, 1868. 79-86.

---. American Hero-Myths, A Study in the Native Religions of the

*Western Continent*. Philadelphia: 1882.

---. *Nagualism, A Study in Native American Folklore and History*. Philadelphia: Proceedings, American Philosophical Society, 1894.

Brockington, Donald. *The Ceramic History of Santa Rosa, Chiapas, Mexico. Papers of the NWAF 23*. Provo, Utah: NWAF, 1967.

Brotherston, Gordon. *Image of the New World: The American Continent Portrayed in Native Texts*. London: Thames & Hudson, 1979.

---. *A Key to the Mesoamerican Reckoning of Time: The Chronology Recorded in Native Texts. British Museum Occasional Papers 38*. London: British Museum, 1982.

Bruce, Robert. "The Popol Vuh and the Book of Chan K'in." *Estudios de Cultura Maya*. Vol 10. Mexico City: Seminario de Estudios Mayas, Universidad Nacional Autonoma de Mexico, 1976-1977. 173-208.

Budge, Sir Ernest Alfred Wallis. *Babylonian Life and History*. Religious Tract Society: London, 1886.

Burrows, M. *What Mean These Stones?* New Haven, Connecticut: American School of Oriental Research, 1941.

Campbell, Joseph. *Oriental Mythology*. Vol. 2 *The Masks of God*. New York: Viking, 1976.

Carmack, Robert M. "New Quichean Chronicles from Highland Guatamala." Estudios de Cultura Maya Vol. XII. Mexico City: Universidad National Autonoma de Mexico, 1981. 83-103.

---. *The Quiche Mayas of Utatlan: The Evolution of a Highland Guatemala Kingdom*. Norman: U of Oklahoma Press, 1981.

Carmack, Robert M. and James L. Mondlach. *El Tituto de Totonicapan: Texto, traduccion y comentario*. Fuentes Para El Estudio de la Cultura Maya, 3. Mexico: Universidad Nacional Autonoma de Mexico, 1983.

Carter, George F. "Plants Across the Pacific." *Memoirs, Society for American Archaeology* 9 (1953): 63-71.

---. "Civilization Puzzle." *Johns Hopkins Magazine* February 1957.

Caso, Alfonso. *La Religion de los Aztecas*. Mexico, D.F.: Enciclopedia Ilustrada Mexicana, 1936.

---. *Calendario y Escritura de las Antiguas Culturas de Monte Alban. Obras Completas de Miguel Othon de Mendizabal* Vol. 1, 1947. 113-45.

---. "Glifos Teotihuacanos." *Revista Mexicana de Estudios Antropologias* Vol. 15. Mexico, 1959. 57-70.

---. *Interpretacion del Codice Bodley 2858.* Mexico City: Sociedad Mexicana de antropologia, 1960.

Ceram, C. W. *Secret of the Hittites.* New York: Alfred A. Knopf, 1956.

Caso, Alfonso, Ignacio Bernal, and Jorge R. Acosta. *La Ceramica de Monte Alban. Memorias del Instituto Nacional de Antropologia e Historia XIII.* Instituto de Antropologia E Historia: Mexico, 1967.

Chadwick, Robert L. "Archaeological Synthesis of Michoacan and Adjacent Regions." *Handbook of Middle American Indians.* Vol. 11. Ed. Gordon R. Ekholm and Ignacio Bernal. Austin: U of Texas Press, 1971. 691-692.

---. "The Archaeology of a New World Merchant Culture." Ph.D. diss. Tulane University, 1974.

---. "Ezekiel 27: an Apparent Transatlantic Expedition Around 500 B.C." Paper presented at the Twenty-fourth Annual Symposium on the Archaeology of the Scriptures held at Brigham Young University on 26 October 1974.

Charney, Desire. *The Ancient Cities of the New World.* Trans. J. Gonino and Helen S. Conant. New York: Harper and Brothers, 1887.

Chimalpahin Quauhtlehuanitzin, Domingo Francisco de San Anton Munon. *Relaciones Originales de Chalco Amaquemecan.* Ed. S. Rendon. Mexico: Fondo de Cultura Economic, 1965.

Christensen, Erwin O. *Primitive Art.* New York: Thomas Y. Crowell Publishing Co., 1955.

Coe, Michael D. "Cycle 7 Monuments in Middle America: A Reconsideration." *American Anthropologist* 59 (1957): 597-611.

---. "Pre-Classic Cultures in MesoAmerica: A Comparative Study." *Kroeber Anthropological Society Papers* 17 (1957): 7-37.

Corona Nunez, Jose. (ed.) *Selden Roll. Antiquedades de Mexico Basedos en la Recopilacion de Lord Kingsborough* Vol. 1. Mexico City: Secretaria de Hacienda y Credito Publico, 1964. 101-113.

Covarrubias, Miguel. *Mexico South.* New York: Alfred A. Knopf, 1949.

---. *Indian Art of Mexico and Central America.* New York: Alfred A. Knopf, 1957.

Cros, Gaston. *Nouvelles Fouilles De Tello.* Paris: E. Leroux, 1910-1914. (Issued in 3 parts, dated 1910, 1911, 1914.) 1914.

Cummings, Byron. "Cuicuilco and the Archaic Culture of Mexico." *University of Arizona Bulletin* 4.8. Tucson: Social Science Bulletin, 1933.

D'Alviella, Count Goblet, Eugene Felicien Albert. *The Migration of Symbols.* New York: University Books Inc., 1956. [A reproduction of the original work published at Westminster in London, in 1894.]

Dahlgren de Jordan, Barbro. *La Mixteca: see Cultura E Historia Prehispanicas.* Mexico: Imprenta Universitaria, 1954.

Davis, John D., and Henry Synder Gehman. *The Westminister Dictionary of the Bible.* Philadelphia: Westminister P, 1944.

Davies, Nigel. *Voyagers to the New World.* New York: William Morrow, 1979.

De Gurgh, William Geoge. *The Legacy of the Ancient World.* London, Baltimore: Penguin Books, 195. 1952.

De Charencey, H. *Les Cites Votanides.* Paris: Ch. Peeters, 1885.

Delgado, Agusin. *Excavations at Santa Rosa, Chiapas, Mexico.* Papers of the NWAF 17. Provo, Utah, 1965.

Diaz-Bolio, Jose. *Le Serpiente Emplumada.* Merida: Registro de Cultura Yucatan, 1952.

Diaz Del Castillo, Bernal. *The Discovery and Conquest of Mexico.* Mexico: Edicionas Tolteca, 1953.

Dinsmoor, William Bell. "An Account of Its Historic Development." *The Architecture of Ancient Greece.* 3rd ed. rev. London: Unwin Brothers Ltd., 1950.

Dixon, Keith A. "Two Masterpieces of Middle American Bone Sculpture." *American Antiquity* 24.1 (1958): 53-62.

Doran, Edwin, Jr. "The Sailing Raft as a Great Tradition." *Man across the Sea: Problems of Pre-Columbian Contacts.* Ed. Riley et al. Austin, U of Texas Press, 1974.

Dressler, Robert L. "The Pre-Columbian Cultivated Plants of Mexico." *Botanical Museum Leaflets* 16.6. Harvard University, 1953.

Drucker, Philip. *Ceramic Sequences at Tres Zapotes, Vera Cruz, Mexico.* Bureau of American Ethnology, Bull. 140, Smithsonian Institution, 1943.

---. *La Venta, Tabasco, A Study of Olmec Ceramics and Art.* Bureau of

American Ethnology Bulletin 153, Smithsonian Institution, 1952.

Ehrle, Franz. *Codice Messicano Borgiano.* Roma: Stablimento Danesi, 1898.

Ekholm, Gordon F. *Excavations at Tampico and Panuco in the Huasteca, Mexico.* American Museum of Natural History, Anthropological Papers 38, 1944. 321-509.

Ekholm, Susanna M. *Mound 30a and the Early Preclassic Ceramic Sequence at Izapa, Chiapas, Mexico.* Papers of the NWAF 25. Provo, Utah: 1969.

Enslin, Morton Scott. *Christian Beginnings, Parts I and II.* New York: Harper and Brothers, 1956.

Fabrega, Jose Lino. *Interpretacion del Codice Borgiano. Anales del Museo Nacional de Mexico.* Vol. 5. Mexico, 1899. 1-260.

Farbridge, Maurice H. *Studies in Biblical and Semitic Symbolism.* Hartford, England: Stephen Austin and Sons, Ltd., 1923.

Ferguson, Thomas Stuart. *Cumorah--Where?* Independence, Missouri: Zion's Printing Co., 1947.

---. "Joseph Smith and American Archaeology." *Bulletin of the University Archaeological Society* 4 (March 1953): 19-25.

---. *One Fold and One Shepherd.* San Fransisco: Books of California, 1958 and 1962.

---. Personal Papers. Manuscripts and Archives, Harold B. Lee Library. Brigham Young University, Provo, Utah.

Ferm, Vergilius. *Ancient Religions: A Symposium.* New York: Philosophical Library, 1950.

Flannery, Kent V, ed. *The Early Mesoamerican Village.* New York: Academic Press, 1976.

Flannery, Kent V. and Joyce Marcus, Eds. *The Cloud People: Divergent Evolution of the Zapotec and Mixtec Civilizations.* New York: Academic Press, 1983.

Frankfort, Henri et al. *The Intellectual Adventure of Ancient Man.* Chicago: U of Chicago Press, 1946.

Frankfort, Henri. *Cylinder Seals.* London: Gregg, 1948.

---. *The Birth of Civilization in the Near East.* Bloomington: U of Indiana Press, 1951.

---. *The Art and Architecture of the Ancient Orient.* Baltimore, Maryland: Penguin Books, 1955.

Freedman, David Noel. "The Babylonian Chronicle." *Biblical Archaeologist* 19.3 (1956): 50-60.

Friedrich, Johannes. *Extinct Languages.* New York: Philosophical Library, 1957.

Furst, Jill Leslie. "The Tree Birth Tradition in the Mixteca, Mexico." *Journal of Latin American Lore.* 3.2 (1977): 183-226.

---. *Codex Vindobonensis Mexicanus I: A Commentary.* Institute for Mesoamerican Studies 4. Albany: SUNY, 1978.

Gadd, C. J. *History and Monuments of Ur.* London: Dutton 1929.

Garcia Payon, Jose. "Una Palma *in Situ.*" *Revista Mexicana de Estudios Antropologicos* Vol. 10. Sociedad Mexicana de Antropologia, 1948-49.

---. "Archaeology of Central Veracruz." *Handbook of Middle American Indians.* Vol. II. Ed. Gordon F. Ekholm and Ignacio Bernal. Austin: U of Texas Press, 1971. 16 Vols.

Gardiner, Alan H. "The Baptism of Pharoah." *Journal of Egyptian Archaeology.* Vol. 36. 1955. 3-12.

Gardiner, Helen. *Art Through the Ages.* New York: Harcourt, 1948.

Gardner, Brant. "The Christianization of Quetzalcoatl." *Sunstone* Vol. 10.11 (Sep 1986): 6-10.

Gardini, Walter. *Influencias de Asia en las Culturas Precolombinas: Estado Actual de las Investigaciones.* Buenos Aires: Ediciones Depalma, 1978.

Girard, Rafael. *Los Chortis Ante el Problema Maya.* Mexico City: Antiqua Libreria Robredo, 1949.

. *El Popol Vuh Fuente Historica.* Guatemala: Minestero de Educacion Publica, 1952.

Gladwin, Harold Sterling. *Men Out of Asia.* New York: Whittlesey House, 1947.

Glass, John B. in collaboration with Donald Robertson. *A Census of Native Middle American Pictoral Manuscripts. Handbook of Middle American Indians.* Vol. 14. Ed. Howard F. Cline, et al. Austin: U of Texas Press, 1975. 81-252.

Glueck, Nelson. "Exploration in Eastern Palestine II." *Annual of the American School of Oriental Research* 15 (1935): 1-202.

Goetz, Delia, and Sylvanus G. Morley, trans. *Popol Vuh: The Sacred Book of the Ancient Quiche Maya.* Norman: U of Oklahoma Press, 1950.

Goodenough, Erwin R. *Jewish Symbols in the Greco-Roman Period.* Vol. 7. Toronto, Canada: McClelland and Stewart, Ltd., 1958.

Graves, Robert. *The Greek Myths.* Vol. 1. New York: George Braziller, 1957.

Grigson, Geoffrey, and Edwin Smith. *Art Treasures of the British*

*Museum.* London: Thames and Hudson, 1957.

Groth-Kimball, Irmgard. *The Art of Ancient Mexico.* London: Thames & Hudson Company, 1955.

Gurney, O.R. *The Hittites.* Baltimore: Penguin, 1952.

Hammond, Norman. "The Earliest Maya." *Scientific American* 236 (1977): 116-33.

---. "Early Maya Ceremonial at Cuello, Belize." *Antiquity* 54 (1980): 176-90.

Hanson, Paul M. *In the Land of the Feathered Serpent.* Independence, Missouri: Herald Publishing House, 1949.

Harris, Franklin S., Jr. *The Book of Mormon Message and Evidences.* Salt Lake City: Deseret News Press, 1953.

Hartner, Willy. "The Earliest History of the Constellations in the Near East in the Motif of the Lion Bull Combat." *Journal of Near Eastern Studies* 24.1-2 (1965): 1-36.

Harvey, Herbert R. "Cultural Continuity in Central Mexico: A Case for Otomanque." *Actas y Memorias del XXXV Congresso International de Americanistas.* Vol. 2. Mexico City, 1964. 525-32.

Hay, Clarence L. et al., eds. *Maya and Their Neighbors.* New York and London: D. Appleton-Century Company, Inc. 1941.

Hays, William C. *The Scepter of Egypt.* New York: Metropolitan Museum of Art, 1953.

Herodotus. *The Persian Wars.* Trans. George Rawlinson. New York: The Modern Library, 1942.

Herrmann, Paul. *Conquest by Man.* New York: Harper & Brothers, 1954.

Heyerdahl, Thor. *American Indians in the Pacific.* London: G. Allen and Univin, 1952.

---. *The Ra Expeditions.* Garden City, New York: Doubleday, 1971.

Hinke, William J. *A New Boundary Stone of Nebuchanezzar I from Nippur.* Philadelphia: U of Pennsylvania, 1907.

Holbrook, Neil K. "Remarks at the Funeral of Thomas Stuart Ferguson." 21 March 1983. Photocopy of typescript in possession of Larry Ferguson.

Holy Bible. King James Version, A Concise Biblical Encyclopedia (Addendum to the Holy Bible, Missionary edition. Distributed by The Deseret Book Company, Salt Lake City, Utah) Cambridge, England: The University Press, 1979.

Hrozny, Bedrich. *Ancient History of Western Asia, India and Crete.*

Prague: Artia, 1953.

Huber, Jay M. "Lehi's 600 Year Prophecy and the Birth of Christ." *Foundation for Ancient Research and Mormon Studies, Preliminary Report, HUB-82.* Provo, Utah: FARMS, 1982.

Humboldt, Alexander von. *Vues des cordilleres et monuments des peuples indigines de l'Amerique.* Paris: F. Schoell, 1810.

Hunter, Milton R. and Thomas Stuart Ferguson. *Ancient America and The Book of Mormon.* Oakland, California: Kolob Book, 1950.

Hunter, Milton R. *Archaeology and The Book of Mormon.* Salt Lake City, Utah: Deseret Book, 1956.

Ixtlilxochitl, Don Fernando de Alva. *Obras Historicas.* 2 vols. Ed. Edmundo O'Gorman. Mexico City: Universidad Nacional de Mexico, 1975.

Jackson, Wilfred. "The Geographical Distribution of the Shell Purple Industry." Memoirs and Proceedings. Vol. 60. *Manchester Literature and Philosophy*, 1916

Jacobsen, Thorkild. *The Intellectual Adventure of Ancient Man.* Ed. H. and H. A. Frankfort et al. U of Chicago Press, 1946.

Jakeman, M. Wells. *The Origins and History of the Mayas.* Los Angeles: Research Publishing, 1945.

---. "The Ancient Middle-American Calendar System: Its Origin and Development." *Archaeology and Early History.* Brigham Young University Publications 1, 1949.

---, ed. and trans. *The "Historical Recollections of Gaspar Antoio Chi: An Early Source Account of Ancient Yucatan."* Brigham Young University Publications in Archaeology and Early History, 3. Provo, Utah, 1952.

---. "An Unusual Tree-of-Life Sculpture from Ancient Central America." *Bulletin of the [Brigham Young] University Archaeological Society* No. 4 (1953): 26-49.

---. *Discovering the Past.* Provo, Utah: Brigham Young University, 1954.

---. *Stela 5, Izapa, Chiapas, Mexico.* University Archaeological Society. Provo, Utah: Brigham Young University, 1958.

James, E. O. *The Ancient Gods: The History and Diffusion of Religion in the Ancient Near East and the Eastern Mediterranean.* New York: Putnam's, 1960.

Jett, Stephen C. "Diffusion Versus Independent Development." Riley et al. 1974. 5-53.

Jimenez Moreno, Wigberto. *El Occidente de Mexico, Sociedad*

*Mexicana de Antropologia*. Mexico: IV Reunion de la Mesa Redonda. Mexico City: Sociedad Mexicana de Antropolgia, 1948. 146-57.

---. *Sintesis de la Historia Pretolteca de Mesoamerica. Esplendar del Mexico Antiguo*. Vol. 1. Ed. Raul Noriega, Carmen Cook de Leonard, and Julio Rodolfo Moctezuma. Mexico City: Centro de Investigacians Antropologies, 1959. 1019-1108

Jobes, Gertrude. *Dictionary of Mythology Folklore and Symbols*. New York: Scarecrow Press, 1961.

Johnson, Frederick, ed. "Radiocarbon Dating." Memoir 8. Menasha, WI: Society for American Archaeology, 1951.

Jordan, Bart. "Pentatuch, Patriarchs, Prism, Planets, and Precession." *New England Antiquities Research Association Journal* 19.3 (1985): 59-61.

---. "Measure Man's Mind and Mind Man's Measure." *New England Antiquities Research Association Journal* 19.4 (1985): 65-78.

Jorgensen, Bruce W. "The Dark Way to the Tree: Typological Unity in the Book of Mormon." *Literature of Belief: Sacred Scripture and Religious Experience*. Ed. Neal E. Lambert. Salt Lake City, Utah: Publishers Press for BYU Religious Studies Center, 1981. 217-32.

Kaufman, Terrence. "Mesoamerican Indian Languages." *Encyclopedia Britanica*. 15th ed. Vol. 11. 1974. 956-63.

---. "Archaeological and Linguistic Correlations in Maya Land and Associate Areas of Mesoamerica." *World Archaeology* 8.1 (1976): 101-118.

Kelemen, Pal. *Medieval American Art*. New York: The Macmillan Co., 1956.

Keller, Werner. *The Bible as History*. New York: William Morrow, 1956.

Kelley, David H. "Calendar Animals and Deities." *Southwestern Journal of Anthropology* 16 (1960): 317-37.

---. "Eurasian Evidence and the Mayan Calendar Correlation Problem." *Mesoamerican Archaeology: New Approaches*. Ed. Norman Hammond. Austin: U of Texas Press, 1974. 135-44.

---. "The World Ages in India and Mesoamerica." *Newsletter and Proceedings of the S.E.H.A* 137. March. Provo, Utah: SEHA, 1975.

---. "Astronomical Identities of Mesoamerican Gods." *Archaeoastronomy Supplement to the Journal for the History of Astronomy* 2. Vol. 11. 1980. s1-s54.

---. "The Maya Calendar Correlation Problem." *Civilization in the Ancient Americas: Essays in Honor of Gordon R. Willey.* Albuquerque and Cambridge: U of New Mexico Press and Peabody Museum of Archaeology and Ethnology, 1983. 157-208

Kelso, James L. "Excavations at Bethel." *Biblical Archaeologist* 19 (1956): 36-39.

Kidder, Alfred and Edwin M. Shook. "Mound E-III-3, Kaminaljuyu, Guatemala." *Carnegie Institution of Washington Publications* 596, 1952.

Kidder, Alfred V., Jesse D. Jennings, and Edwin M. Shook. *Excavations at Kaminaljuyu, Guatemala.* Carnegie Institution of Washington Publication 561, 1946.

Kingsborough (Edward King) Lord. *Antiquities of Mexico.* 9 vols. London: Henry G. Bohn, 1841-48.

Kirkham, Frances W. *A New Witness for Christ in America.* Independence, Missouri: Zion's Printing, 1951.

Kluckholm, Clyde. "Suppose Columbus Had Stayed Home." *Saturday Review* 22 September 1956. 9-10, 37.

Kramer, Samuel Noah. "Enki and Ninhursag." *Bulletin of American Schools of Oriental Research.* New Haven, Connecticut: Supplementary Studies 1, 1945

---. *From the Tablets of Sumer.* Indian Hills, Colorado: The Falcon's Wing Press, 1956.

Kroeber, Alfred. L. *Anthropology.* New York: Harcourt, Brace, 1948.

Landa, Diego de. *Relacion de las Cosas de Yucatan.* Trans. and ed. Alfred M. Tozzer. Papers of the Museum of Archaeology, Harvard University. Vol. 18. 1941.

Lange, Kurt and Max Hirmer. *Egypt, Architecture, Sculpture Painting in Three Thousand Years.* London: Phaidon, 1957.

Laughlin, Robert M. *The Great Tzotzil Dictionary of San Lorenzo Zinacatan.* Smithsonian Contributions to Anthropology 19. Washington, D.C.: Smithsonian Institution Press, 1975.

Las Casas, Fray Bartolome de. *Apologetica Historia de las Indies.* 2 Vols. Biblioteca de Autores Espanoles, Nos. 105: I 106: II. Madrid.

Layard, Austen Henry. *Discoveries among the Ruins of Nineveh and Babylon.* New York: G.P. Putnam, 1853.

Lecomte Du Nouy, Pierre. *Human Destiny.* New York: Longmans,

Green, 1947.

"Legends 'Brought Back Home.'": Rare Booklet Found; Leaders, Scholars are Given Copy. *Church News,* Church Section. 26 May 1985, page 11.

Leonard, Irving Albert. *Don Carlos de Siguenza y Gongora.* Berkeley, California: U of California Press, 1929.

*Life,* Editors of. *The Epic of Man.* New York: Time Incorporated, 1961.

Lindemann, Hannes. "Alone at Sea for 72 Days." *Life* 43 22 July 1957. 92-108.

Lloyd, Seton. *Foundations in the Dust.* London: Oxford University Press, 1947.

---. *The Art of the Ancient Near East.* New York: Frederick A. Praeger, 1961.

Lothrop, Samuel K., William F. Foshag, and Joy Mahler. *Pre-Columbian Art.* London: Phaidon, 1957.

Loud, G. *Khorsabad II.* Chicago: Oriental Institute Publication, No. 40, 1938.

Lounsbury, Floyd G. *Maya Numeration, Computation, and Calendrical Astronomy. Dictionary of Scientific Biography.* Vol. 15. Supplement on Ancient Science. Ed. Charles Gillespie, 1978.

Lowe, Gareth W. *Summer Excavations at Chiapa de Corzo, Chiapas.*Publication 2 (Summary Notes 1). Provo, Utah: NWAF, 1957.

Lowe, Gareth W., Thomas A. Lee, Jr., and Eduardo Martinez Espinosa. *Izapa: An Introduction to the Ruins and Monuments.* Provo, Utah: Papers of the NWAF 31, 1982.

Magelby, Kirk A. "A Survey of Mesoamerican Bearded Figures." *Foundation for Ancient Research and Mormon Studies, preliminary Report,*MAG-79. Provo, Utah: F.A.R.M.S., 1979.

Mason, J. Alden. *The Ancient Civilizations of Peru.* Baltimore: Penguin, 1957.

Matheny, Raymond T. *El Mirador, Peten, Guatemala: An Interim Report.* Provo, Utah: Papers of the NWAF 45, 1980.

---. *Investigations at Edzna Campeche, Mexico: Vol. 1, Part 1: The Hydraulic System.* Provo, Utah: Papers of the NWAF 46, 1983.

May, Herbert Gordon. *Material Remains of the Megiddo Cult.* Chicago: Oriental Institute Publication, No. 26, 1935.

MacNeish, Richard S. *An Early Archaeloogical Site Near Panuco, Vera*

*Cruz.* American Philosophical Society, n.s. 44, Pt. 5., (1954): 543-646.

McVicker, Donald. "The Place of the Salt: Archaeological Survey and Excavation in the Valley of Ixtapa, Chiapas, Mexico." Ph.D. dissertation, University of Chicago, 1969.

Means, Philip Ainsworth. *History of the Spanish Conquest of Yucatan and the Itzas* Vol. 1. Cambridge: Papers of the Peabody Museum of American Archaeology and Ethnology, 1917.

Meggers, Betty J. "The Transpacific Origin of Mesoamerican Civilization: A Preliminary Review of the Evidence and its Theoretical Implications." *American Anthropologist* 77 (1975): 1-27.

Meggers, Betty J., Clifford Evans, and Emilio Estrada. *Early Formative Period of Coastal Ecuador: The Valdavia and Machalilla Phase.* Smithsonian Contributions to Anthropology 1, 1965.

Melgarejo Vivanco, Jose Luis. *Codex Vindobonensis.* Jalapa Veracruz: Instituto de Antropologia, 1980.

Mendizabal, Miguel Othon de. *Obras Completas.* 6 vols. Mexico: 1946-47.

Meservy, Keith H. "Discoveries at Nimrud and the 'Sticks of Ezekiel 37.'" *Newsletter and Proceedings of the S.E.H.A.* 142 (1978): 1-10.

*Mesoamerican Notes 5.* Department of Anthropology, Mexico City College, 1957.

*Middle American Research Records.* Pub. 15. Louisana: Tulane University, Middle America Research Institute, 1951.

Montet, Pierre. *Les Reliques de l'Art Syrienne dans l'Egypte du Nouvel Empire.* Paris: P. Geuthner, 1937.

Moran, Hugh A., and David H. Kelley. *The Alphabet and the Ancient Calendar Signs.* 2nd ed. Palo Alto, California: Daily Press, 1969.

Morley, Sylvanus G. *The Ancient Maya.* Palo Alto, CA: Stanford University Press, 1946.

Morley, Sylvanus and Delia Goetz. *Popol Vuh.* Norman, Oklahoma: U of Oklahoma Press, 1950.

Morton, William H. "Umm el-Biyara." *Biblical Archaeologist* 19 (1956): 26-36.

Moscati, Sabatino. *The Face of the Ancient Orient: A Panorama of Near Eastern Civilization in Pre-Classic Times.* Garden City, New York: Doubleday, 1962.

Navarrete, Carlos. *Explorations at San Agustin, Chiapas, Mexico.* Papers of the NWAF 3, Provo, Utah: NWAF, 1959.

Nelson, Fred W., Jr. "Thomas Stuart Ferguson, 1915-83." Paper presented at the 32nd annual symposium, SEHA, Provo, Utah, 22 Oct. 1983. Photocopy in possession of Larry Ferguson.

"New Information about Mulek, Son of the King." F.A.R.M.S. Update (Feb. 1984).

*New Standard Bible Dictionary.* New York: Funk and Wagnall, 1936.

Nibley, Hugh. *Lehi in the Desert and The World of the Jaredites.* Salt Lake City, Utah: Bookcraft, 1952.

---. *An Approach to the Book of Mormon.* Salt Lake City, Utah: Deseret Book, 1957.

Nibley, Preston. *The Witnesses of the Book of Mormon.* Salt Lake City, Utah: Deseret Book, 1946.

Noguera, Eduardo. "Cultura de El Openo." *Mexico Prehispanico.* Mexico: Instituto nacional de Antropologiae Historia, 1946. 150-54.

Noriega, Raul. *Desciframientos de Inscripciones Ciclograficas del Mexico Antiguo.* Mexico City: Conference en la Asociecion Mexicana de la Periodistas,, 1958.

Norman, V. Garth. "The Seven Golden Candlesticks of the Apocalypse." *Papers of the teenth Annual Symposium on the Archaeology of the Scriptures.* Ed. Ross T. Christensen. Provo, Utah: Extension Publication of Brigham Young University, 1964. 47-66.

---. *Izapa Sculpture,* Part 1: Album. Papers of the NWAF 30. Provo, Utah, 1973.

---. *Izapa Sculpture,* Part 2: Text. Papers of the NWAF 30. Provo, Utah, 1976.

---. "Astronomical Orientations of Izapa Sculptures." M.A. thesis. Brigham Young University, 1980.

---. "San Lorenzo as the Jaredite City of Lib." *Newsletter and Proceedings of the S.E.H.A.* 1530. June. Provo, Utah: SEHA, 1983.

Nowotny, Karl Anton. *Tlacuilolli. Die Mexikanischen Bilderhandschriften.* Stil und Inhalt miteinen Katalog der Codex-Borgia-Gruppe. Berlin: Ibero-Amerikanische Bibliothek, Monumenta Americana 3, 1961.

Oppenheim, A. Leo. "Assyro-Babylonian Religion." *Ancient Religions: A Symposium.* Ed. Vergilius Ferm. New York:

Philosophical Library, 1950. 63-79.

Ordonez y Aguiar, Ramon de. *Historia de la Creacion del Cielo y de la Tierra.* Mexico: Imprenta de M. Murguia, 1907.

Palmer, David A. *In Search of Cumorah: New Evidence for the Book of Mormon from Ancient Mexico.* Bountiful, Utah: Horizon Publisher, 1981.

Parrot, Andre. *Discovering Buried Worlds: The Tower of Babel.* New York: Philosophical Library, 1955.

---. *The Arts of Assyria.* New York: Golden Press, 1961.

---. *Sumer, the Dawn of Art.* New York: Golden Press, 1961.

Percival, Bonnie E. "Tree of Life Symbolism: A Selected Diachronic Analysis." Ms. Provo, Utah, 1984.

Peterson, Frederick. *Ancient Mexico: An Introduction to the Pre-Hispanic Cultures.* New York and London: G.P. Putnam's Sons and George Allen and Unwin LTD, 1959.

Petrie, Sir Flinders. *Scarabs and Cylinders With Names: Illustrated by the Egyptain Collection in University College.* London: Egyptian Research Account and British School of Archaeology, 1917.

---. *The Photographic Encyclopedia of Art.* Vol 1 Paris: tel, 1935.

Pierce, Norman C. *Another Cumorah, Another Joseph.* Salt Lake City, Utah: Norman Pierce, 1954.

Piggott, Stuart. *Prehistoric India to 1000 B.C.* Baltimore, Maryland: Penguin, 1950.

---, ed. *The Dawn of Civilization. A compilation of England's leading archaeologists.* London: Thames and Hudson, 1961.

Pina Chan, Roman. *Las Culturas Preclasicas de la Cuenca de Mexico.* Mexico City: Fonda de Cultura Economica, 1955.

---. *Tlatilco.* Vols. 1 and 2 of *Investigaciones.* Instituto Nacional de Antropologia e Historia, Mexico, 1958.

Porter, Muriel Noe. *Tlatilco and the Pre-Classic Cultures of the New World.* Viking Fund Publications in Anthropology 19. New York, 1953.

---. "Excavations at Chupicuaro, Guanajuato, Mexico." American Philosophical Society. Transactions 46, part 5, 1956.

Pritchard, James Bennett. *Palestinian Figurines in Relation to Certain Goddesses Known Through Literature.* New Haven, Connecticut: American Schools of Oriental Research. Series 24, 1943.

---. *The Ancient Near East in Picture.* Princeton: Princeton University Press, 1954.

---. *Archaeology and the Old Testament: The Ancient Near East—an Anthology of Texts and Pictures.* Princeton: Princeton University Press, 1958.

Proskouriakoff, Tatiana. *Olmec and Maya Art: Problems of their Stylistic Relation. Dumbarton Oaks Conference on the Olmec.* Washington, D.C.: Dumbarton Oaks Research Library and Collection, Trustees for Harvard University, 1968. 119-134.

Rawlinson, George. *The Seven Great Monarchies of the Ancient Eastern World.* New York: A.L. Burt, 1870.

Recinos, Adrian. *Popol Vuh: the Sacred Book of the Ancient Quiche Maya.* English version by Sylvanus G. Morley and Delia Goetz. Norman, Oklahoma: University of Oklahoma Press, 1950.

Recinos, Adrian, and Delia Goetz. *The Annals of the Cakchiquels.* Norman, Oklahoma: University of Oklahoma Press, 1953.

Reko, Blas. P. "The Royal Stars of the Hebrews, Aztecs and Quiches." *El Mexico Antiquo* 3.3-4 (1934): 49-56. Mexico City: Sociedad Alemana de Mexicanistas.

---. "Star-Names of the Chilam Balam of Chumayel." *El Mexico Antiguo* 3.9-10:1-52; 11-12:13-84; 4. 21-67, 95-129, 163-178, and 255-283. Mexico City, Sociedad Alemana de Mexicanistas, October 1935-May 1939.

Reynolds, George. *A Complete Concordance of the Book of Mormon.* Edited and arranged by Philip C. Reynolds: Salt Lake City, Utah: Deseret Book, 1957.

Richards, Le Grand. *A Marvelous Work and A Wonder.* 1st ed. Salt Lake City, Utah: Deseret Book, 1950.

---. *Israel! Do You Know!* Salt Lake City, Utah: Deseret Book, 1954.

Ricketson, O. G., Jr. and E. B. Ricketson. *Uaxactun, Guatemala, Group E., 1926-1937.* Carnegie Institution of Washington Pub. 477. 1937.

Ricks, Joel Edward. *Book of Mormon Geography.* Logan, Utah: Joel Edward Ricks, 1939.

---. *The Nephites in Story.* Logan, Utah: Joel Edward Ricks, 1940.

Riley, Carroll L. et al., eds. *Man across the Sea: Problems of Pre-Columbian Contacts.* Austin: U of Texas Press, 1971.

Rouse, Irving. *Migrations in Prehistory: Inferring Population Movement from Cultural Remains.* New Haven, Connecticut: Yale University Press, 1986.

Ruz Lhuillier, Alberto. "Exploraciones en Palenque: 1950." *Anales del*

*Instituto Nacional de Antropologia e Historia* 5.24-45 (1952).

Sahagun, Bernardino de. *Historia General de las Cosas de Nueva Espana*. Mexico City: Editorial Parrua, 1946.

---. *Florentine Codex: General History of the Things of New Spain*. Trans. from Aztec into English, with notes and illustrations by A. J. O. Anderson and C. E. Dibble. Book 10. *The People*. Santa Fe: School of American Research and University of Utah, 1961.

Samuel, Maurice. *The Professor and the Fossil*. New York: Alfred A. Knopf, 1956.

Sanders, William T. *Ceramic Stratigraphy at Santa Cruz, Chiapas, Mexico*. Provo, Utah: Papers of the NWAF 13, 1961.

Santillana, Giorgio, and Hertha von Deschand. *Hamlet's Mill*. Boston: David R. Godine, 1969.

Sauer, Carl O. *Agricultural Origins and Dispersals*. Bowman Memorial Series 2. New York: American Geographical Society, 1952.

Sawyer, Alan R. *The Nathan Cummings Collection of Ancient Peruvian Art*. Greenwich, New York: New York Graphic Society, 1954.

Schele, Linda. *Maya Glyphs: the Verbs*. Austin: U of Texas Press. 1982

Schneider, Harold K. "Prehistoric Transpacific Contact and the Theory of Culture Change." *American Anthropologist* 79 (1977): 9-25.

Sejourne, Laurette. *Burning Water*. New York: Vanguard Press, 1956.

Seler, Eduard. *Codex Borgia, Line Altmexikanishche Bilderschrift der Bibliothek der Congregatio de Propoganda Fide*. 3 Vols. Berlin, 1904-09.

Shao, Paul. *Chinese Influence in Pre-Columbian American Art*. Ames, Iowa: Iowa State University Press, 1978.

---. *The Origin of Ancient American Cultures*. Ames, Iowa: Iowa State University Press, 1983.

Shearer, Tony. *Beneath the Moon and Under the Sun*. Albuquerque, New Mexico: Sun Publishers, 1975.

Shook, Edwin M. *The Present Status of Research on the Pre-Classic Horizons in Guatemala. Civilization of Ancient America, Selected Papers of the 29th International Congress of Americanists*. Ed. Sol Tax, 1956. 93-100.

Shook, Edwin M. and Alfred V. Kidder. *Mound E-III-3, Kaminaljuyu, Guatemala*. Carnegie Institution of Washington. Contribution 596, 1952.

Sjodahl, J. M. *An Introduction to the Study of the Book of Mormon*.

Salt Lake City, Utah: Deseret News Press, 1927.

Smith, A. Ledyard. *Uaxactun, Guatemala, Excavations of 1931-37.* Carnegie Institution of Washington 588, 1950.

Smith, Joseph, Jr. *The History of the Church of Jesus Christ of Latter-day Saints.* Ed. B. H. Roberts. 2nd ed. rev. 7 vols. Salt Lake City, Utah: Deseret Book, 1951.

Smith, Joseph Fielding. *Teachings of the Prophet Joseph Smith.* Salt Lake City, Utah: Deseret Book, 1938.

Smith, Joseph Lindon. *Tombs, Temples, and Ancient Art.* Norman, Oklahoma: U of Oklahoma Press, 1956.

Smith, Marian W. (ed.) "Asia and North America, Transpacific Contacts." *American Antiquity* 8.3, Pt. 2, Memoirs of the Society for American Archaeology 9, 1953.

Smith, Mary Elizabeth. *Picture Writing from Ancient Southern Mexico: Mixtec Place Signs and Names.* Norman, Oklahoma: U of Oklahoma Press, 1973.

Smith, Robert E. *Ceramic Sequence of Uaxactun, Guatemala.* Vol. 1 and 2. Middle American Research Institute. Tulane University Publication 20. New Orleans: Tulane University Press, 1955.

Smith, Robert F. "Sawi-Zaa Word Comparisons." Ms. September 1977. 1-9.

Smith, William Anton. *Ancient Education.* New York: Philosophical Library, 1955.

Solis Alcala, Ermilo. *Diccionario Espanol-Maya.* Merida, Mexico: Editorial Yihal Maya Thon, 1949.

Sorenson, John L. "Preclassic Metal." *American Antiquity* 21 (1954):64.

---. *A Chronological Ordering of the Mesoamerican Preclassic.* Middle American Research Institute 2.3. New Orleans: Tulane University Press, 1955. 43-68.

---. "Bible Prophecies of the Mulekites." *A Book of Mormon Treasury: Significant Articles from the Pages of the Improvement Era.* Ed. Doyle L. Green and Marva C. Josephson. Salt Lake City, Utah: Bookcraft, 1959. 229-37.

---. "The Significance of an Apparent Relationship Between the Ancient Near East and Mesoamerica." Riley et al. 1971. 219-241.

---. *An Ancient American Setting for the Book of Mormon.* Salt Lake City, Utah: F.A.R.M.S. and Deseret Book, 1985.

Sperry, Sidney B. *Our Book of Mormon.* Salt Lake City, Utah: Stevens & Wallis, 1947.

---. *The Book of Mormon Testifies.* Salt Lake City, Utah: Bookcraft, 1952.

---. *Book of Mormon Compendium.* Salt Lake City, Utah: Bookcraft, 1968.

Spinden, Herbert Joseph. *Maya Art and Civilization.* Indian Hills, Colorado: Falcon Wing Press, 1957.

Steward, Julian H., ed. *Irrigation Civilizations: A Comparative Study (Symposium).* Washington, D.C.: Pan American Union, 1955.

Stirling, Matthew, ed. *Stone Monuments of Southern Mexico.* Bureau of American Ethnology. Bulletin 138, 1943.

Stoddard, Darrell J. *The Tree of Life Symbol as a "Fountain of Living Water."* Ms. Provo, Utah, 1968.

Tax, Sol, ed. *The Civilizations of Ancient America.* Chicago: U of Chicago Press, 1951.

Tedlock, Dennis, trans. *Popul Vuh: The Definitive Edition of the Mayan Book of the Dawn of Life and the Glories of Gods and Kings.* New York: Simon and Schuster, 1985.

Thompson, J. Eric S. "Maya Hieroglyphic Writing." *Carnegie Institution of Washington,* 589, 1950.

---. "Aquatic Symbols Common to Various Centers of the Classic Period in Meso-America." *Tax.* 1951. 31-36.

---. *The Rise and Fall of Maya Civilization.* Norman, Oklahoma: U of Oklahoma Press, 1954.

---. "Symbols, Glyphs, and Divinatory Almanacs for Diseases in the Maya Dresden and Madrid Codices." *American Antiquity* 13 (1958): 297-308.

Tolstoy, Paul. "Cultural Parallels Between Southeast Asia and Mesoamerica in the Manufacture of Bark Cloth." Trans. New York Academy of Science. Series 2, Vol. 25. 646-662.

Torquemada, Juan de. *Monarquia Indians.* Mexico City: Editorial Chavez Hayhoe. 3 vols. 1943.

---. *Los Veinte y un Libros Rituales y Monarchia Indiana.* Madrid, 1723. Facsimile edition, Mexico City: Editorial Salvador Chavez Hayhoe, 1943.

Torre, Jose Castillo. *Por La Senal de Hunabku.* Mexico City: Libreria de Manuel Porrua, 1955.

Toynbee, Arnold. *An Historian's Approach to Religion.* New York: Oxford University Press, 1956.

Tozzer, Alfred M. *Landa's Relacion de las Cosas de Yucatan, a translation.* Peabody Museum, Harvard University. Anthropological Ethnological Papers 18.

Tufnell, Olga, et. al. *Lachish IV: The Bronze Age.* London: Oxford University Press, 1938.

Urrutia, Benjamin. *Shiblon, Coriantumr, and the Jade Jaguars.* Proceedings of the S.E.H.A. 150.0. Aug. Provo, Utah: Society for Early Historic Archaeology, 1982.

Vaillant, George C. "A Bearded Mystery." *Natural History* 31 (1931): 243-52.

---. *Artists and Craftsmen in Ancient Central America.* Museum of Natural History, Guide Leaflet Series 88, 1935.

---. "Excavations at El Arbolillo." *Anthropological Papers of the American Museum of Natural History* 35, pt. 2, 1935. 137-279.

---. *Aztecs of Mexico.* New York: The American Museum of Natural History, 1944.

Van Buren, Elizabeth Douglas. *The Flowing Vase and the God with Streams.* Berlin: H. Schoetz & Co. gmbh, 1933.

---. *Gods of Mesopotamia.* Rome: Vatican, 1939.

Velt, Harold I. *The Sacred Book of Ancient America.* Independence, Missouri: Herald House, 1952.

Vestal, Kirk Holland, and Arthur Wallace. *The Firm Foundation of Mormonism.* Los Angeles: L L Company, 1981.

Veytia, Mariano. *Historia Antiqua de Mexico.* Mexico: Imprenta Juan Ojeda, 1836.

Vincent, David. "Studies Zapotec Units of Measure." U.A.S. Newsletter 47.2, Jan. 1958, Provo, Utah: The University Archaeological Society.

Vigneau, Andre. *Encyclopedie Photographique de L'Art.* Paris: Editors "Tel," 1949.

Von Hagen, Victor Wolfgang. *Maya Explorer, the Life of John Lloyd Stevens.* Norman, Oklahoma: U of Oklahoma Press, 1947.

Von Wuthenau, Alexander. *Unexpected Faces in Ancient Mexico: The Historical Testimony of Precolumbian Artists 1500 B.C.-A.D. 1500.* New York: Crown, 1975.

Ward, William Hayes. *The Seal Cylinders of Western Asia.* Washington, D.C.: The Carnegie Institute of Washington, 1920.

Warren, Bruce W. *The Sociocultural Development of the Central Depression of Chiapas, Mexico: Preliminary Considerations.* Ann Arbor, Michigan: University Microfilms International, 1978.

---. "A Cautious Interpretation of a Mesoamerican Myth:

Reflections upon Olmec-Jaredite Roots." *Newsletter and Proceedings of the S.E.H.A.* 154.0, July 1983, Provo, Utah: SEHA.

---. "A Fourth Century A.D. Migration in Mexico as Related by Ixtlilxochitl." Newsletter and Proceeding of the S.E.H.A. 160-0, Mar. 1986, Provo, Utah: SEHA.

Warren, Bruce W. and John A. Tvedtnes. "In Search of the Historic Nimrod." *Newsletter and Proceedings of the S.E.H.A.* 155.0, Nov. 1983, Provo, Utah: SEHA.

Washburn, J. A., and J. N. Washburn. *An Approach to the Study of Book of Mormon Geography*. American Fork, Utah: Alpine Publishing, 1939.

Watts, Alan Wilson. *Myth and Ritual in Christianity*. London: Thames and Hudson, 1954.

Wauchope, Robert. "Implications of Radiocarbon Dates from Middle and South America." Middle American Research Institute 2.2. New Orleans: Tulane University Press, 1954.

Webster, David L. "The Fortifications of Becan, Campeche, Mexico. In *Archaeological Investigations on the Yucatan Peninsula*. Middle American Research Institute 31. New Orleans: Tulane University Press, 1974.

Welch, John W. "Chiasmus in the Book of Mormon." *Brigham Young University Studies* 10 (1969): 69-84.

Westheim, Paul. *The Art of Ancient Mexico*. Garden City, New York: Doubleday-Anchor Books, 1965.

Widtsoe, John Andreas. *Joseph Smith.* Independence, Missouri: Press of Zion's Printing and Publishing Company, 1951.

Willetts, William. *Foundations of Chinese Art*. New York: McGraw Hill, 1965.

Wilson, John A. *In The Intellectual Adventure of Ancient Man*. Chicago: U of Chicago Press, 1946.

---. *The Culture of Ancient Egypt*. Chicago: U of Chicago Press, 1956.

Wirth, Diane E. *Discoveries of the Truth*. Santa Clara: Vanguard Graphics, 1978.

---. *A Challenge to the Critics: Scholarly Evidences of the Book of Mormon*. Bountiful, Utah: Horizon Publishers & Distributors, Inc., 1986.

Wolf, Eric R. *The Sons of the Shaking Earth*. Chicago: U of Chicago Press, 1959.

Woodbury, Richard, and Aubrey S. Trik. *The Ruins of Zaculeu*.

Guatemala United Fruit Company. Richmond, Virginia: William Byrd Press, 1953.

Wooley, Sir Leonard. *Ur of the Chaldees*. New York: Scribner's, 1938.

Wright, G. Ernest. *Biblical Archaeology*. Philadelphia: Westminster Press, 1957.

Ziegler, Wesley. *An Analysis of the Book of Mormon*. Pasadena, California: Publication Press, 1947.

# INDEX

**MAP 1**

**RELATIVE POSITIONS OF MORMON'S CUMORAH AND MORONI'S CUMORAH**

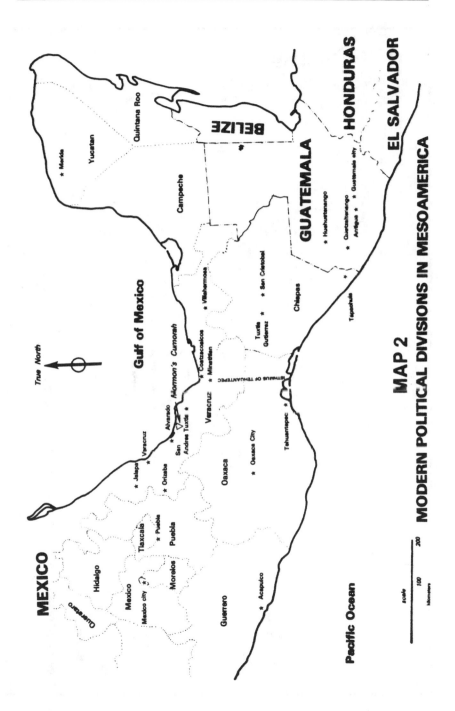

**MAP 2**

**MODERN POLITICAL DIVISIONS IN MESOAMERICA**

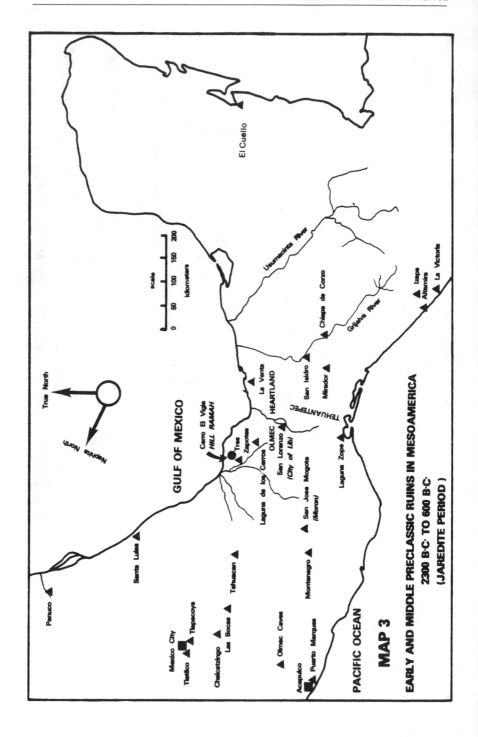

MAP 3

EARLY AND MIDDLE PRECLASSIC RUINS IN MESOAMERICA
2300 B.C. TO 600 B.C.
(JAREDITE PERIOD )

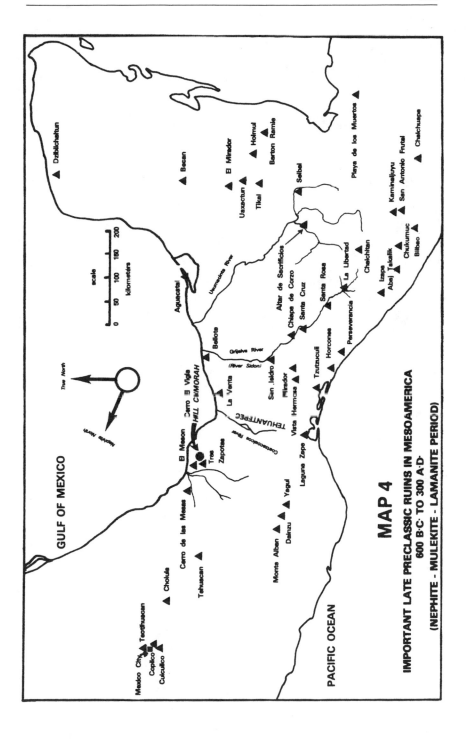

GULF OF MEXICO

PACIFIC OCEAN

MAP 4

IMPORTANT LATE PRECLASSIC RUINS IN MESOAMERICA
600 B·C· TO 300 A·D·

(NEPHITE - MULEKITE - LAMANITE PERIOD)

scale

0  50  100  150  200

kilometers

True North

Magnetic North

Mexico City
Teotihuacan
Copilco
Cuicuilco

Cholula

Cerro de las Mesas

Tehuacan

Monte Alban
Dainzu
Yagul

El Meson
Tres Zapotes

Cerro El Vigia
HILL CUMORAH

La Venta

Laguna Zope

Vista Hermosa

TEHUANTEPEC

Coatzacoalcos River

San Isidro

Mirador

Tzutzuculi

Dzibilchaltun

Becan

El Mirador
Holmul
Barton Ramie

Uaxactun
Tikal

Seibal

Playa de los Muertos

Aguacatal

Usumacinta River

Bellote

Grijalva River
(River Sidon)

Altar de Sacrificios

Chiapa de Corzo
Santa Cruz

Santa Rosa

La Libertad

Chalchitan

Izapa
Abel Takalik

Kaminaljuyu
San Antonio Frutal

Chalchuape

Chukumuc
Bilbao

Horcones

Perseverancia

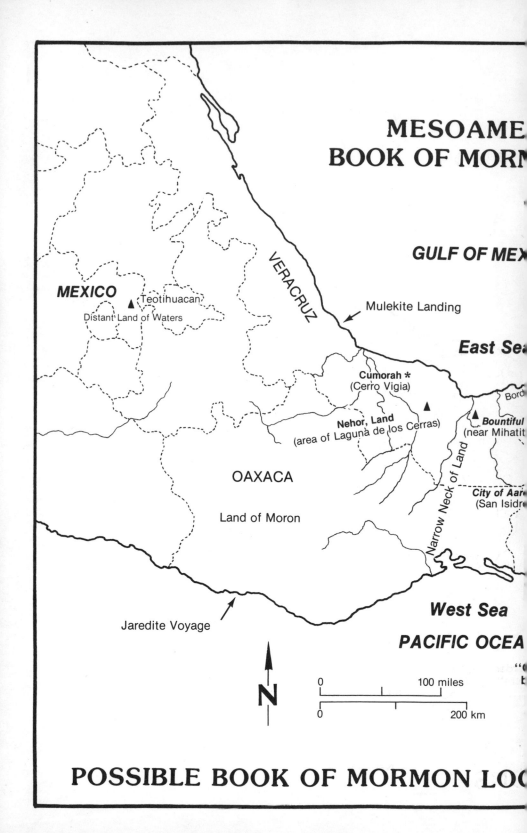

MESOAME
BOOK OF MORM

GULF OF MEX

MEXICO
▲ Teotihuacan
Distant Land of Waters

Mulekite Landing

East Sea

VERACRUZ

Cumorah *
(Cerro Vigia)

▲

Nehor, Land
(area of Laguna de los Cerras)

▲ Bountiful
(near Mihatit

Bord

OAXACA

Narrow Neck of Land

City of Aar
(San Isidr

Land of Moron

West Sea

Jaredite Voyage

PACIFIC OCEA

N

"
b

0          100 miles

0          200 km

POSSIBLE BOOK OF MORMON LO